FROM MY GUY

FROM MY GUY TO SCI-FI

Genre and Women's Writing in the Postmodern World

Edited by
HELEN CARR

PANDORA

London   Winchester   Sydney   Wellington

First published by Pandora Press, an imprint of the Trade Division of
Unwin Hyman, in 1989
Selection and Introduction copyright © Helen Carr 1989

Feminist Criticism Twenty Years On copyright © Cora Kaplan 1989
Putting on the Style copyright © Alison Light 1989
Tracking Down the Past copyright © Rosalind Coward &
Linda Semple 1989
Romantic Readers copyright © Helen Taylor 1989
The Science Fictiveness of Women's Science Fiction
copyright © Roz Kaveney 1989
Women's Biography and Autobiography
copyright © Carolyn Steedman 1989
Feminist Literary Strategies in the Postmodern Condition
copyright © Carolyn Brown 1989
Poetic Licence copyright © Helen Carr 1989
Private Spaces to Public Places copyright © Naseem Khan 1989
Themes and Trends in Caribbean Writing Today
copyright © Merle Collins 1989
Futures in Feminist Fiction copyright © Sara Maitland 1989
Feminism, Writing, Postmodernism copyright © Leslie Dick 1989

PANDORA PRESS
Unwin Hyman Limited
15/17 Broadwick Street, London W1V 1FP

Unwin Hyman Inc
8 Winchester Place, Winchester, MA 01890

Allen & Unwin Australia Pty Ltd
P.O. Box 764, 8 Napier Street, North Sydney, NSW 2060

Allen & Unwin NZ Ltd
(in association with the Port Nicholson Press)
Compusales Building, 75 Ghuznee Street, Wellington, New Zealand

British Library Cataloguing in Publication Data

From my guy to sci-fi: genre and women's writing in the
postmodern world.
1. Fiction in English. Women writers, to 1980.
Critical studies
I. Carr, Helen
823'.009'9287

ISBN 0-04-440408-5

Typeset in 10 on 11 point Palatino by
Computape (Pickering) Ltd, North Yorkshire
and printed in Great Britain by Cox & Wyman Ltd., Reading

CONTENTS

ACKNOWLEDGEMENTS

———◆———

This book came out of a series of talks at the Institute of Contemporary Arts in 1988. The idea of the talks came to me when I was asked by Thames Television to write the booklet to accompany a series of programmes produced and directed by Jill Fullerton-Smith on *Women Writers*, which looked at six best-selling women writers, each working in different genres. The ICA series was jointly organised by the University of London Department of Extra-Mural Studies (now the Birkbeck College University of London Centre for Extra-Mural Studies) and the ICA, and supported financially by Thames Television and Pandora Press. I should like to thank all those involved in making that series the success it was: in particular, Jill Fullerton-Smith, Maggie Millman and Paul Gerhardt at Thames Television; Erica Carter at the ICA; Mary Kennedy at the Department of Extra-Mural Studies; and Philippa Brewster at Pandora Press; the speakers, all of whom I am delighted have contributed to this volume; and last, but by no means least, the audience for those talks, whose lively contributions have found their way into the rewritten versions of some of these pieces, and whose insights I have tried in some measure to represent in my introduction. The title of this book, as of the series, was Erica Carter's inspiration: I am most grateful.

I should also like to thank the following for permission to reprint copyright material: Carcanet Press for permission to reprint 8 lines of 'The Journey' from Eavan Boland's *The Journey and Other Poems*, 1986, and 15 lines of 'Search for My Tongue' from Sujata Bhatt's *Brunizem*, 1988: Faber & Faber Ltd and Alfred A. Knopf Inc for 10 lines of 'Salvage' from Amy Clampitt's *The Kingfisher*: Penguin Books for 17 lines of 'Resigned' by Amrita Pritam from Adil Jussawalla (ed.) *New Writing in India*, 1974: and Sheba Feminist Publishers for the fable 'The Female Swan' from Suniti Namjoshi's *Feminist Fables*, 1981.

Finally, I should like to thank Philippa Brewster again, this time for her patience and her many invaluable suggestions while this book has come together: to thank Steven Connor for discussions and advice on postmodernism: and to thank my family for so ably falling into the roles of token average readers, proofreaders, spell-checkers, word processor specialists, experts on popular culture and critics of my arguments as the occasion demanded.

PART I

—◆—

The Critical Scene

INTRODUCTION: GENRE AND WOMEN'S WRITING IN THE POSTMODERN WORLD

HELEN CARR

We all resemble errant E.T.s, infantile, scathed, lacking 'home' and love. We lack today an amatory code, an amatory myth, but it would be an imposture should we wish to propose new ones. We can but live a plurality of possible myths. . . . In other words, the remedy to the amorous crisis is creation, from archaeology to fiction.
(Julia Kristeva)[1]

I would ask you to write all sorts of books, hesitating at no subject however trivial or however vast . . . when I ask you to write more books I am urging you to do what will be for your good and for the good of the world at large.
(Virginia Woolf, *A Room of One's Own*)[2]

Books about women's writing and books of women's writing are much more plentiful and various than when Virginia Woolf wrote *A Room of One's Own* in 1928. But even so, *From My Guy to Sci-Fi* is unusual in two ways. Firstly, the contributors are not solely either creative writers or literary critics. In this collection women's writing today is discussed by a diverse group of academics, journalists and practising writers, who bring very different approaches, preoccupations and emphases to what they have to say. And secondly, these essays are not only concerned with texts for which they claim literary merit, as would probably have been the case ten years ago. Nor are they just about popular fiction, as some more recent books have been. The book brings together high and low culture, mainstream and marginal, mass appeal and avant-garde. At what Cora Kaplan calls this 'historic moment for feminist critique' it takes a fresh and open look at what feminists can say about women's writing in its new rich plenitude.

The book's unusual format is perhaps an indication of its origins. *From My Guy to Sci-Fi* came out of a series of well-attended, enthusiastic and argumentative meetings at the Institute of Contemporary Arts in London, at which these essays or versions of them were given, under the same general title as the present book. But before the ICA events, in production if not in dissemination, was a series of programmes for Thames Television on *Women Writers*, for which I wrote the booklet. I suggested the ICA series as one of a range of educational events organised in conjunction with this television series. Superficially the two series might seem rather different: the television programmes looked at six bestselling women writers, and although each was drawn from a different genre, they didn't consider the significance of genre as such. No one involved in the talks, except for myself, had anything to do with the television series. But in a more important way the existence of those programmes, broadcast by Thames Television to a mass audience, was fundamental to the conception of the talks. What the broadcasting of those TV programmes made clear was that the discussion of women's writing because it was by women, which little more than a decade ago was rare, marginal and academically suspect, is now part of the currency of our culture.

All these essays are conscious of this new currency. In her analysis of our present 'historic moment' Cora Kaplan suggests that second wave feminism really took off in 1969. Certainly, the first piece of feminist literary criticism that I read, or indeed heard of, appeared in the United States that year – Kate Millett's exciting and provocative *Sexual Politics*. Mary Ellmann's *Thinking About Women* had come out the year before, but I didn't discover that until much later.[3] Now nearly every established academic publisher has a list of feminist criticism. Today all accounts of women's writing begin with the awareness that feminist literary criticism has a history. Publishing women's writing has become profitable and sometimes big business. Yet some of the premisses of that early criticism have changed. The political climate in most parts of the Western world is in many ways more radically opposed to the values of second wave feminism, especially to its attack on competitiveness and aggression, than it was in 1969. Many younger women would not call themselves feminists even though they express what in the 1970s would have been thought feminist views. They don't want to talk about oppression, certainly not to consider themselves victims. How do we understand the position of women and the constraints of gender today, and how does that shape our interpretations and expectations of women's writing and of women's criticism now?

Much of the discussion following these sessions of talks, especially the first at which both Cora Kaplan and Alison Light spoke, was about the transformations within the last two decades, and the differences between generations of feminists. The changes are perhaps encapsulated by the very fact that the series chose to concentrate on genres, rather than, as it might well have done ten years ago, either on specific women writers or on the general relation of women to literature and language. So I want here briefly to suggest why this series looked at what feminist criticism in the late 1980s has to say about genres, and in so doing pick up on some of these discussions.

Firstly, it's no longer possible or fruitful to try to discuss women's writing as a single category in the way one could or at any rate did in the mid 1970s. We now realise that we can't talk of women as a monolithic category. There are questions of race, class, sexuality and historical context, and in writing different modes and contexts of literary production, different conventions and functions, all of which must be considered. To think of women or their writing as a single homogeneous group is nearly as impossible as to talk of 'mankind' or 'great literature'. Some early feminists have been criticised for assuming that their white, middle-class, heterosexual values formed a consensus. In their search to establish the distinctiveness of a women's tradition of writing it was perhaps too easy to give a mirror image of the Eurocentric establishment. We are now much more aware that the business of feminist criticism should be, as Marilyn Butler says, 'decentring criticism, on the principle Gertrude Stein laid down, "act so that there is no use in the centre"'.[4] Looking at

genre is a way of escaping the pressure to construct an alternative canon of great women writers – not easy to do, as
someone pointed out acerbicly in the discussion on postmodernism, which kept relentlessly returning to *Jane Eyre*. The
essays here discuss a range of texts, written and read by women
from different racial, class and educational positions, written and
read for a variety of purposes and in a variety of ways: Asian
women writers, Mills & Boon and Harlequin, women's telling of
their own or other women's life stories, and so on. Women's
writing has now to be seen as pluralistic, protean and diverse.
Taking the question of genre is one way of focusing on the
interaction of the complex strands that form it.

The word genre, of course, has two very different sets of
associations. Often it's now used in the context of popular
literature, where it frequently implies 'not literature', but rather
some low-level formulaic production. But its older use is by
formalist academic literary critics, for whom it means established
literary forms such as the epic, tragedy, comedy, realist novel
and so on. As Tzvetan Todorov points out in *The Poetics of Prose*,
up until the eighteenth century in the classical tradition inherited
by the Renaissance, a genre had very definite rules, and the
writer's art was shown in their faithful observation.[5] The Romantics' emphasis on originality and organic form changed all that.
Great writing was to be unique and *sui generis* – literally, creating
its own genre. But now once again we are aware of the importance of genre, not as a set of rules that ought to be followed, but
as a framework that is always there to some degree. All texts are
dependent on and grow out of other texts. All texts are variations
on previous models. The importance of the rules may be, as
Rosalind Coward and Linda Semple suggest, that they are there
to be broken. But they are there nonetheless, though perhaps we
should now call them codes: they are what make storytelling
possible.

This collection might be described as a thoroughly postmodern
mingling of literary and popular genres; that's true, but perhaps
because questioning the validity of definitions of high and low
culture has always been part of the feminist critique. Jonathan
Culler defines genre as groups of norms and expectations that
help readers assign functions to the various elements in the
work.[6] The reader knows what to expect and why: each genre

has its codes and conventions. As Rosalind Coward said in the discussion following the talks on detective fiction, if a clock strikes nine in a crime novel, we read that possible clue in the appropriate way. It will be different from our response to the stroke of a clock in a gothic novel, where it would be more likely to be midnight and chilling the blood, or in a modernist text, as for example in *Mrs Dalloway*, when the striking of Big Ben is a comment on the nature of time and its social divisions. And to put it in more general terms, if we read crime novels we expect a mystery, an investigator and a solution. If we read a romance we expect a hero, a heroine and true love. Since the norms and expectations of each genre are enmeshed with the norms and expectations of society as a whole, they seem a particularly fruitful point to focus upon – how gender enters into and is constructed by the form of the genre, and how and perhaps why those constructions may change.

Each genre – whether the sonnet or sci-fi, revenge tragedy or soap opera – has grown out of specific social situations and conditions of literary production. Norms and expectations are not inscribed for ever within the text, but are always dependent on the readers' knowledge of the codes. We are not necessarily always sure which conventions to read by. Angela Carter's novels became much more acceptable in Britain after the discovery of South American magic realism: her readers discovered that she was writing in a genre that could be named and to whose apparent random mixture of fantasy and reality some order could be assigned.[7] No one reading *Frankenstein* in 1818 could have thought they were reading science fiction, but with a history of science fiction we read it differently now.[8] Genres represent a set of conventions whose parameters are redrawn with each new book and each new reading. The concept involves a contract between reader and writer. Once we think of a text as an example of a genre, we can no longer approach it only as an artefact to be analysed in some contextless critical purity. We need to ask who reads such books, why and in what way, seeing them as what Helen Taylor describes as texts-in-use. Looking at genres brings together a range of levels in which these forms operate in our culture, from the pragmatics of production to issues of ideology and language.

Questions about the relationship of women to our language,

where the masculine is the norm, have always been central to feminist criticism. Genres are perhaps, in one way, best understood as particular forms of discourse, that is, special systems within language. And, of course, there are other norms in our language and in these genres besides those of gender. Mills & Boon heroes aren't allowed to be black. Caribbean writers have had to return to their own patois to evade the British values inscribed in the English they were taught to use at school. Some early feminism criticism saw women's texts as swamped, invaded, imprisoned by these norms, reproducing oppressive ideologies – the detective novel kowtowing to the establishment, the romance reinforcing the subordinate, male-dependent position of women. Helen Taylor quotes Germaine Greer's description of romance as 'dope for dope'. The essays here are more concerned to show how women as writers or readers can rework or subvert genres, either consciously or unconsciously, imagining new possibilities for themselves. While genres in a literature dependent on aristocratic patronage were slow to change, genres in our present complex market economy are fluid and mixed, constantly transforming and reinventing themselves, cross-fertilising and regenerating.

The sense of writing as a source of potential transformation and radical change has always been present in feminist thought. But it has often been in tension with the apparently deterministic drive of much of twentieth-century language theory. Structuralist and post-structuralist views of language have in many ways been creatively absorbed not just by feminists but by our culture generally. Women felt freed by the idea of language as a system which constructs arbitrary differences, which have more to do with the power relations in a given society than with absolute meanings. It made it possible to question the definitions of womanhood and femininity embedded in the words we speak. Yet such a theory leaves uncertainties: if language is speaking us, rather than we speaking language, how do we transform those definitions? Ideas about women and language came up several times in the discussions. Overall, there seemed to be a shift from an emphasis on how language privileges the masculine and demeans the feminine to a sense that we can change language as we can rework genre. The most pervasive theory of language among feminists to date has been that of the

French psychoanalyst, Lacan, according to whom all language is always phallocentric, always privileging the masculine, always looking to the phallus, the slash of differentiation between he/she, as the ultimate difference. It's a theory which has been used very fruitfully by feminists, but like most theories to emerge from France in the last three decades, much better at theorising the state of oppression than the means of escaping it. I believe it is essential to understand how power works before one can change its structures, so I don't want to discount the Lacanian moment. But my feeling is that in that form its moment has passed. For one thing, like most psychoanalysis up until now, it has little to say about race or class. In these sessions language as a factor in colonial and racial oppression emerged even more strongly than in gender. And in English society, seventy-five years after *Pygmalion* it is still the case that language is one of the most powerful instruments of the class system. What we need is a theory which allows us to look at sexual and other forms of difference in less fixed and determined ways.

The focus on genre allowed another important and evolving debate to emerge: what part pleasure does or should have in our reading. One participant argued very fiercely in the session on the detective novel against allowing ourselves to be gripped by the tawdry charms of the mystery plot. It was, she said, an unworthy way to spend our time, trapping us in bourgeois, patriarchal views of crime and morality. But she had few supporters. On the whole the arguments went quite the other way. Few wanted to interpret popular fictions as the opium of the masses, but instead to emphasise the importance of play, desire and fantasy. But here as in other sessions there remained something of a generational gap, with women in their twenties insisting that the earlier phases of the Women's Movement had been too puritanical. They argued that older feminists were still too influenced by the patronising attitudes inherited both from literary critics like Leavisites and from the left generally, which assumed, as the Marxist Frederic Jameson put it, that mass culture existed merely for 'the legitimation of the existing order'.[9] You will of course be able to make up your mind yourself as you read these essays. I certainly feel that the crucial questions of why we enjoy reading, what are the pleasures that it can bring, what are the desires it speaks, and what are its powers of transformation are all opened up here.

This isn't of course new. As long ago as 1979 Mary Jacobus was noting that feminists had become more likely to 'stress pleasure than suffering'.[10] Much work on popular culture has used psychoanalytic theory to understand desire in texts and language, or Gramscian notions which see popular culture not simply as repressive but as a site of struggle. The latter is perhaps a particularly useful model, because it can be used to bring together the need to combat oppressions, a commitment to political change, with the language of desire. In the session on postmodernism Carolyn Brown argued that women should now resist a patriarchal culture through ruses, play and irony instead of through anger and confrontation, whose day she believed had passed. She provoked a storm of opposition, which certainly suggested her prediction was premature. Perhaps both strategies are necessary.

What overall came out of these discussions was the paradoxical conjuncture of a celebration of the achievements of the women's movement with anxiety in the face of a reactionary political climate. Yet in the discussion at the first session, there was unease about any simple explanation of our contemporary moment by slipping back into the reassuring format of 'on the one hand this' and 'on the other that', of concern at the reactionary balanced by the promise of the progressive. The comforting familiarity of these traditional binaries of advance/regress, improvement/impairment, progress/decline doesn't fit our contemporary experience, with its multitudinous, pluralistic range of images of women and diverse and contradictory political shifts. As Alison Light says, these changes are not to be so easily labelled and appraised.

This world of uncertain directions and kaleidoscopic, contradictory images is increasingly labelled as postmodernist. Some contributors define postmodernism in various ways and for various purposes later in this book, but I want to mention it at this early stage because issues raised, or at any rate implied, by postmodernism are of crucial importance for a feminist critique. The word postmodernist sometimes seems just to stand for the twentieth-century version of nineteenth-century *fin de siècle* decadence: Disneyland or *Dallas*, Warhol or war-games. Like modernism, it is a movement which can be either intensely reactionary or deeply radical: but the ideas and impulses behind this cultural mood are central to an understanding of present political context, not just in Britain, but throughout the Western world. Postmodernism is about fragmented images, and its manifestations are so diverse that often it's hard to read what the fragments say. We're frequently reminded that it first emerged as an architectural term for those that rejected what was known as the international modernist style – which had in its turn rejected the architectures of the past and insisted on the need for a new style for the Modern age; postmodernist architecture is an eclectic pastiche, a medley of past styles – look down any British high street at mock–mock-Tudor shopping centres, Crystal Palaces crossed with Covent Gardens, brick Palladio hotels. Some of the early pioneers of postmodernism in poetry were the American poets of the Black Mountain College led by Charles Olson, who believed the world went wrong with Plato's imposition of universals, that we should return to particulars, to the tangible rather than the ideal, and to geography rather than history. What these and other postmodernist forms have in common is the loss of faith not just in progress but in any of the organising structural narratives of Western civilisation. History is no longer a movement along the files of time. It is a set of myths inhabiting the present. Some Marxists denounce hotly the abandonment of belief in a history whose central trajectory is the Western-model class struggle.[11] They see postmodernism as an evasion of politics. But postmodernism, apolitical as it sometimes is and often appears, neoconservative as in some circumstances it may be, is politically significant in broader terms. If modernism was the movement that registered the cracking of the European hierarchies of bourgeois/proletarian, male/female, white/other, high art/low culture, postmodernism is the recognition that we are in a multicultural world in which all the traditional hierarchies are in question.

The story of this transformation is sometimes told as if what had vanished, to be replaced by this video show of broken images, were rock-like certainties of meaning and direction. I don't think it's as simple as that. Those hierarchies were never really unproblematic. They were founded not on confidence but on deep anxieties that emerged as misogyny, homophobia, racial and class fear. What the change marks is the end of the European assumption that our culture is the only path of civilised progress, and that the white, bourgeois, male represents true humanity. It follows the collapse of European colonisation and the growth of global media and production systems, the realisation that Western culture and traditions are only one of many. As Carolyn Brown argues in her essay, the critique that the Women's Movement made of our masculine-dominated culture is in many ways the same as the postmodernist attack on what they call 'the master narratives' of Western culture. But something paradoxical has happened in the lifetime of second wave feminism: its own critique has undermined the terms in which its rebirth was announced. Second wave feminism was perhaps the last of the radical movements that could emerge self-consciously modelled on the idea of a clear oppressor and oppressed, following the pattern of the class struggle, the colonial wars of liberation, and the black civil rights movement. The very universality of the oppression by gender that feminism attacked meant that the movement had rapidly to transform itself into something more complex and more diffuse. None of us are just women: we come from specific class, racial, economic, educational positions. The amount and location of power, the extent and nature of oppression in each of our lives varies enormously, and can only be understood in the context of all contingencies. And in the last two decades for many middle-class women in Western cultures, the overt disadvantages of being a woman have undoubtedly diminished. This is not to say that issues of political equality are no longer important, but that one has to remain aware that one of the gains, if that's the right word, for women has been that it is now much easier for a woman to become an oppressor. The political challenge is central as it always was. The Women's Movement was in some senses, I think, the most far-reaching of the liberation movements, because it argued fundamentally against a society structured on exploitation rather than co-operation. Those insights and that critique are as vital now as they have ever been.

Feminist theory at the moment is fluid and diverse. As Suzanne Moore has said recently, theories are always about what has passed.[12] They limp behind the present moment. Theories can only be models, essential but ephemeral. Yet sometimes they can seem like fractels, those wonderful equation-based computer drawings, which can go on to infinity by endlessly reproducing themselves, taking over the world in the same reductive pattern. The world is very different from twenty years ago: the bases of power have shifted, and so have ways of understanding them. Old certainties have gone, though new and perhaps equally repressive authoritarianisms have emerged, which in their term must be challenged. Harold Bloom, writing in the mid 1970s, saw a feminist critique as the destruction of all that he valued in the Western civilisation.

> Nor are there Muses, nymphs who know, still available to tell us the secrets of continuity, for the nymphs are certainly now departing. I prophesy though that the first true break with literary continuity will be brought about in generations to come, if the burgeoning religion of Liberated Woman spreads from its clusters of enthusiasts to dominate the West. Homer will cease to be the inevitable precursor, and the rhetoric and forms of our literature then may at last break from tradition.[13]

It's perhaps Bloom's rigidly linear model which makes despair his only conceivable response. We live in a richer world than he thinks, not one with a single vein of precious ore that we must mine, but with a range of 'differences of view', as Virginia Woolf called them, of traditions and possibilities.[14] The contributors to this book have different approaches, interests, backgrounds and viewpoints: it's the belief in the value of those differences which makes it possible for them to engage creatively with the question of the place of writing, of women's writing and of feminist writing in the future of our global culture. I don't want to attempt to sum up either those discussions or the essays here. The strength and excitement of these essays is their openness, their querying, their sense of living in a changing and evolving moment, of looking forward not backward, of drawing on past feminist theoretical critiques in order to move on to new ways of understanding.

Notes

1 Julia Kristeva, 'Histoires d'Amour', in Lisa Appignanesi (ed.), *ICA Documents I: Desire*, Institute of Contemporary Arts, London, 1984, p. 21.

2 Virginia Woolf, *A Room of One's Own* (1928), Penguin Modern Classics, Penguin Books, London, 1945, pp. 107, 108.

3 Kate Millett, *Sexual Politics* (1969), Sphere Books, London, 1971.
Mary Ellmann, *Thinking About Women* (1968), Virago Press, London, 1979.

4 Marilyn Butler, 'Feminist Literary Criticism, late-80s style', *Times Literary Supplement*, 11–17 March 1988, p. 283.

5 Tzvetan Todorov, trans. Richard Howard, *The Poetics of Prose* (1971), Basil Blackwell, Oxford, and Cornell University Press, NY, 1977.

6 Jonathan Culler, *The Pursuit of Signs: Semiotics, Literature, Deconstruction*, Routledge & Kegan Paul, London, 1981, p. 123.

7 Angela Carter herself has mixed feelings about this identification. See her interview with John Haffenden in *The Literary Review*, November 1984, and also the review I wrote of the film of *The Magic Toyshop*, based on an interview with her, in *Women's Review*, nos 14/15, December 1986/January 1987.

8 Mary Shelley, *Frankenstein* (1818), Penguin Books, London, 1985. Maurice Hindle's introduction to this edition deals very interestingly with this novel as science fiction.

9 Frederic Jameson, 'Ideology, Narrative Analysis and Popular Culture', in *Theory and Society*, no. 4, Winter 1977, p. 144.

10 Mary Jacobus, 'The Difference of View', in Mary Jacobus (ed.), *Women Writing and Writing about Women*, Croom Helm, and Barnes and Noble, 1979, p. 11.

11 See for example Terry Eagleton, 'Capitalism, Modernism and Postmodernism', *New Left Review*, no. 152, 1895, pp. 60–73.
Frederic Jameson, 'Postmodernism, or the Cultural Logic of Late Capitalism', *New Left Review*, no. 146, 1984, pp. 53–93.

12 Suzanne Moore, 'Here's looking at you, Kid', in Lorraine Gamman and Margaret Marshment (eds), *The Female Gaze: Women as Viewers of Popular Culture*, The Women's Press, London, 1988.

13 Harold Bloom, *A Map of Misreading*, Oxford University Press, Oxford and New York, 1975, p. 33.

14 Virginia Woolf, 'George Eliot', in *The Common Reader I*, Hogarth Press, London, 1984, p. 171.

FEMINIST CRITICISM
TWENTY YEARS ON

———◆———

CORA KAPLAN

I'm going to describe how I saw the situation of feminist criticism in the mid 1970s, and compare it with what is happening now.[1] Picking up on what Helen Carr has said in her introduction, one of the other great differences between women, besides those of race and class, is that of national culture. My national culture of origin is American, and when I gave this paper at the ICA in January 1988, I had just been back for a month, to the big Modern Language Association conference, which is where most teachers of literature in tertiary education find themselves in Christmas week in the United States, either giving papers or listening to them or trying to get a job – it's a meat market as well. One of the striking things that you could see there, and something which was the theme of rather many sessions at the MLA this year, was the notion of a sort of coming of age or generational change. There was even a session in which older feminist critics and younger feminist critics talked across the generations. Perhaps we could use this notion here, or at least the sense, not of coming of age, something which in the late 1970s feminist criticism was talking a lot about, but of ageing.

As we come up to twenty years of second wave feminism in the West, dating it probably not from 1968 as people want to do for neatness, but really, I would think more accurately, from 1969, which is certainly the date that's been taken in the United States, we feel that it's borne upon us to think about our history. Now that's a very interesting and ironic thing. Postmodernism declares that history is dead, and that all history read under the light of the 1980s is not history at all but simply belongs to a kind of curious present moment, with the loss of the notion of historical depth. And yet feminists, I think, are actually quite nervously trying to see where it is they have got to, and thinking that twenty years is a good traditional chunk of time in which to start to re-evaluate what's happened to them in all kinds of different areas, culture of course being one.

I think that one thing is that history comes on you with a great thump, like middle age; you suddenly look in the mirror and, Christ, there it is. You can't get away from it, you've got to deal with it. It isn't always a mirror you have to look in; it's very often your students' faces. I realise that the students I've been teaching in the last few years have known nothing but Thatcherism, and in the United States, nothing but Reaganism, really ever since they entered secondary school. As this has been their world ever since they came into adolescence and a sense of themselves as autonomous beings and as people who could think, there's an awful lot to be explained to them. You can't simply hand them texts from the last twenty years of feminism and assume that those texts all have somehow an easily accessible contemporary reading, and make the same sense for them as they did – and do – for you. You have to give them a historical account of the production of those texts; an account, I'm afraid, which also includes explaining to them what a social movement is about, what it feels like to be part of it, and more than that, what happens and what it feels like when it seems to disperse and come to an end in that particular form. Offering students that history is very sobering, partly because it is extremely hard to convey – hard to convey because the present moment doesn't legitimise that past; in fact today, on the left as well as on the right, there is no political euphoria. And it's hard to explain political euphoria. It's like trying to explain what it's like being in love. You either make people irritable or envious (I know, I've been trying to explain to them, so I know this is the effect it has on people). But in any case trying to do that in pedagogic terms with students in classes has been very instructive.

As my classes at Sussex often include mature students, older women and men, who actually lived through that moment, those discussions have become very interesting. You realise you can't simply hang on to the historic moment. It isn't just that you have to tell the younger students how it was, you have to objectify that moment and your place in it. Among other things you need to be very self-critical about how you turned it into a mythic moment of euphoria. I don't mean you should say it was naive or awful, but you need both properly to present its political excitement and possibilities, and also to critique your own history of it, and those histories which simply see it as a narrative decline or a narrative progress. So I think one of the things about the 1980s, especially 1988 and 1989, is that it is at many different registers a historic moment for feminist cultural critique. In saying this I'm drawing the net wider to include much more than the literary in that definition of culture, because I think that one has to do so.

I suppose what I want to pose is a few questions about difference, the difference between the late 1960s and the 1970s and now, without actually periodising too closely, or, as was very popular towards the end of the 1970s, trying to look at different kinds of feminist criticism, to distinguish, as Elaine Showalter did, gynocriticism, the criticism of women's writing from a critique of men's writing, and so forth. I don't want in that way to attempt to define categories or different orders of feminist criticism by whether it looks at different objects, either men's writing or women's writing, popular writing or the canon, or indeed, as I think Elaine Showalter very usefully did, to employ the different strategies of talking about woman as a reader or gender as a component of readership and gender as a component of writing. I don't think one can take pleasure in such categorising at the moment, as if we have so much feminism we can begin to give it some shape and tidy it up, as if it was a kitchen (to use a nice woman's image). I think it's extraordinarily untidy at the moment, both for positive reasons and for reasons that have to do with the general impoverishment of feminist political culture and alternative and radical political culture in the West. I am talking principally about the cultures I know – Britain and the United States and France a little bit. So instead of that kind of categorising I want just to remind those of you who were around then, and for those of you who weren't to try to suggest to you, what was the triangular shape of the relationship between the development of a feminist criticism, feminism as a social movement and women's writing; that is, the creative space and the new renaissance of women writing self-consciously as feminist writers inside that moment.

My talk at the MLA was about women's imaginative writing, and how that has shifted, but one of the things I started out by saying was that it seemed to me that in the 1970s those of us engaged in the feminist critical project, whatever bits of it we were looking at, if we were involved in the Women's Movement we *all* read poetry and novels as they came out much more than we read them now. We read them because those texts were part of the ongoing debate of the social movement of which we were part. In the middle of the 1970s you read a contemporary novel, whether it was American or British, because that novel was part of the different positions, of the ebb and flow of debate.

Feminist criticism, you must remember, was not institutionally located at all in Britain until the late 1970s and though in the United States that process began a few years earlier, it still took a long time. 1969 to 1979 was the period in which feminist cultural criticism gained a foothold within the institutions, and again there are cultural differences between the United States and Britain. Feminism in terms of its base in tertiary education started out in the United States in the humanities, which was much more open to it for various reasons, whereas here in Britain it started out more in the social sciences, and the humanities, and particularly English Literature, were the last bastion of resistance. This has been particularly the case within the universities, the highest point of the tertiary pyramid, where there were not only fewer interventions but also fewer women academics on the faculty who might be interested in teaching that kind of thing. In many though by no means all the polytechnics there were rather more women teaching literature; often they seemed to be less isolated if they displayed an interest in feminism than their university equivalents. In fact English as a field of study in Britain has been one of the most conservative of the humanities in certain ways and still is taught extremely conservatively at many British universities, though not so much any more at polytechnics. So most of the feminist critical work that was initially being done was extra-institutional. Even if you taught at a university, your work on feminist criticism was outside the institution; you did it at conferences and events organised by the Movement. And even in the United States where there was more of a growing institutional base, what you spoke into, in those early years, were conferences which were political in nature, rather than academic or purely professional. And, as I've said, when you read the imaginative writing that was being produced, again that was very much as a part of the ongoing debate about what different positions were developing within feminism, what strategies of action and practice. For example, those powerful debates between black and white feminists in the United States, as there were around class here in the mid and late 1970s. And then, with a few years gap, because of the different ways in which the social movements have developed in the two countries, there have been vigorous arguments around race within British feminism. All that engaged imaginative writing and feminist critical practice came out of much wider debates within feminism. As a feminist critic, at the back of all that you were doing and thinking about was this sense that you were creating a space not solely for a critical project, but for the imaginative project itself. Women who were talking about women's writing, whether it was older works like *Jane Eyre* and other nineteenth-century writing, or rethinking gender in Shakespeare, or bringing out old writers, or looking at the new edge of the representation of women in film and television, or at feminist theatre, were creating a space for the production of a cultural practice, a unified and dialectical cultural practice that spoke into and out of the imaginative project.

Of course in some ways in our culture the political awareness feminism has brought is clearly there. We now have a feminist language. We have the word 'sexist' which we definitely didn't have; we have a language about male power and sexual difference. I watched an episode of *Coronation Street* recently where most of the episode was given up to a women's strike in a small garment-making unit, and every single thing those women said assumed a women's language, a language around a gendered relationship between workers and power.[2] It was an anti-Thatcherite episode, an episode you couldn't have imagined on *Coronation Street* twenty years ago. Now that's partly market forces, with *Coronation Street* now being in competition with *Eastenders*, as *LA Law* is with *Cagney & Lacey*. But it was still a wholly different kind of women's talk which went on in that episode: it was about differentials, it was about male power, it was about women's solidarity or lack of it. There were the genteel and less genteel women, shop floor and union women, black and white women all there. That's not just a transformation of images but of audience awareness: putting that out to a huge audience of people who were expected to understand on some level – certainly to be educated to some extent but essentially to understand a public language which wasn't accessible or available or developed or had meanings twenty years ago.

It isn't just popular culture that assumes a feminist language. I would want to see what's happening on television as having a dialectic relationship with a new flowering of book culture, a flowering which the success of the feminist presses bears out. That same book culture was the medium for black movements and for feminism, and it's the proliferation of books, the development of new reading audiences, the intervention of women in popular genres which has further expanded that interaction. Those books then sell in vast quantities, which has then made it possible for those themes and ideas to get taken up by the more highly capitalised television and film, so there's now a dialogue between books and visual culture, which it is very important to recognise. Though again, so far as books are concerned, there are cultural differences between Britain and the United States. I thought the response to James Baldwin's death in December 1987 exemplified this. I wrote an obituary for *Marxism Today* in which I said that for me he changed the shape of writing in the 1960s, which is what Toni Morrison also said at greater length and with much eloquence in an obituary she wrote in the United States.[3] He made possible in part the space in which writers like Alice Walker and Toni Morrison could talk about sexual orientation, sexual politics and race all together. Black writers in general, but James Baldwin more than any single person, made a space for putting those issues together, made it possible to write about them in a popular way, and made it possible for a writer to be a political figure. What is striking is how in British cultural life the writer as political figure is entirely absent. No one knew how to write about Baldwin and his homosexuality, which was suppressed in all the articles about him. No one knew how to write about him as a great writer who was great because he was a politically engaged writer. In the United States it's quite different, both for black and feminist writers. People expect writing to be political. Feminist and black writing have changed the field of writing and the expectations of what writing is, and even under Reaganism that was an unchanged fact. But that hasn't happened here. That's why I say you have to look at different conjunctions. But unless you keep that history in mind and in play, you lose the sense of what change has been, and to lose a notion of real change is to lose the notion of future change too.

But in spite of this cultural awareness and politicised writing, that triangular relationship seems to have gone. That's what it felt like to me at the MLA this last visit. I've been to the MLA only three times, in 1979, 1983 and again in 1988. In 1979 there was a great, moving excitement about women's things. There were the beginnings of the alternative MLA, which was the feminist MLA. In 1983 it felt a little more established, but this time when you looked at the papers it felt as if 40 per cent of them had something about gender in them, and yet only a small proportion of them really seemed to be moved by any strong sense of what feminism was about. Gender has become a respectable thing to study. In the United States it has been institutionalised and professionalised, and now has a much higher 'academic' profile. I think that in many ways is a good thing and not a bad thing, I hasten to add. I'm not knocking it, and I don't think it's become part of the dominant. Now of course I didn't actually go to every one of those 40 per cent of papers about gender to discover what the politics were. Maybe all the ones on the Renaissance were political and quite a lot of ones on contemporary women's writing were not. It wouldn't be obvious from the titles or periods which papers had more of a political clout than others. There are courses which have feminism in the title which aren't very political, and others which are, called gender studies or women's studies. It's not so easy to separate them out into political or apolitical. I don't mean political narrowly, but in the sense that what is being taught connects up with what you might be doing now around those questions, that it is being taught in relation to a dynamic of what you might *do* or *produce* or *be* in some future conjuncture, rather than just as an object of study.

Yet feminist criticism seemed at the MLA this time to have been cut off both from cultural production itself, from what women are actually writing, and from a political movement. I remember that at earlier MLAs there were a lot more living women writers, both being discussed and on the platform. This time the MLA had a rule so that Alice Walker and other writers who wanted to appear and read their work, couldn't do so unless they paid the admission fee, which at the MLA is ninety dollars. Many of them of course didn't want to do that, as in any case they weren't getting paid to speak. There seemed a big division between the most exciting new writing by black American writers, and feminist writers, trying now to write in their literary texts chronicles of different kinds of history and gender. I was thinking there about Toni Morrison's book *Beloved*, which is out here now, which is about a slave narrative.[4] Although at one level it's about a woman escaping from slavery in the nineteenth century, it's also a historical novel in which the history of feminism is mapped as another text. Another similar novel is *Dessa Rose*, by the black writer Sherley-Anne Williams.[5] There are also the two big blockbuster novels by Marge Piercy and Valerie Miner about the Second World War, which take account of a lot of feminist research on the Second World War.[6] What seems to be happening is that these novels are using all that feminist historiography and cultural critique actually as a basis for a new kind of historical novel, one that uses all the research that's come out. But feminist critics aren't reading them. Or if they're reading them it's not with the same attention or the same centrality any more. It's as if the project about cultural practice and imaginative practice, and the practice of criticism have somehow got cut off from each other.

Now I know someone's going to come back and say that's all the fault of post-structuralism and the fault of the kind of criticism that critics like myself have used – that if we'd only stuck with an older humanism those things would still be integrated. I don't think it's that simple, and I think it's something that needs discussing. Just as I think all genre can be appropriated for different political ends, so that a genre isn't by itself reactionary or radical, it seems to me that different kinds of critical intervention have all been very productive within feminism in different ways, but all can be appropriated to a more conservative and a more locked off or to a more open and radical way of thinking. It's partly the general politics of the time that's doing that cutting off; partly it is the establishment and the professional legitimation in some spheres. But partly in other ways, it seems to me, it's a problem which does go back to the question that I hope is going to be posed by the rest of these essays, which is what kind of novels should a feminist write now? There's a new book out by Hazel Carby called *Reconstructing Womanhood: The Emergence of the Afro-American Woman Novelist*, in which one of her nineteenth-century figures poses the question: if you are a black woman interested in furthering the cause of black women, why write a novel?[7] I think that's the question that needs to be opened up, together with, why write criticism? It's important because I think in a sense that while we're sure of what we're doing while we're talking about looking at gender in current cultural practices that have appropriated feminist language, and the backlash against it in popular culture, it's not so clear any more what we are doing with traditional literary forms, and with feminist critique in general. That seems to me to have a certain uncertainty around it, and the uncertainty is about the dissolution of that earlier very strong three-way dialogue.

Notes

1 This is an edited transcript of the actual talk Cora Kaplan gave.
2 *Coronation Street* is a long established British TV soap opera set in Manchester. *Eastenders* is a more recent soap opera set in the East End of London. Both deal with working-class life, and when *Eastenders* was first introduced it was spectacularly successful. Now both shows have lost out badly to the Australian import *Neighbours*.
3 Cora Kaplan, 'James Baldwin', *Marxism Today*, January 1988.
4 Toni Morrison, *Beloved*, Chatto & Windus, London, and Knopf, NY, 1987.
5 Sherley-Anne Williams, *Dessa Rose*, William Morrow & Co, NY, and Macmillan, London, 1987.
6 Valerie Miner, *All Good Women*, Methuen, London, 1987 and Crossing Press, Trumansburg, NY, 1987.
Marge Piercy, *Gone to Soldiers: a novel of the Second World War*, Michael Joseph, London, 1987, and Summit Books, NY, 1987, Fawcett, NY, 1988.
7 Hazel Carby, *Reconstructing Womanhood: The Emergence of the Afro-American Woman Novelist*, Oxford University Press, Oxford, 1987.

PUTTING ON THE STYLE: FEMINIST CRITICISM IN THE 1990s

ALISON LIGHT

Has feminist criticism come of age? Or is it rapidly disappearing over the hill?[1] If we take Cora Kaplan's date of 1969 as the birth of second wave feminism, should we be sounding a twenty-one gun salute as 1990 approaches, or looking, with some trepidation, into the future? Speaking to a room packed with women at the Institute of Contemporary Arts in London, it might have been tempting to start lighting the candles, and yet it was impossible not to be struck immediately by the very different generations of feminists there, on the platform and in the hall, whose lively presence suggested a rich potential for disagreement, as well as a cause for celebration. A relative newcomer to feminist literary work myself, I spoke alongside Cora Kaplan, who had herself been the moving force behind my returning to university in 1981 as a maturish student, and the tutor who had encouraged my interest in women's writing. Apart from my seniors and mentors, the room was also crowded with women ten or fifteen years younger than me, and I found myself wondering how far we could have a common project, or even a common language in which to talk about feminist literary criticism – let alone feminism.

As one of that 'middle' generation in her early thirties, I came just too late for the great euphoric moments, those times in the late 1960s and early 1970s when feminism might be learnt through a recognisably shared and coherent public moment of collective identification. My own starting point, via a women's writing group, was rather more at arm's length from the campaigning activities of the Women's Liberation Movement, and it was through academic work that I first encountered the solidarity that is possible between women with shared political goals. The support and encouragement I found was no less liberating for keeping me on the whole off the streets and enticing me into the library; nor was it, in any case, divorced from what went on in the bedroom. Yet whilst I am living proof, if I may put it so grandiloquently, of the expansion of feminist ideas in the 1980s, I am also aware of an opposite, conflicting feeling amongst colleagues, amongst friends; a feeling that feminism is now somehow adrift, unanchored and cut off in crucial ways from the everyday texture of women's lives, a sense that the crude but powerful notion of being 'post-feminist' may have some real purchase. We may have arrived in full force on the cultural scene, even packing some of the more sophisticated metropolitan venues, but we may nevertheless be even more separated from other forms of cultural practice and from effective forms of political intervention. How in the 1990s will our literary and cultural work relate to 'the great outside'?

It seems indisputable that 'the woman question' is now taken seriously and has a credibility that it simply didn't have when I was a student in 1981. Certainly this is true in the polytechnic where I work and where we have a number of courses running which are informed by feminist ideas. Feminism is at once everywhere and nowhere. It doesn't have a unified body any more (even in the sense of being recognisably the 'Women's Movement' – that phrase has gone out of fashion), or a national conference, but yet if it seems fragmented, those fragments are, I think, symptomatic of a much wider spread of feminist ideas and feminist politics too. There is an attention to sexual difference across a number of forms of cultural practice and production that wasn't there seven or eight years ago. And certainly you could argue that feminism is much less cloistered, much less contained within academia: that it doesn't belong to privileged groups of people in the same kinds of ways.

When I was suggesting this to myself, it seemed impossible that on the face of it things should have changed so much so fast, so I dragged out of a file a letter which I wrote in 1979, just before I gave up work to become a student again. I was working as a technician at the BBC and the letter, written in a moment of

cheek and some feminist anger to the Head of Productions and
Planning – whom I'd never met – proposed that he should put on
a magazine programme for women. His reply was a very kindly
rebuke, and a fairly patronising one, saying that obviously 'we'
don't need programmes about women; they are covered by other
programmes; these are human issues, not female ones – you
know how the argument goes. And he finished by hoping that
he wasn't being too discouraging, but (in so many words) would
I please go back to the tape-deck? That was 1979. I was contrast-
ing this in my mind to reading in the *Guardian* a few days earlier
the producers of a new women's magazine programme, *Woman
In View*, saying more or less the complete opposite: that women
nowadays are 'into everything', everyone wants women's 'stuff'.
What a severe contrast! Clearly, the idea of women, and the idea
of feminism, has become immensely marketable, and this is not
the least significant of the shifts which we might like to bear in
mind during our discussions.

In 1979 the books of feminist literary criticism – even that term
was a bizarre and unwieldy one – could be numbered on one
hand. In my case it included pioneer works like Ellen Moers's
Literary Women and Elaine Showalter's *A Literature Of Their Own*;
and actually having those two books on my shelf at home caused
my then boyfriend and I to split up, they were such obtrusive
volumes.[1] We were working, I think even then, very much from
an awareness of absences; what we wanted to do was put
women in where there were no women. We were trying to write
whole new histories and were part, if you like, of a counter-
culture. It did feel like that – even I can remember that. That
situation has changed in ten years almost unimaginably. Now it
seems that feminism has in some ways become a growth industry. Despite educational cuts, feminist courses continue to be put
on the books (a new MA in 'Gender Divisions' is being launched
at Middlesex Polytechnic, I believe), feminist publishing seems
to be thriving, and there is a currency of reference, and a much
more popular awareness too, of what it means to think about
feminism and to think about sexual difference. It no longer
sounds outlandish or just plain silly to talk about 'sexual politics'.

It obviously isn't the case that we don't still fight the old battles
and have the same old arguments in our lives and in our places of
work as we always did. Nor that for many women the feeling of

living outside the mainstream isn't still their most powerful one. Nevertheless it does matter hugely, and it certainly matters to me in my teaching, that we now have a whole panoply of outlets: that books exist and can be referred to, that departments exist, that there are women's bookshops, cafés, discos, holiday homes, taxi services – that we are no longer working in the dark as lonely rebels. More importantly perhaps, some of the people I teach, who, as Cora Kaplan pointed out, may have been born in 1968, have also grown up with feminism. For them, feminism, far from being a new taking-off point, a moment of great self-discovery as it was for me, is in fact a bit of a bore, something they have lived with – often literally in the form of their mothers – for the last twenty years. And that is again an important historical shift.

To put it rather less negatively, I'm constantly stunned by the articulacy of younger women, their fluency within a certain kind of political discourse; it wasn't one that I had when I was at university, and I have a real respect for it. There are good things about having been able to take feminism for granted. Yet over and against this articulacy, this confidence and this self-possession, I've also got to think that, even in my few years, the women's group at the Polytechnic is no more, the sexual harassment campaign has folded, that personally I don't belong to any women-only groups or know of any at the Polytechnic (though they exist on a larger circuit). There are real severances here. That sense of plenty is also met by a sense of loss.

One of the ways in which I find it problematic simply to celebrate the growth of feminist literary criticism in the 1980s is that I have frequently been quite unexcited by some of the recent volumes we have produced and even, on occasion, alarmed by what already looks like a tiredness of sentiment creeping in. Any political movement has to guard against being imprisoned in its own pieties, and against electing, for the enjoyment of security, the comfortable belief in being one of the chosen few. Feminist literary criticism is, as we know, quite capable of creating its own canons and schools, which can intimidate and exclude new writers and thinkers, tying them up in knots of deference and immobilising them as effectively as the kowtowing to crusty professors did in the bad old days. If the day ever comes that any woman feels she cannot put pen to paper without being conversant with Lacan's mirror phase (examples, of course, are unfair) then we may as well stop the bus and get off. Twenty years of work, however rich, cannot take on the mantle of incontrovertible authority. Repeating such truths as we have ought to make us more aware of how radically incomplete they are. Being a feminist, as I understand it, should not be like being in church: there are no blasphemies, no ritual incantations, no heretics and no saints.

We might want to think too about the possibility of our being part of a much more transforming set of changes which have been taking place in the last decade or so. Our political reach as teachers, students, critics, may be losing its hold, not simply because of the danger of our work congealing into a new kind of academic or political orthodoxy, but because academic work itself, and the whole sphere of education, is being radically decentred. This would entail a lengthy discussion, but there is a sense in which education, in the way in which many of us have understood it and experienced it, has, I think, become marginal to some notions of cultural production; 'prosperity', in the words of one enthusiastic practitioner, is now 'the core of the curriculum'.[2] Educational philosophies, which have seen learning as something apart from, or in excess of economic controls and financial accountability, have recently been subject to the most rigorous attack since the very idea of public education first gained ground in the last century. The generation of intellectual argument, of critical and wayward intelligences, and alternative knowledges, may well be shifting elsewhere, back to where education always was for many people for many centuries – outside of the realm of official institutions and the library. So the proliferating discussions of the idea of gender difference in the media, popular cinema, the press, are also part of this shift whereby education is no longer necessarily where the action is, or indeed where the knowledge is, where people are learning their social values, or learning to think about sexuality, learning to think themselves masculine or feminine. So that's a larger cultural displacement in whose wake feminist academia may also be caught.

It may go some way to help account for the sense of loss and of disenchantment which older feminist teachers seem to be feeling when we really consider the very different status too that the whole idea of working with books has for young people now.

Like many other grammar school girls, I know myself to have been made by books; all my earliest identifications were with girls (or boys) in stories, and books were the way out of my home and, for better or for worse, out of my class. Nowadays girls are as likely to fall asleep dreaming of becoming a car mechanic like Charlene in *Neighbours*, as they are wondering what Katy did. And they haven't just swapped one narrative for another: a television serial takes place in quite a different universe from a story-book. We are only just beginning to think about the differences. In the 1970s feminist criticism was still very much in love with the library, and I suspect that we still have a great deal invested in it. It is hard to see how we can continue to change without some loss on our part.

If there is any mileage in the thinking about the relegation of education, or of certain notions of what education might do for people or offer people, and if we wanted to say that for many people education is now on the sidelines of their imaginative life, that television, for instance, is a much more powerful source of learning for children than print, then that need not become an argument for a kind of 'new realism' for feminists; that we should all rush off to produce television programmes – I don't think that is desirable, even if it were possible. It might mean, however, that if feminist literary criticism is to survive into the 1990s (and I'm quite agnostic as to whether it should or not) it has got to be informed by a sense of the marginality of some of its own ideologies, and areas of production, and at the same time – which is difficult – to be aware also of the new and multi-faceted ways in which sexual difference is still on the cultural agenda.

Whereas in the past we saw ourselves as doing a restoration job, countering absences with our own new presence, now it seems we are having to deal with a plethora of representations, a flood of presences, in which the strong, independent woman greets us from a poster on the tube escalator in her new Barrett show home, and may even get to be Prime Minister. It seems worth considering whether for many people feminism has not indeed become a kind of contemporary *style*, and that it is primarily through the mediated form of images, rather than through more orthodox and more acceptably political activities, that a sense of being feminist, or of knowing feminism, may now take root. At its worst we might want to dismiss this as what public relations calls 'image-management', where feminism appears as style, emptied of its history and its political theory to be appropriated by consumer capitalism in the most opportunist way. That's partly why we may feel slightly uneasy at the glossy feminist paperbacks in the ICA lobby. But it is an inadequate response.

A more provocative approach might take the new miniskirt, the wearing of the 1980s mini, and what that might mean for people nowadays. In one piece Suzanne Moore suggested ways in which the new miniskirt might be worn differently from the old. The new miniskirt is worn with a kind of streetwise air, and a sense of being wise to sexual politics which makes the wearing of the 1960s mini appear naive and childlike: little girls in short skirts. It is as though the contemporary mini can be worn, as it were, in a post-feminist way.[3] What fascinated me was that in the course of marking essays on magazine analysis I came across *Playboy* (November 1987), which an enterprising student had submitted, and there was an article with a very similar argument. Photographs of women in extremely short skirts were accompanied by a text in which the influence of feminism was mentioned, and which proposed that the miniskirt could now be worn by women who may choose to look inviting but also choose to say no. Both pieces can be read as a curious follow-up to that earlier rallying-call of the Women's Movement – the woman's right to say 'no' – but more significantly, to carry with them the rather disturbing notion that feminism can be a sort of choice; something you can take or leave, something you might (literally) try on for size, something, moreover, you can play with.

The model of fashion journalism is not a flippant one, though I suspect it is still for many feminists an uncomfortable, even upsetting place to turn to. Perhaps for some of us our deepest fear is not so much that feminism will become a new orthodoxy, as that it won't. Fashion gives us a very useful set of insights into the playing with images which seems to characterise how this culture understands itself. It thrives on immediacy, on visual impact, on dispensability, on redefining and recycling the new, and it often brings together dissonant, even contradictory styles and references. The new mini, for example, is frequently worn with leggings. Contemporary fashion mixes its messages into a montage in which no single style is discernible, and from which no simple political position can be read off.

Think of the difference between the covers of magazines like *Cosmopolitan* in the late 1970s, through to something like *Options* in the 1980s which rejected the libertarian sexuality (though one never free from the need for male approval) of the Cosmo girl in favour of a cooler, more professional grown-up woman for whom sex is one of many [sic] options. Both were clearly informed by feminism, however modified. Yet compare these with magazines like *Blitz*, or *The Face*, or *i-D*, where the interest of the magazines is with the appeal of the images themselves. *i-D*, as its title suggests, assumes that identity is something which can be played around with, that it is fragmented and fragmentary, that all you can do is choose between different appearances, different styles. It is visually both sophisticated and knowing. How do we find points of connection here with a feminist struggle which has always to some extent needed a unified narrative of the past, and a coherent and collective set of aims? Should we find this montage and flux alarming or cheering? Can it still be 'politicising'? Or doesn't that matter?

In fact at thirty-two I am already a member of that older generation who finds it disconcerting if a woman has cropped hair and wears bomber-jackets and isn't a feminist. When I had my ears pierced, it was ironically a blow for freedom, and involved no little moral fervour. The idea that it is possible to juggle with appearances couldn't be further from one version of a politics which looks for a complete identity and way of being in political activities. I have always found the notion of a lifestyle politics, in which feminism is something which you eat, drink, and put on your walls, both seductive and coercive. Ultimately I find any refusal of dogmatism heartening. Not to be tied to authorities of our own making – to be post-feminist in that sense – will be quite a relief. But if deconstruction can be liberating, it can also be debilitating. All these changes do seem to rely upon certain kinds of individualism, and to signal the end of a sense of collective purpose, or of community interest. At the same time they increase our awareness of how fictional the coherence of past struggles actually was. Does that also mean the end of what we have always meant – at least in the industrialised West – by 'politics'? Certainly, neither the mythologising of the heady days of pure feminist sisterhood, nor the simple invocation of 'pleasure' and 'play' as the highest good seem satisfactory ways forward.

Often it is the very accessibility and omnipresence of potentially positive images which now cause us problems. The 1980s television duo, *Cagney & Lacey*, is a good case in point. This is a series which could not have been imagined before the impact of the modern Women's Movement. The police detective heroines are good friends, strong-minded and articulate, and have managed to encounter most of the issues on the feminist agenda in the course of their immensely popular adventures: rape, abortion, child abuse, have all been the subject of special programmes. The unequal position of women at work, the tension between private lives and public position, the relationship of women to power – all these have been constant themes in the series. It would be hard, I think, to underestimate the force of such images and the powerful appeal they made across a heterodox audience of millions of viewers. The actresses themselves were all but mobbed when they appeared recently on the Terry Wogan chat show on prime-time BBC TV; the audience, which was noticeably female, screamed, cheered and applauded, especially when Cagney swore on the air.

Our own analyses are thankfully now able to take such phenomena seriously; it is no longer liable to cause uproar and amazement in feminist circles if you admit to reading romances. Indeed, *Cagney & Lacey* featured on the covers of both the feminist periodical *Spare Rib*, and the alternative London magazine, *City Limits*. Why then is there a feeling of stalemate about some of our discussions? Are we not still inclined towards a rather noble idealism in our own writing, one which can lay the dead hand of ideological soundness on our analyses? It's as though, having switched off the television, we feel duty-bound to point out the inadequacy of such images (the limitations of *Cagney & Lacey*'s liberalism, for example, or of their being representatives of 'law and order'), and our delight is quickly swamped by distaste. If we're not careful, the only pleasure we can allow ourselves is that of the kill-joy. Yet it is this disjunction which needs speculating upon; analysis won't make it go away: the contrareity is actually what is interesting.

Part of the trouble, ironically, is precisely the widespread take-up of feminist ideas. In the last twenty years we've seen feminism wrenched out of context, distorted and commodified, as well as welcomed by people, and in places, where we would least expect allegiance to our movement. This seems a painful, but inevitable part of political growth. In fact, I would argue that it is really at this point that our politics comes alive. In any case, unless we want to retreat into a nunnery, we cannot keep our positions pure, and the vexed question of just how ideologically unsound *Cagney & Lacey* is, will have to remain unanswered. If we rightly don't want to indulge either in an undiscriminating populism, or in a patrician disdain for 'mass' culture, then I suspect that we need to see that it is precisely the unresolvable and the unmanageable contradictions in these images which makes them appealing in the first place. We cannot tidy up the mess of identifications and conflicting meanings which such images offer women; the best we can do is to revel in the mixture, and try to understand its composition as accurately as we can. If that's sitting on the fence, then I suggest we lay in a good supply of cushions.

Given the tendency for such images to be dissevered from the places and the histories of their production, the usefulness – and the difficulties – of genre studies, in its new sense as the study of the popular, is apparent. Genre studies seems to me to be useful precisely as a way of prising free and remapping a multiplicity of cultural forms and images. It can give us a way of moving beyond the fixity and authority of any one form of representation, of breaking open great traditions, allowing us to realign questions of value, of what constitutes high culture or low, the serious and the trivial, the masculine and the feminine; genre can invert and dissolve some of those oppositions in favour of a much broader set of pluralities, driving a wedge into a closed world of clerical distinctions. But genre studies can also be a baggy monster, or a convenient holdall into which we throw a pile of very loosely connected items, divorcing them from their individual meanings. I think it is worth pondering the pros and cons of a book on women and detection, for example, which has room for both Miss Marple and her knitting, and *Cagney & Lacey* toting their New York hardware. Or where the 'Gothic' can be so expanded as to include eighteenth-century novels, nineteenth-century potboilers, Harlequin romances, and contemporary soap operas. Genre studies is a fashionable and easily marketable form of literary criticism, especially when it comes in the shape of the edited collection of individual essays, though as a contributor to this volume it may seem ungracious of me to say so. It is, we have to admit, a cheap and speedy way to publish. It can give a deceptive equivalence to what are actually very different appearances in literary and cultural history. Perhaps it would be more radical to consider what Agatha Christie, for example, has in common with other writers of the 1930s – her breezy dialogue which smacks of the West End stage, her 'Little Englandism' – than with crime writers from divergent pasts and different cultural milieux. Genre studies can too easily succumb to the lure of contemporaneity and the thrill of immediacy.

I would like to see feminist criticism in the 1990s develop ways of coping with what in the West is offered to us as a 'culture of plenty', a culture of abundance and choice, which is certainly how Margaret Thatcher sells her own ideological bargain and packages consumer capitalism for us. When I think of the work within feminism which has most excited me in the last five or six years, it's actually been writing which doesn't fit into disciplines, nor, strictly speaking, into genre studies either; work which is anti-nomian, which sits perhaps uneasily in amongst a mix and match of perspectives and theories, and which isn't dutiful nor deferential. A book, for example like Carolyn Steedman's *Landscape For A Good Woman*, which despite being about biography and autobiography, manages to show how troublesome and fragile such categories are.[4] Beatrix Campbell's *Iron Ladies* also springs to mind.[5] I suspect that if feminist criticism of whatever kind is going to survive, it will need to keep on opening itself out, and move beyond its own boundaries.

Finally, with retrospectives of the 1960s already upon us, it does seem that our capacity to turn the past into images is growing, together with our need to do so. Perhaps because we are finding it harder and harder to feel those continuities from our present-day lives back into our past, we create a constant barrage of anniversaries and red-letter days to keep us in touch. Ironically, the past seems to be coming closer all the time, just when our connections with it are more and more severed. With twenty years of recent, self-conscious history already being chronicled, a feminist politics can have a wider sweep of reference now and many more channels for its expression, however much it is arguably less rooted and less anchored. I wonder then how we might feel about a feminism which ends up delighting and inspiring the young women of the year 2000 only in the form of videos, or weekend stays in their local Heritage Centre where they can experience 'how we were then'?

Notes

1 Ellen Moers, *Literary Women*, The Women's Press, London, 1978.
  Elaine Showalter, *A Literature of Their Own*, Virago, London, 1978.
2 John Rae, 'Prosperity – that's the core of the curriculum', *Evening Standard*, Tuesday 1 December, 1987, p. 7.
3 Suzanne Moore, 'Mini-politics: Saying No In Public', *New Statesman*, 18–25 December, 1987, p. 26.
4 Carolyn Steedman, *Landscape For A Good Woman*, Virago, London, 1986.
5 Beatrix Campbell, *The Iron Ladies: Why do Women Vote Tory?*, Virago, London, 1987.

PART II

---◆---

Decoding the Genres

TRACKING DOWN THE PAST: WOMEN AND DETECTIVE FICTION

———◆———

ROSALIND COWARD and LINDA SEMPLE

Introduction

Until very recently all the critical writing about Thrillers – an all-purpose generic term which includes mysteries, detective fiction and spy stories – would lead you to believe that the vast majority of important work in this area was produced by men. The litany begins with Edgar Allan Poe who is often regarded as the 'Father of Detective Fiction'. Next comes Arthur Conan Doyle whose Sherlock Holmes made detective fiction so hugely popular. Ronald Knox laid down the ten golden rules for writing detective fiction for the Detection Club in 1929.[1] In the 1930s, the United States produced its own distinctive variant of detective fiction, what has become known as the 'Hard-Boiled' school with its wise-cracking Gumshoe anti-heroes. Francis Iles is said to have written the first 'inverted' crime novel, *Malice Afore-thought* (where you know whodunnit but the puzzle is how). And, very frequently, it is a list of men's names which is given when critics are asked who has made the genre great – Simenon, Erle Stanley Gardner, Michael Innes, Rex Stout and Mickey Spillane.

The Golden Age tends to present problems for this kind of criticism.[2] It is traditionally dated from the first novel of Agatha Christie (*The Mysterious Affair at Styles* in 1920) to the last by Dorothy L. Sayers (*Busman's Honeymoon* in 1937), a definition which draws attention to the importance of women writers at this time.[3] After all, it would be impossible to talk of this period without mentioning at least three other women writers – Ngaio Marsh, Margery Allingham and Josephine Tey. The problem is duplicated in contemporary times. All criticism is agreed that detective fiction has received a most extraordinary boost from three women writers – P. D. James, Ruth Rendell and Patricia Highsmith. Not only have they revived the popularity of crime fiction but many critics also claim that their writing has blurred the earlier distinctions between 'genre fiction' (seen as lowbrow and inferior) and serious literature.

Some critics have of course remarked on the presence of women writers in the area of detective fiction. But it is only recently that anyone has begun to point out both the extent and the significance of this presence. At every moment in the history of detective fiction there is a plethora of women writers, many of whom have been allowed to go out of print, but whose numbers hint at a hidden tradition.[4] This search for a hidden tradition of women crime writers has in part been fuelled by the revival of interest in women writers in general. Feminist criticism argued that many women writers had disappeared from print simply because their gender allowed negative critical values to operate. Their discovery led to the successful foundation of the Virago Modern Classics and Pandora's 'Mothers of the Novel' series. Far from an absence of women writers, numerous examples could be found of women neglected simply because critics would not take women's writing seriously.

Detective fiction itself can provide a clear example of this devaluation of women's writing with the fate of the 'Had I But Known Novel' – a description given by Ogden Nash in the *New Yorker* magazine. According to Nash and subsequent critics, this genre is almost invariably written by women and involves a female sleuth who unwittingly places herself and others in danger. Somewhere towards the end of the book, the heroine usually utters some variant of the remark, 'Had I but known then what I know now I would not have . . .' The phrase was rapidly taken up by reviewers and critics as a way of dismissing novels with this structure. It meant that they dismissed much of Mary Roberts Rinehart's output (whose work included the best selling *The Circular Staircase*) as well as Daphne du Maurier's *Rebecca*.[5] Even today, in more traditional critical approaches to detective fiction, a novel can be dismissed as a 'Had I But Known', a dismissal simultaneously suggesting inadequacy and female authorship.

But the current revival of interest in detective fiction is fuelled by another element as well as the critical revival of women's fiction. Perhaps more important has been the renaissance of detective fiction writing itself spearheaded by women. Not only has 'quality' detective fiction been dominated by P. D. James, Ruth Rendell and Patricia Highsmith but, more unexpectedly, there has been the immense success of *feminist* crime novels. With the appearance first in the United States and then in Britain of what seemed a whole new style of thriller – early Kate Fansler mysteries by Amanda Cross and *Murder in the English Department* by Valerie Miner – there were suddenly novels satisfying both as thrillers and for the political questions they raised.[6] In *Murder in the English Department*, for example, the investigation of the murder was also the investigation of sexual politics in academia.

Writers like Mary Wings and Barbara Wilson have both furthered the cause of this kind of writing with their plausible feminist sleuths – Emma Victor and Pam Nilsen respectively. And both have demonstrated how well feminist politics can be integrated into the structure of detective fiction. Barbara Wilson's *Sisters of the Road* is a vivid example of this; the novel blurs the usual distinctions between sleuth and victim in order to make powerful points about women's vulnerability to male violence.[7] Both these writers heralded the appearance of a sort of genre within a genre when women writers, like Katherine V. Forrest and Sarah Dreher, also integrated lesbianism (and even lesbian erotica) into their plots.[8]

This renaissance of crime led by women writers has pushed several questions to the forefront of our consciousness. One is whether women in fact have always dominated crime writing and their importance has simply been neglected because of sexism within critical attitudes. And if it is the case that women have always excelled, not just recently, then why is it that women are so good at crime? A third question follows. Is there anything in the genre and in women's particular relation to the genre which might have warned us that contemporary writers could use it to such political ends?

Tracking Down the Past

There is certainly plenty of support for the thesis that women have not only been present in detective fiction but that they have been enormously important, perhaps even dominant within the genre. At every moment in the history of detective fiction women writers have been found, many of whom were remarkably popular and influential in their period although lost to subsequent generations. Anna Katherine Green, an American writer, wrote *The Leavenworth Case* in 1878, popularly believed to be the first detective novel written by a woman.[9] *The Leavenworth Case* is hard going for the contemporary reader, being overwritten and full of clichés but Anna K. Green can be given some credit for having introduced the first 'elderly spinster' detective, Amelia Butterworth, in her other novels.

In fact it would be possible to produce earlier contenders for the title of first woman detective novelist; cases can be made for *East Lynne* by Mrs Henry Wood (1861), *Lady Audley's Secret* by Mary Braddon (1862) and *The Dead Letter* by Seeley Regester (1866). Only the latter has a true tale of detection at its centre; the others could just as easily be described as gothic, romantic or sensation fiction. But this fact only illuminates the difficulty of rigid definitions of the genre. Late nineteenth-century detective fiction is often characterised by the blurred lines between gothic, romance, macabre and detection. An example of this is Wilkie Collins' *The Woman in White*, with its graveyard scenes, madness, secret Italian brotherhood and devoted love.[10] It was only in the 1880s and 1890s that detective fiction began to acquire the attributes of a distinctive genre, whose narrative format was predictable and geared economically towards the solution of a crime.

Women writers made their mark as soon as the genre began to take on its characteristic form, L. T. Meade co-wrote popular medical crime stories, and Baroness Orczy attempted to rival Conan Doyle with the creation of *Lady Molly of Scotland Yard*, Lady Molly didn't catch on in the way Sherlock Holmes did, but Baroness Orczy's other detective novel, *The Old Man in the Corner*, is certainly worthy of some critical attention.[11] Not only does it have as its heroine a female journalist but the overall design of the book is extremely ingenious. The journalist meets up with an old man in a café who claims to have the answers to several notorious unsolved crimes. Like Sherlock Holmes the old man has done this simply by the process of logical deduction and no active involvement. The denouement of the book enmeshes the investigations of the journalist and the old man in an extremely interesting, perhaps even radical way.

Shortly afterwards, another woman writer rose to prominence. Marie Belloc Lowndes is best known for her novel *The Lodger* (1913) which is a brilliant exercise in suspense writing, involving a woman's suspicions that Jack the Ripper is lodging in her house.[12] Alfred Hitchcock recognised the powerful control of suspense when he used the novel for the bases of one of his earliest films. It is also one of the few novels from this early period which has recently been reprinted. It is interesting to note that several of the novels by women from this time were made into films, such as *The Wheel Spins*, which became *The Lady Vanishes* and *The Circular Staircase*, which became *The Bat*, a fact which bears witness to the popularity of these books.[13]

From the 1930s onwards, it is only an act of wilful blindness which could overlook the enormous importance of women writers. We have already mentioned the best known from the Golden Age. But there were many other excellent writers whose careers (extending into the 1940s and 1950s) challenge the conventional definitions of the Golden Age – Elizabeth Daly, Josephine Bell, Christianna Brand, Charlotte Armstrong, Hilda Lawrence, Ursula Curtiss, Mignon G. Eberhardt and Gladys Mitchell to name but a few. It is not difficult to make out a case for Christianna Brand as at least an equal of Agatha Christie in her complex plotting amongst closed communities – an evacuated hospital in *Green For Danger* and a family in *London Particular*. Nor is it far-fetched to suggest that some of these forgotten writers actually used the detective fiction form much more adventurously and productively than the more well-known writers. Josephine Bell, for example, wrote with the personal knowledge of a doctor specialising in drug-related problems and produced a brilliant study of London dockside, working-class life in *The Port of London Murders*. Hilda Lawrence, on the other hand, subverted the conventional detective novel narration in *Death of a Doll* to give the novel over to more atmospheric and psychological concerns.[14]

It would be possible, but not very illuminating, to continue at this stage with yet more examples of these many gifted women crime writers who had been allowed to go out of print. But there are more useful issues to turn over in relation to this hidden wealth. Perhaps the most important is whether or not the prominence of these writers carries any critical or political significance. Does the sheer volume of women writers in this genre tell us anything about women or detective fiction? In other words, is there anything special in the form which attracts women? And do these large numbers of women indicate a 'progressive' presence, one that might have hinted at feminist writers' ease with the form? In short, is there any point of contact between these early women writers and the current wave of contemporary women writers?

Are Women Writers always progressive?

There's a branch of feminist criticism which insists that detective fiction was extremely conservative until the emergence of the new feminist writers of the 1970s and 1980s. There's obviously some accuracy in this. Classic detective fiction usually starts with a disruption of the status quo and proceeds to a discovery (and eradication) of the perpetrator of this disruption. Usually the 'establishment' – the police, and the judiciary – are the forces which restore order and stability. In 'classic' detective fiction, the disruption takes place in closed hierarchical communities, is solved by the police or an amateur detective who is also an establishment figure, and ends with the restoration of the old hierarchies, The thriller from this position could be seen as the last bastion of racism, imperialism, outmoded class attitudes, sanitised violence, sexism, too much respect for authority and an unhealthy tendency to see moral issues in absolute terms. Attributing to detective fiction such conservative forms tends to imply rather negative reasons for women's prominence in the genre. It would suggest that women writers are best within safe, repetitive genres with conservative implications.

But these views are founded on two errors. One is a too-scanty knowledge of the history of detective fiction and women's place within it. The other is a far too rigid interpretation of the detective fiction genre. On the contrary we would assert that the boundaries of the detective fiction genre, like any genre, are relatively fluid and do not necessarily have conservative implications. Only an extraordinarily fertile and productive genre could have spread worldwide as detective fiction has done, with such very different developments, from the Catalan writer Maria Antònia Oliver who writes collectively, to such avant-garde writers as Alain Robbe-Grillet in France and Umberto Eco and Leonardo Sciascia in Italy, who rework the genre to explore the nature of narrative itself. What's more, in the British tradition women seem to have always been at the forefront of a radical use of the genre, both in form and content. After all, even Agatha Christie, often upheld as the most conservative of writers, created at least three radical departures from the form in *Ten Little Niggers*, *Murder on the Orient Express* and *The Murder of Roger Ackroyd*.[15] Even Roland Barthes with his lifelong commitment to avant-garde, anti-realist writing recognised the subversiveness of *The Murder of Roger Ackroyd* where the narrator is also the murderer.[16] And in *Ten Little Niggers* the murderer is one of his own victims, and in *Murder on the Orient Express* the victim is killed by twelve separate but co-operating murderers. And many of the women novelists from earlier periods integrated contemporary issues, like abortion and illegitimacy, as in *London Particular*, into their novels in much the same way as the new feminist writers are integrating current issues affecting women.

In arguing that it is inaccurate to drive a wedge between earlier women detective novelists and the new, progressive wave, it might be thought that we are moving towards the other extreme, suggesting that women's writing is always of necessity more progressive. This would not be an isolated critical position since some feminists have suggested that women's language and women's perceptions somehow necessarily entail a more progressive or subversive form of writing. It would, however, be stretching a point in relation to detective fiction. Not all women have written more progressive or pro-women fiction than men. As with any area of writing, there have always been both the worst offenders against feminist sensibilities and the most unlikely allies. Sometimes a writer falls into both categories, Dorothy L. Sayers could write passages of, to us, extraordinary anti-semitism and racism, and then produce a brilliant novel like

Gaudy Night where she tackles the dilemmas of an intellectual woman and her conflicts with domesticity.[17] Many women feel *Gaudy Night* does ultimately let the side down since the novel culminates in Harriet Vane accepting Lord Peter Wimsey's proposal. Yet the book is in other ways a vindication of the academic anti-domestic woman in a period when such women were generally regarded as peculiar and freakish. In the novel the acts of madness and violence are committed on behalf of domesticity and an extreme version of normality.

Even among contemporary writers, it is not always the case that women writers necessarily take radical stances either on the subject matter or form of detective fiction. A striking phenomenon in recent crime fiction has been the attempt at a feminist reworking of the 'Hard-Boiled' school of detective fiction. Given the extreme individualism, violence and outrageous social attitudes towards women and other minority groups which writers like Mickey Spillane, Dashiell Hammett and Raymond Chandler often display, it is hard to imagine a form less susceptible to a feminist interpretation. But there have been many attempts to appropriate the genre, the two best-known being Sara Paretsky and Sue Grafton. Sue Grafton's novels have a female private investigator who adopts the aggressive, gun-slinging attitudes of her male predecessors. Instead of a man bursting through the door and pumping his adversary full of bullets, it's a woman.

But in spite of the sympathetic, independent heroines and (especially in the case of Sara Paretsky) the politically satisfying plots, their acceptance of the individualistic and machismo codes of violence are highly problematic. It is highly problematic for feminists to replace the tough gun-toting man with a female equivalent and include little or no criticism of the violence in the Gumshoe novels. Ironically it is a man, Robert B. Parker, who has gone furthest in retaining the pleasures of the style and language of a Gumshoe novel while questioning the individualism and violence which normally sustains it.[18] His central investigator, Spenser, is constantly endangered and compromised by his overenthusiasm for violence; his girlfriend Susan spars with, and criticises him, for his unreconstructed attitudes. But it is worth noting that early in the genre, a woman writer, Marion Mainwaring, had written a wickedly funny parody of Mickey Spillane in her novel, *Murder in Pastiche*.[19] She invents a character called Spike Bludgeon, whose commentary on the murder takes over from the absurd delicacies of Miss Fan Sliver (herself a parody of Patricia Wentworth's Miss Silver); 'Well, he hadn't lost his eye, but he'd got the head it came in smashed. Smashed to such a pulp the eye would never be much good to him again' (p. 131).

But having said that women do not necessarily write more progressive fiction than their male counterparts, it is nevertheless the case that many of the women writers even in the earlier period inclined towards potentially radical areas of investigation. Many took issues that were of paramount importance to women in those periods and turned them into the subject of the crime novels. Illegitimacy, abortion, the isolation of mothering, the powerlessness of women and the displacement of unmarried women recur in these novels long before the new wave of political thrillers. Lucy Malleson, writing as Anthony Gilbert in the 1940s, explored, for example, illegal abortions and women's powerlessness. In *The Spinster's Secret* she deals with a lonely, impoverished old woman who witnesses a crime but who no one believes.[20] The result is an impressively radical novel where sleuth and victim merge and where the image of the genteel spinster detective (like Miss Marple and Miss Silver) is given a rather shocking addition of realism. It is interesting that P. D. James's *A Taste for Death* has a sub-plot concerning old age and dependency which strongly evokes Anthony Gilbert's earlier treatment.[21] *The Spinster's Secret* shows clearly how the earlier writers had a strong grasp of the social position of women and its relevance to crime writing.

Women's powerlessness and isolation is a theme which runs through many contemporary feminist thrillers. Rebecca O'Rourke's *Jumping the Cracks*, for instance, foregrounds the vulnerability and marginality of a woman living outside the conventions of heterosexual families.[22] Her 'heroine' accidentally turns detective simply because her marginality feeds doubts about what she has seen. But in the 1950s Celia Fremlin had already made such concerns the central focus of her novels, exploring the breakdown between reality and fantasy resulting from social isolation. In *The Jealous One*, she took the obsessions of a bored and isolated housewife whose grasp on her own self-worth is severely undermined by a new neighbour.[23]

Perhaps her most impressive novels integrate the issue of mothering into this investigation of isolation and paranoia. In *The Hours Before Dawn*, her central character is a young mother whose endless broken nights wear her down and make her prey to anxious, if not to say paranoid, fantasies about her lodger. As is often the case with Celia Fremlin, the plot revolves around the question of how far the central character's fears and imaginings are justified. But in exploring this fragile boundary she has much to reveal about the obsessions and fantasies of so-called normal people, and about the pressures which would tip an individual into paranoid fantasies.

The anxieties around mothering are a recurrent theme throughout crime fiction written by women in the 1940s and 1950s. Katherine Farrar made it central to *The Missing Link*, a novel in which a baby reared according to the strict dictates of the childcare manuals is abducted.[24] The ostensible plot is the quest for the baby; who could have taken it and why? But the underlying theme is mothering. What is the natural 'maternal bond' if a loving mother can jeopardise her child by adhering to rigid 'scientific' advice. And in exploring the theme, the novel is highly critical of the inhumanity of science. The vulnerability of mothers crops up again and again in the early novels. Charlotte Armstrong in *Mischief* uses it as the basis of a brilliant 'night of suspense' novel when a woman leaves her child with an unknown babysitter.[25] And Josephine Bell's *Easy Prey*[26] has a plot which strangely prefigures the more recent *A Dark-adapted Eye* by Barbara Vine (Ruth Rendell).[27]

The coincidences between earlier crime fiction and contemporary writers demonstrate not plagiarism but the fact that questions of female powerlessness, the vulnerability of mothers and the disregard of unmarried women are no less relevant now than they were in the 1940s. Obviously these issues are raised in different ways and often have very different resolutions. Many of the earlier novels mentioned have apparently conservative resolutions, in particular the vindication of the nuclear family as can be seen in *The Hours Before Dawn* and *The Missing Link*. But given the periods in which they were written, all raise and explore the issues affecting women in highly sensitive ways. Contemporary feminist writers may have added whole areas of other concerns like pornography, rape and sexual violence. But this addition has only strengthened the link between women's issues and crime fiction, exploring as it does the whole area of victimisation, which is so much more significant to women than to men.

The Sleuth, the Law and the Country House; are the conventions conservative?

What is crucial in all the novels mentioned so far is attention to psychological detail. All the writers have used the fear and vulnerability which women routinely experience as the basis for a psychological investigation of crime – why people commit crimes and what are the effects on the victims. In this respect, the earlier novels are direct precursors of contemporary novels with their explicit themes of female victimisation and it is not difficult to make out a case for the radicalism of some of these early novels. But this is to leave aside questions of form. In particular it is to leave aside the question of whether or not the conventions of the detective fiction genre are conservative. Is it the case that while the themes explored by these novels (both the early and the contemporary ones) could be considered as radical, the fixed structure of detective fiction will always pull back towards a hierarchical, establishment world and a faith in traditional authority?

The Sleuth

To answer this question, it is useful to explore some of the main conventions which have led to the accusation of a conservative form, in particular those of the sleuth and of the closed community of suspects. In the pre-feminist days, it was certainly the case that many of the women writers worked with a particular 'establishment' image of the detective. Margery Allingham, Ngaio Marsh, Agatha Christie, Dorothy L. Sayers all created male sleuths, many of whom shared certain characteristics, being upper-class, often intimate with the police but also literate and well-educated. They were god-like figures whose intellectual powers helped them solve problems with the deductive reasoning that was often understood to be decidedly male. Even a more recent writer like P. D. James had used these conventions in her Adam Dalgleish figure. But even this 'classic' image is decidedly contradictory. Dorothy L. Sayers' Lord Peter Wimsey and Margery Allingham's Albert Campion are both often presented as 'effeminate'; their deductive powers are also frequently presented as passive, rather than traditionally masculine, active qualities.

Indeed it is this very quality of passivity which undoubtedly made it relatively easy for women writers to produce sympathetic female sleuths from very early on in spite of the problem of credibility.[28] We have already mentioned Amelia Butterworth and Lady Molly of Scotland Yard. There were plenty of others like the Edwardian Miss Van Snoop (Emma Van Deventer), Harriet Vane (Dorothy L. Sayers), and Dame Beatrice Bradley (Gladys Mitchell). Miss Marple and Miss Silver are both the ultimately passive sleuths. Not only female, they are old and frail. Yet simply their powers of observation and deduction allow them to solve the crimes. This image of the detective who solves problems by the power of reason could be seen as an externalisation of the process of reading detective fiction itself. In the classic detective novel, the reader is often fed (though rarely explicitly) the vital information about the criminal amidst a welter of other misleading information. One of the pleasures of the unfolding narrative is whether the reader will be able to solve the mystery before the detective. Yet the pleasure is a delicate one. Solving the crime too early is unpleasurable; real satisfaction comes from the work of trying to foresee the end but not quite having done so (that is the privilege of the sleuth).

This delicate tension between the desire to know and understand but the simultaneous desire to delay and not know too soon, is another reason why some of the critics of crime fiction's conservatism may have got it wrong. It is true that classic crime fiction tends to end with certainties. The criminal is revealed and the world is given some stability again. The fact that the classic detective tended in the past to be an establishment figure might seem to imply that the forces of law and order were always good and unproblematic. Yet it is possible to make a convincing argument that the outcome of the detective fiction is often secondary to the process of the unfolding of the crime or its effects. There are numerous examples of detective fiction where the build up to the crime occupies over half the book. And there are just as many examples where the revelation of who done it is perfunctory, a necessary ending, but hardly adequate to the complex plotting and interactions which preceded it. The journey in detective fiction is often more interesting than the destination.

The Law

Such an assertion is bound to lead us to the conclusion that the form is not as restrictive as is sometimes thought. On the journey all sorts of unexpected things can happen. After all, crime involves the disruption of normalities, and detective fiction is often the consequences of these disruptions. While detective fiction is of course explictly about the restoration of law, it is important to remember that it is also crucially about the breaking of the law, and about transgression of the normal rules. Looked at from this perspective, women's attraction to the form seems more interesting. Women who, in real life, are less often criminals than victims, are clearly drawn to a genre dealing with transgression of the law. Or, as Christianna Brand put it so tantalisingly in a brief autobiography at the beginning of *Cat and Mouse*, 'In her final job, she went in such fear of a fellow worker that she sublimated an urgent desire to murder her, by writing a crime novel.'[29]

Even if other critics are unwilling to accept the detective novel structure as a play between breaking and restoring the law, it is anyway possible to argue that many writers registered their ambivalence about law and order, even in the earlier days of the genre. Even Agatha Christie frequently represents the police as bumbling and inefficient, much more likely to get it wrong than right. Indeed, the whole phenomenon of the amateur detective takes a slight distance on aspects of the establishment. Lord Peter Wimsey agonises about handing over a criminal to certain execution: an unusual moment where 'what will happen after' is raised in a detective novel. And there are innumerable instances of women subverting the conventions of the establishment figure competently sorting out the crime. Anthony Gilbert's Arthur Crook is a shabby, impoverished, rather unpopular detective, the antithesis of the literate, aristocratic amateur. He is typical of a whole sub-genre which has its apotheosis in the 1960s with Joyce Porter's lazy, scrounging Inspector Dover.

It should be clear from the preceding discussion that contemporary feminist writers moved into an area partially prepared for their own ambivalences towards law and the establishment. Obviously there are new problems for the feminist writers. Since feminism sees the law as often defending the interests of men and controlling the behaviour of women, there is no comfortable way in which the law can exist in the background as the embodiment of a shared morality. Most of the contemporary writers have favoured the tradition of the amateur sleuth, most often someone accidentally caught up in crime, whose redress to the police force is problematic if not to say impossible. But some of the new writers, like Katherine V. Forrest, have written police novels precisely to explore the contradictions within the law. Katherine V. Forrest's central character is a detective with the Los Angeles police, and the novels are in essence 'police procedurals', that is minute details of the progress of a police investigation. But Kate Delafield is a lesbian and this sets her automatically at odds with the social assumptions of her colleagues. In *Murder at the Nightwood Bar*, she is torn between her police duties and her personal affinity to the lesbian bar where investigations are focused.[30] Her personal contradictions are made part of the novel's tensions.

The Country House

The final convention which is cited to demonstrate the conservatism of detective fiction is the convention of a closed circle of suspects, a convention at its most fixed in Patricia Wentworth's country-house novels. It has been said that this convention leans writers towards fixed, closed, unchanging communities – villages, weekend parties at country houses, schools and institutions. The uncovering of the crime is then seen as the restoration of social stability, usually to its previously hierarchical state. But again this assumption of the straitjacket of form tends to neglect what goes on within the form. Women writers appear to have used this convention to extremely interesting effect producing a number of notable detective novels concentrating on a closed community of women. *Gaudy Night*, *Miss Pym Disposes* and *Spotted Hemlock* were all set in women's colleges. Christianna Brand used a hospital and particularly a nurses' home as the focus of suspicions in *Green for Danger*, a novel which prefigures P. D. James's setting for *Shroud for a Nightingale*. Hilda Lawrence set her highly atmospheric *Death of a Doll* in a women's hostel, a novel paralleled by the Japanese writer Masako Togawa's *The Master Key*, set in an apartment block for single women – another instance of the worldwide appeal of so many aspects of the genre.[31]

In all these novels, there is a complexity and richness of characterisation; the relationships between women are presented as deep, often passionate, in a way few other novels of the period achieved. Is this perhaps why there is such a high incidence of lesbian relationships portrayed in these novels? It would be possible to argue that both the closed communities of women and the lesbianism are presented as 'unhealthy' breeding grounds for criminal acts. But this neglects both the sympathetic portrayal of women's relationships and the interesting handling of lesbianism which often comes through in novels like *Death of a Doll* and *Miss Pym Disposes*. Needless to say, given such precedents, this convention far from being restrictive has been a blessing for new writers. The closed community of women has allowed a fiction which could reflect and explore the full complexities of relationships between women.

Many of the contemporary writers have worked within rigid conventions – Amanda Cross with academic and analytic communities, Val McDermid with a girls' school and Antonia Fraser with a convent. But others have extended the notion of community in more radical directions as in Barbara Wilson's *Murder in the Collective*, or Gillian Slovo's community of political activists.[32] Katherine V. Forrest and Mary Wings have both extended the notion of community to cover a community of sexual preference. Of course, an uncritical use of the convention is not without its problems, some of which are embodied in Val McDermid's *Report for Murder*.[33] The novel is set in a girls' private school and the narration is unable to resolve the desire to represent a women's community in a favourable light with the need for a potentially criminal community. Because of this tension, the mantle of criminal falls all-too-obviously to the only available man. The earlier writers had no such squeamishness about representing women as criminals with the result that sometimes the earlier novels have much deeper and more interesting investigations of jealousy, passion and love between women.

Conclusion

In attempting to add both a historical and a new critical slant to the current vogue for crime fiction among women we hope to have demonstrated why this vogue has been so successful. We have argued that many earlier women writers had already used the form to raise and explore social issues affecting women. Indeed we have argued that women's concerns, far from being alien to this genre, are often the very stuff of the crime novel – violence, sexual violence, conflict between individuals and authority, and conflict between men and women. That such potentially radical concerns have often been at the heart of the form should therefore lead to no surprise that the form can be used specifically for radical ends.

Moreover, we have argued that although certain conventions within detective fiction pull towards tradition and repetition, and towards that particular brand of individualism and faith in authority, nevertheless there is nothing necessarily conservative in the form. Different writers do, and have always done, very different things with these generic constraints. And women seem to have been at the forefront of pulling detective fiction away from the predictable and towards a more psychological and social exploration of crime. Women clearly have a ready attraction to and competence in the crime genre, an attraction which probably reflects the fact that the crime novel works over current fears and preoccupations about violence, victimisation and protection. Perhaps it is women's necessarily close contact with these issues which partially explains their importance in the history of the genre.

Notes

1 Ronald Knox, 'Introduction', in Ronald Knox and H. Harrington (eds), *The Best Detective Stories of the Year 1928*, Faber & Gwyer, London, 1929.

2 The most obvious male critics who have written thus are Julian Symons and Colin Watson.

3 Agatha Christie, *The Mysterious Affair at Styles* (1920), Fontana, London, 1987.
Dorothy L. Sayers, *Busman's Honeymoon* (1937), Hodder & Stoughton, London, 1988.

4 Two notable critics who have helped to reverse the trend are Dilys Winn and Jessica Mann. Honourable mentions also to H. R. F. Keating and the foremost US critics Otto Penzler, Allen J. Hubin, Howard Haycroft and both men who were Ellery Queen.

5 Mary Roberts Rinehart, *The Circular Staircase* (1909), Dent, London, 1987.
Daphne du Maurier, *Rebecca* (1938), Penguin Books, London, 1986.

6 See for example Amanda Cross, *In the Last Analysis*, Gollancz, London, 1964.
Valerie Miner, *Murder in the English Department* (1982), Methuen, London, 1988.

7 Barbara Wilson, *Sisters of the Road*, The Women's Press, London, 1987.
Mary Wings, *She Came Too Late*, The Women's Press, London, 1986.

8 Katherine V. Forrest, *Murder at the Nightwood Bar*, Pandora Press, London, 1988.
Sarah Dreher, *Stoner McTavish*, Pandora Press, London, 1987.

9 Anna K. Green, *The Leavenworth Case* (1878), Dover & Constable, London, 1981.

10 Mrs Henry Wood, *East Lynne* (1861), Dent, London, 1987.
Mary Braddon, *Lady Audley's Secret* (1862), Oxford University Press, Oxford, 1987.
Seeley Regester, *The Dead Letter*, Beadle & Co., London, 1866.
Wilkie Collins, *The Woman in White* (1860), Penguin Books, London, 1974.

11 Baroness Orczy, *The Old Man in the Corner* (1909), Hogarth Press, London, 1989.

12 Marie Belloc Lowndes, *The Lodger* (1913), Pan Books, London, 1947 and Academy Chicago Publishers, Chicago, 1988.

13 Ethel Lina White, *The Wheel Spins* (1936), Dent, London, 1987.
Mary Roberts Rinehart, op. cit.

14 Christianna Brand, *Green For Danger* (1944), Pandora Press, London, 1987.
— *London Particular* (1952), Pandora Press, London, 1988.
Josephine Bell, *The Port of London Murders* (1938), Pandora Press, 1987.
Hilda Lawrence, *Death of a Doll* (1948), Pandora Press, London, 1987.

15 Agatha Christie, *Ten Little Niggers* (1939), Fontana, London, 1985.
— *Murder on the Orient Express* (1934), Fontana, London, 1985.
— *The Murder of Roger Ackroyd* (1926), Fontana, London, 1985.
16 Roland Barthes, *Writing Degree Zero*, Cape, London, 1984.
17 Dorothy L. Sayers, *Gaudy Night* (1935), Hodder & Stoughton, London, 1988.
18 See for example Sara Paretsky, *Indemnity Only* (1982), Penguin Books, London, 1986.
Sue Grafton, *A is for Alibi* (1986), Papermac, London, 1988.
Robert B. Parker, *Looking For Rachel Wallace* (1982), Penguin Books, London, 1988.
19 Marion Mainwaring, *Murder in Pastiche* (1955), Pandora Press, London, 1987.
20 Anthony Gilbert (pseud. of Lucy Malleson), *The Spinster's Secret* (1946), Pandora Press, London, 1987.
21 P. D. James, *A Taste for Death* (1986), Sphere, London, 1988.
22 Rebecca O'Rouke, *Jumping the Cracks*, Virago Press, London, 1987.
23 Celia Fremlin, *The Jealous One*, Gollancz, London, 1965.
— *The Hours Before Dawn* (1959), Pandora Press, London, 1988.
24 Katherine Farrer, *The Missing Link* (1952), Penguin Books, London, 1955.
25 Charlotte Armstrong, *Mischief* (1950), Pandora Press, London, 1988.
26 Josephine Bell, *Easy Prey* (1959), Pandora Press, London, 1988.
27 Barbara Vine (pseud. of Ruth Rendell), *A Dark-adapted Eye*, Bantam, NY, 1986, and Penguin Books, London, 1987.
28 For a fuller discussion of the history of female sleuths there is *The Lady Investigates* (1981), by Mary Cadogan and Patricia Craig, Oxford University Press, Oxford, 1986.
29 Christianna Brand, *Cat and Mouse*, Michael Joseph, London, 1950.
30 Katherine V. Forrest, op. cit.
31 Josephine Tey, *Miss Pym Disposes* (1946), Penguin Books, London, 1988.
Gladys Mitchell, *Spotted Hemlock*, Michael Joseph, London, 1958.
Christianna Brand, op. cit.
P. D. James, *Shroud for a Nightingale* (1971), Sphere, London, 1988.
Masako Togawa, *The Master Key*, Penguin Books, London, 1985.
Detective fiction is the most popular genre of novel in Japan, having been introduced there in the 1920s by a writer who called himself Edo Gawa Rampo, who discovered the form through the works of Edgar Allan Poe.
32 Barbara Wilson, *Murder in the Collective*, Seal Press, Seattle, and The Women's Press, 1984.
33 Val McDermid, *Report for Murder*, The Women's Press, London, 1987.

References and Further Reading

Other relevant essays and books on mystery fiction, in addition to those in the notes, include:

Gamman, Lorraine, 'Watching the Detectives: The Enigma of the Female Gaze', in Lorraine Gamman and Margaret Marshment (eds), *The Female Gaze: Women as Viewers of Popular Culture*, The Women's Press, London, 1988.

Ginsburg, Carlo, 'Morelli, Freud and Sherlock Holmes: Clues and Scientific Method', *History Workshop Journal*, vol. 9, Spring 1980, pp. 5–36.

Mann, Jessica, *Deadlier Than The Male*, David & Charles, London, 1981.

Munt, Sally, 'The Investigators: Lesbian Crime Fiction', in Susannah Radstone (ed.), *Sweet Dreams: Sexuality, Gender and Popular Fiction*, Lawrence & Wishart, London, 1988.

Sayers, Dorothy L., 'Aristotle on Detective Fiction', in *Unpopular Opinions*, Gollancz, London, 1946.

Todorov, Tzvetan, trans. Richard Howard, 'The Typology of Detective Fiction', in *The Poetics of Prose*, Basil Blackwell, Oxford, and Cornell University Press, NY, 1977.

Winn, Dilys, *Murderess Ink*, Workman Publ. Inc., NY, 1979.

ROMANTIC READERS

———◆———

HELEN TAYLOR

We are living through a period of fashionable romance. All the world loves a lover, and all TV producers love a romantic hit. We have witnessed the phenomenal success of glitz-serials like *Dallas* and *Dynasty*; the massive advance for Sally Beauman's *Destiny*; huge sales of novels by Shirley Conran, Jilly Cooper, Barbara Taylor Bradford; the televisation of novels such as *Sins*, *Hollywood Wives* and *Lace*. The late 1980s are a period of fashionable romance – Interflora, *Guardian* valentines, party frocks, Andy and Fergie, and *The Thorn Birds*.[1] In the look-don't-touch atmosphere of AIDS panic and *Fatal Attraction*'s warning to would-be adulterers, the romance is in style. Barbara Cartland, laughed out of court some years ago for arguing that virginity was in fashion and romance leading to wedlock the highpoint of women's lives, is now claiming to be vindicated. So, along with homophobia and section 28, career feminism and silk camisoles, romance – white, Anglo-Saxon, middle-class, heterosexual, displayed in designer underwear and exotic locations – speaks for a postmodern generation hooked on style and image.[2] Mega-publishing, flashy prices, the writer-as-product and huge book advances have displaced genteel radio discussions of 'books and authors'. Tom Wolfe, talking of 'great vices' of decades, argues that while the great vice of the 1970s was pornography, of the 1980s it is the graphic depiction of the acts of the rich. As a character in Caryl Churchill's *Serious Money* puts it, 'Sexy greedy *is* the late 80s'.

So, in sexy-greedy times, what makes big bucks is of interest. Romantic novels are huge business – both the blockbuster writers I've mentioned, and the twelve titles a month published by Mills & Boon (which is owned by the same conglomerate as

Harlequin and Silhouette) outsell any Booker prizewinner or Delia Smith cookbook. For instance, Taylor Bradford's *A Woman of Substance* has sold worldwide twelve million copies so far.[3] Mills & Boon romances sell annually 220 million books, 20 million in Britain alone.[4] Mills & Boons are not distributed through ordinary bookshops but through those which are also major national newsagent chains such as W. H. Smith and John Menzies, and in supermarkets and corner shops. They are deliberately marketed as a product with a recognisable label rather than as individual books by particular authors. Family sagas are marketed and publicised not so much on their authors' literary qualities, as on their resemblance to other family sagas which have sold well and which readers will be expected to know:

'Tailor-made for fans of McCulloch's *Thorn Birds*'
(Barbara Taylor Bradford, *A Woman of Substance*)

'a marvellous blend of *Gone With the Wind* and *The Thorn Birds*'
(Reay Tannahill, *A Dark and Distant Shore*)[5]

Romantic fiction is believed to be read mainly by women and it is therefore crucial for feminists to examine its success and appeal for women readers. But we should make no assumptions about who these women are. The genre of romance is a complex one with many sub-genres within it. And it is certain that the readers of this large, varied group of writings are a mixed and contradictory group about whom far too many easy generalisations are always being made.

Feminist debates about romance have all acknowledged the existence and significance of these woman readers, either self-consciously and with some embarrassment, or with scholarly enthusiasm and utter seriousness. As many critics have observed, it is *other* people who read romances – your grandmother, mother, friend, you as a teenager. I know of no feminist critic who compulsively reads romances on a scale romantic publishers claim (4–5 a week) though many of us are now dedicating ourselves to such reading – with, of course, knees together and pencil in hand to make scholarly notes. But the serious press addresses the issue still in whimsical, ironic and rather dumbfounded ways. For example, 'Living' *Observer Colour Magazine* (3 April 1985): 'Nobody discusses [romantic fiction] at dinner parties and no one is seen to read it in public. Consequently, not much is known about closet romance readers. Who are they? They're not just spinsters or librarians. They could be housewives, career women or others.' Those words reveal a very common squirming, giggling embarrassment at the whole subject – not to mention ignorance about readership. Secret and closet it may be for *Observer* journalists, but for many women in hairdressers, on buses and in offices – and, of course, libraries and private homes – romance reading is publicly engaged in, albeit with the full knowledge of the scorn and derision it receives from husbands, sons and male employers. It still seems incredible to liberal journalists and feminist critics that in postfeminist Britain, Mills & Boon sell more copies of a single novel than a dozen of the 'bestsellers' in respectable bookshops, and that romance reading has risen steadily since the beginning of the Women's Liberation Movement in the early 1970s. Many share a puritanical dismay at the popularity of texts which appear to confirm all the worst aspects of patriarchal capitalist society: missionary-position male dominance, female submission at work, play and in bed; the norm and ideal of white heterosexual marriage, the suspect nature of celibacy, careerism and feminism; the privatisation of love and the idealisation of the young male/female couple as the supreme model relationship. It does seem, in the gloomiest reading, that romance is indeed, in Germaine Greer's words, 'dope for dopes', a way of keeping women quiet, complaisant, heterosexual and home-and-family-oriented. Not many role models here for those falling in love over the age of thirty, single parents, lesbians, celibates, 'Citizens'–style communal households and Asian girls destined for arranged marriages. In many accounts of romance by critics of the popular such as Q. D. Leavis and Richard Hoggart, as well as recent male left critics of popular culture, the genre has been ignored or ridiculed and, by association, the romantic reader patronised and despised.

The last decade's focus on, and celebration of romance itself has led to the circulation of new and different meanings for the romantic novel for women, and to a new breed of romantic writers and developments within the genre itself. An indication of this is the current vogue for romantic films – supposedly for an older adult audience, focusing on feelings rather than sexual explicitness: best represented in Claude Lelouche's remake of his 1967 *A Man and A Woman* called (not too imaginatively) *A Man and A Woman 20 Years Later*. Very much a product of the 1980s it is pastiche-ridden, ironic, self-reflecting, self-conscious, subscribing to and gently undermining the ideology of romantic love. Feminism, too – in all its forms – has had considerable impact on the genre of romance, if not the impact socialist-feminists might wish. Ann Jones demonstrates ways in which the Mills & Boon romance now has heroines continuing to work after marriage. She cites the novel *Maelstrom*, in which both lovers are – improbably – petroleum engineers and the heroine continues to work, albeit with a less reckless petroleum company than before marriage; and Jones suggests that women initiate more declarations of love and sexual moves than a decade ago.[6] But this goes only so far. The ideology of masculinity remains – men are still older, richer, wiser, more sexually experienced than the heroine, and the happy ending is not yet open for revision.

Then there is that group of bestselling novels about wealthy or rags-to-riches women offering role models of the new 1980s woman in designer jackets, which could be labelled 'the sexy-greedy saga'. Susan Howatch's *The Rich are Different* has a blurb which reads 'A great future and the struggle to control a worldwide business empire; an ambitious and beautiful woman who is one of the most provocative heroines in fiction; a love that spans ecstasy and anguish': while that of Jackie Collins's *Hollywood Wives* describes a 'close-up look at life among the ladies who owe their carefully preserved figures, fingernails, matching Mercedes and palatial homes to the men who make the movies'.[7] Writers like Shirley Conran, Danielle Steel, Sally Beauman. All these women, like their heroines, are celebrated in their publicity hand-outs and interviews as ideals of contemporary career feminism – Thatcherite models who demonstrate the fact that you too can get a multi-million advance if you work fourteen hours a day, regard yourself as a serious novelist, but accept the necessity for your novel to be packaged and marketed as a commodity. Taylor Bradford, a stunning example of this, talks in a manner to warm Edwina Currie's heart of her '5 Ds': desire, dedication, determination, discipline, and drive. One might add a sixth; the sugar daddy to pay the bills and housekeeper while you are tied to your writing desk. Her latest novel is aptly called *To Be the Best*.[8]

Many of these family dynastic sagas seem to offer a counter to the romantic-gothic which positions its heroine too often as victim of male power and aggression. In the sexy-greedy saga, woman is survivor – certainly the butt of male anger, dominance and violence – but able to avenge herself through dramatic and often sensational upward economic and class mobility. Like her author, she is methodical, tidy, and works long hours without distraction. Her independent nature and means are epitomised by that resonant title *A Woman of Substance*. She may lose the man she really loves, and several others she quite fancies along the way, but as compensation she has a tidy sum in her bank accounts, usually a mansion and estate at her disposal, if not a worldwide business empire. As Barbara Taylor Bradford says revealingly in the 1988 Thames Television *Women Writers* series, 'I write about . . . women who are achievers and survivors rather than victims . . . I like strong women . . . I think in this day and age women can have it all'. The Blessed Margaret could not have put it better herself.

There is feminist reworking and pastiche of the romance: novels like Margaret Atwood's *Lady Oracle* (1976) about a gothic novelist, Marilyn French's *The Bleeding Heart* (1980), and Jill Tweedie's *Bliss* (1985). Also, the interesting collection of stories edited by Jeanette Winterson, *Passion Fruit: Romantic Fiction with a Twist* (1986).[9] There is a growing market for new lesbian romances; hitherto (as a list of Virago's top sellers reveals) lesbians in large numbers have had to rely on *The Well of Loneliness*, with all its reactionary and contradictory heterosexist biologistic assumptions about 'inversion'.[10] The relationship of lesbian to heterosexual romance is problematic, and deserves a detailed study. But United States publishers like Naiad Press recognise the gap in the market, producing titles like *The Marquise and the Novice*, and Jane Rule's now-filmed *Desert of the Heart*. One Naiad publication, *For Keeps* by Elizabeth Nonas, uses one of the heterosexual formulas of rejected lover, taking a few false turns, coming to terms with her mother's death and lover's rejection, ending in the arms of Lauren and True Love:

As they ate and talked, Kate still had butterflies in her stomach. The potential for their life together filled the room.

'So.' Kate looked at Lauren. When she had read in novels about a character's heart pounding so loudly she couldn't hear, she had never believed it possible. Until now.

'Want to get married?'

'I thought you'd never ask.'[11]

Michèle Roberts discusses the difficulties of writing lesbian romance: 'A conventional lesbian romance may be so concerned with establishing the finding of the lost, good, nurturing mother that it can make no space for the exploration of "bad" feelings, angry feelings, just as the conventional heterosexual romance smoothes over all conflict between the man and the woman . . . I'd like to read a romance about a lesbian sadist!'[12] It will be interesting to watch developments in this very new, so perhaps by definition still derivative, sub-genre.

All of these have opened romance up for revision and re-vision: all recognise the variety of ways in which the romance can speak as perhaps nothing else does to our desire, fantasies and longings for a better world and for states of individual and collective transcendence. If many of these works – including both lesbian and heterosexual feminist romances – seem to subscribe to bourgeois individualist values and fail to undermine patri-archal capitalism, we can either decide to attack them – usually with sardonic humour – or more usefully examine their power for women, if only to imagine more resonant feminist alter-natives. The answers they give to life's problems may not be the ones feminists would give, but clearly the questions they raise are ones which matter to women, and the form or formula in which they are asked – the genre of romance and its sub-genres (historicals, family saga, lesbian romance and so on) – obviously work.

What has been exciting in the last five or six years is the way some feminists have revised the 'dope for dopes' dismissal, by seriously addressing the appeal of romance reading and especially considering the nature of the readers – who are, as all audience research accounts show, an extremely heterogeneous bunch. Apparently they come from all classes, races, ages and possibly both sexes (though overwhelmingly women). Mills &

Boon romances are translated into dozens of languages and sell in Japan, India and Africa as well as Western countries. As Inga Lubbock, Mills & Boon PR spokesperson, said, 'There's a huge trade in English Mills & Boons on the Costa del Sol, because Mrs Buggins goes for her hols and doesn't know what to read so she picks up an English Mills & Boon; whereas Mrs Perez somewhere in Madrid wants to pick up a Spanish one'.[13] It is a formidable task for a critic to account for the pleasures of reading a Mills & Boon when discussing a Sri Lankan and a Canadian reader in the same breath – or Inga Lubbock's Mrs Buggins and Mrs Perez. In terms of the unashamedly Westernised cultural contexts and references of the commercial romance (however generalised and simplified) it seems obvious that these books will be read and understood in different ways in each country, class and race to which they are distributed. (I recall Maya Angelou's line in *I Know Why The Caged Bird Sings* about her teacher Mrs Flowers, who was 'Like women in English novels who walked the moors (whatever they were)'.[14]

The main feminist response to this mixed and non-unified readership is understandably to use European-inflected psycho-analytic models. Recent critics have tried to explain the appeal of romantic fiction in terms of women's unconscious desires, fantasies and fears. Rosalind Coward argues that the fantasy which romantic fiction satisfies is a reactionary one: women's desire for heterosexual domination and evasion of active sexual identity. Women are offered the promise of safety with dependence, power with subordination.[15] Ann Barr Snitow argues that romances 'make bridges between contradictions', and 'soothe ambivalence'; she sees a brutal male sexuality converted to romance. Sexual feeling is celebrated in a universal timeless battle between man and woman. As she says 'Pleasure for women is men'.[16] There have been debates about whether the appeal of romance for women is pornographic; questions about whether the hero represents the bad, dominant father/husband or the idealised, yearned-for father who controls and subdues the heroine in a loving and protective way; or whether the hero is for women the lost *mother*, enfolding, all-nurturant, loving and attentive to one's every childish need and desire.[17]

Some critics have seen romances as offering less regressive pleasures. Tania Modleski, in her influential study *Loving with a*

Vengeance, looks at three different genres – the Harlequin/Mills & Boon romance, the gothic novel, and soap opera.[18] (The third is a curious choice – the family saga would have been more logical.) Modleski argues that all these genres reveal rather than cover over the contradictions and difficulties in women's lives, and fulfil the Utopian function of entertainment which is to offer the reader/viewer visions and models of energy, abundance, intensity, transparency, community and transcendence or self-forgetfulness. So women are able to use these texts to work through conflicts in their lives; for example, she says the gothic romance uses female doubles (often the dead first wife or mad wife in the attic/basement etc.) as a way of exorcising women's fear not only of being like their mothers but actually *being* their mothers. Soap opera, she argues, offers women a vision of extended rather than nuclear family, with several generations of a large family in one place involved with each other's lives – a progressively *collective* rather than privatised fantasy. Alison Light argues similarly, saying that though not progressive, the reading of romantic fictions may be transgressive – a forbidden pleasure, like cream cakes. Cora Kaplan, in a fascinating discussion of *The Thorn Birds*, suggests that the romantic narrative 'can constitute one of women's few entries to the public articulation and social exploration of psychic life.'[19] But all of these accounts have generalised from the texts themselves, and do not address real readers; they were speculating about the 'implied' reader and about the common fantasies which apply to all readers, presumably from Taiwan to Tallahassee.

In a recent work which has shifted the ground somewhat, Janice Radway (*Reading the Romance*) examined a group of romance readers.[20] She contacted a woman well-known to the United States' romance publishers, a shop assistant in a Midwestern town. This woman, called 'Dot' for the purposes of the book, reads romances voraciously, recommends them to her customers, and in recent years has produced a newsletter summarising plots and giving ratings to new books. Interviewing Dot and her customers, Radway discovered that for the women of 'Smithton', reading romances was a 'declaration of independence' from their families and domestic work – a way of saying 'This is my time, my space. Now leave me alone.' They read romances to relax, to escape from intolerable or dreary pressures, to learn about exotic places, customs, foods and so on. Because of the short length and clear simple plots, women can pick them up and put them down between domestic tasks or breaks at their paid work; and they are extremely discriminating about the books. Knowledgeable about individual writers and styles, they select carefully (hence Dot's newsletter) and even read in the store the first few and the last pages to see if the style suits them. They also have a considerable knowledge of the way the genre itself has developed into different forms, especially in relation to the treatment of sexuality. (For example, they could date the beginning of a more sexually explicit, bodice-ripping genre to one work, Kathleen Woodiwiss's *The Flame and the Flower*, 1972.)

The importance of Radway's book lies first in her analysis of an actual group of readers, and the documentation of their reading habits and conscious, or stated, reasons for reading romances and selecting the ones they do. More important, for my purpose, is the fact that the book exposes the complexity both of the romance market and also the uses women make of books and the habit of reading. Radway's work gives a vivid picture of what has been called 'texts in use' rather than 'the text itself'.[21] Romances – like other kinds of text – have meaning only within particular historically and culturally precise contexts. That is, the process of reading itself is not an abstraction between a fixed book and a generalised universal reader, rather it is an *exchange*, a relationship between an active, critical reader, with all her educational, social and cultural baggage of experience, and a text, with all its literary, historical and cultural references, not to mention the ways it has been produced, packaged and marketed. In terms of Radway's sample, for instance, 'reading the romance' is an exchange between Dot, a sophisticated and highly critical romance reader, housewife and worker in a Midwestern town in the Reaganite 1980s, and the specific romantic novel, with its variation on a limited formulaic plot and stock characters drawn from a long and well-developed tradition of romance writing (from the troubadours on), together with a 1980s emphasis on greater sexual explicitness and gestures at female independence, all packaged in a standardised format with high gloss quasi-photographic cover illustration and mass-marketed through drugstores, supermarkets and chain stores. So while the book itself may remain the same (and often it is translated into other languages, which will change it radically) the reading process in Turkey or Taiwan has to be radically different – producing a very different text.

Radway, like other critics, focused her attention mainly on the Harlequin romance. Although she throws open the possibility of group experience of reading, on the whole she sees the pleasures produced by romance reading as individual and privatised, not social and collective. But there is one sub-genre of romance which seems to offer precisely that vision of community which most feminists deny the orthodox romance.[22] The family saga – *Penmarric* by Susan Howatch, *A Dark and Distant Shore* by Reay Tannahill, Zoë Fairbairns' feminist *Stand We at Last* – usually covers several generations rather than one heterosexual couple; begins with marriage and the end of the heightened romance episode; often covers more than one family, and certainly more than one protagonist.[23] Those fantasies which Tania Modleski accords to soap opera are continually appealed to: continuity, community, self-forgetfulness, energy and abundance. Very different from the paranoid or masochistic nature of those romances which focus on the young, childless heterosexual couple to the exclusion of historical and social contexts. The historical and cultural elements of the sagas are often laughably like history and sociology-by-numbers, with an author's research of orthodox and usually reactionary sources paraded as a guarantee of authenticity. Nonetheless there *is* a sense of human love, passion and family continuity, change, development all inscribed in, and mediated by historical changes and continuities. And *regional* specificity is also an important part of these sagas. In *Gone with the Wind*, Scarlett O'Hara's venture-capitalist spirit and triumphs and disasters in love are demonstrably shaped by the American South's crisis and the conditions of war and Reconstruction.[24] Barbara Taylor Bradford's Emma Harte, however Cinderella-ised, does take us through some aspects of late nineteenth-century working-class Yorkshire experience, tells us something of anti-Semitism in the Leeds of the early twentieth century, and places family and individual experience in the context of two cataclysmic wars. *Penmarric* vividly describes both Cornwall's topographical characteristics and also its industrial crisis around the mining industry – something the tourist brochures rarely discuss. Certainly historical novelists vary in the quality of their historical research and of their writing, and there is a spurious authority given many blockbusters with literary epigraphs and references and the use of family trees and discussions of real historical moments to flesh out the fictional events and characters. But that said, these novels address women in historical, social, collective contexts, and although indubitably class and family romances at many levels, focus on discontinuities, fragmentation, broken marriage, unwanted or unhappy children, deaths and new beginnings. They also often transgress social and sexual taboos – both literally (in *Penmarric* and Sally Beauman's *Destiny* an incestuous marriage goes un-punished or unrevealed) and metaphorically (as in the many quasi-incestuous relationships in *The Thorn Birds*, especially between 'Father' Ralph and Meggie).[25] Wholeness and com-pletion but also breakdown and disappointment. The reader is not lulled into complacency, and endings are often open and ambiguous, inviting active critical thought and engagement.

So the genre is more complex than is usually acknowledged, and the nature of the readership it addresses necessarily so. And there are numbers of questions about romantic reading which still need to be taken up. Questions such as the difference a reading context makes: is the romantic novel produced by a reader very different if it is read during childbirth between contractions, on an aeroplane flying to an illicit liaison, or at night in bed beside a partner of twenty years? How can we classify readers in terms of class, age, race, region, nation and sexual orientation? How does a black lesbian read a white heterosexual romance? Do different aspects of the text make different kinds of impact? One example from my research into reader-viewer response to the book and film of *Gone with the Wind*. Hearing from women of different generations about their experiences, I was struck by how many women reading it during the Second World War noted the scene when Scarlett pulls down Tara's green velvet curtains to make a dress – a scene described by them as one of wonderful excess and also resourcefulness. Dress material was rationed during the war and so of course the velvet curtains story was extremely resonant for such readers. Not so for post-rationing generations.

We still know very little about the different kinds of readership for any of the sub-genres of romance. Even within one apparently simple group, the Mills & Boon romance, we do not know about the composition, reading habits, preferences and so on of those who regularly choose the 'Doctor–Nurse' over the 'Masquerade historical' or 'Temptation' romance. Nor do we know much about the impact of the highly personalised mail order service it offers women readers, or the significance of the packaging-like-soap-powder which is so crucial to their success. The long family saga is probably read by the sort of women who adore long historical romances like *Gone with the Wind*, but do they choose only such fiction, and if not, what else do they read? I had assumed all women readers read with care the sex scenes in romances, until I interviewed a woman who reads 'historicals' and claims she and her friends skip them as 'they're all the same'. Is there something about the whole experience of reading a very long book, over days and weeks, which makes for a different reading experience from skimming in one night the 180 pages of a short romance? These are some of the problems students of romance and romantic reading need to address before we begin to get a historically and sociologically precise idea of what reading means in women's lives.

In researching responses to *Gone with the Wind*, I have become aware of the complexity of women's relationship to reading–viewing itself. The variety of ways women have read books and viewed films at different periods of their lives, and with very different uses, lays wide open the question of how a critic can assign single meanings either to a particular text or indeed to the process of reading itself. First, each reader has her own reading history – one specific to her class, education, race, generation and so on. For example, I interviewed two women. One was middle-class, and when a child was caught between her grandmother who read to her because she thought education was crucial for girls, and her mother who feared excessive reading would ruin her eyes and thus chance of marriage. A working-class woman was regarded as 'mad' by her non-reading parents, and found solace and reading ideas by escaping to the library. (I think female librarians are key figures in many women readers' lives.) Both women read and loved *Gone with the Wind*, though taking different class-inflected perspectives on it. The presence or absence of books in girls' homes as they grow up marks future attitudes to and ease with books. Many of my *Gone with the Wind* correspondents who had acquired an expensive copy of the book in wartime regard it as a prized object (much sellotaped, re-covered, etc.) and indeed for many it is one of the only books – certainly one of the only hardbacks – they *own*. Especially, in the genre of romance, mothers' and other family attitudes are central. It is well known that romances are circulated between mothers, daughters, sisters and friends, hence a collective experience of romance (private jokes and key words etc.), but if your class position meant a general frowning on romance reading, a covert, secretive and highly privatised pattern sets in (the sort the *Observer* journalist identified, probably from her own experience with a torch under the bedclothes). There is a considerable difference in my correspondents' memories of *Gone with the Wind* reading: the woman who waited to read the shared copy bought collectively in a wartime factory, and then the excited group discussions and debates about the inconclusive ending, compared with the solitary feminist reading it in the 1980s, squirming with anger and embarrassment at her mixed pleasure in the narrative and horror at its overt racism.

Again, the conventions of the romantic novel are historically very specific, especially in relation to the treatment of female sexuality and definition of femininity – so each reader will respond in some measure within her time. Several women who read *Gone with the Wind* in the 1940s and 1950s record that it was thought to be a 'fast' 'brown paper' novel, and was on the Catholic Index of Forbidden Literature; a couple of readers chose it as a school prize together with a sober Christian text to appease parents and teachers. Rhett's frankness about his whore, and the famous ravishing scene when he carries Scarlett to bed, are key memories of forbidden pleasure for many older women. Melanie is likely to be admired more highly than Scarlett by earlier generations (a survey of college students in the 1950s found Melanie was the role model, in the late 1970s, Scarlett). By older women Scarlett is viewed as deviant and wonderful: 'She may not be admirable, but what a woman'; 'an uneasy figure for my baby boom generation' – as one woman said; 'an object lesson in how to get it wrong and lose your man'; and a role model in gutsy independence for a 1970s and 1980s feminist, who is nonetheless uncomfortable with her attitude to the class and race positions of the black characters. And within those generations is a range of specific reading experience, therefore production of text and memory. Again, thinking of those first readers in the late 1930s and early 1940s, there is a considerable heterogeneity which no critic can ignore. Rudolf Hess apparently spent much of the Nuremberg trial reading his way through *Gone with the Wind*, while one of my respondents read it to drown her sorrows the week in 1939 when Hitler and Stalin signed their non-aggression pact. Did they produce the same text? Some women first read it in air raid shelters or larders under the stairs with torches during blackouts – women in the thick of war reading of other women surviving theirs. A very different experience this from a contemporary woman in her twenties, never having come closer to a real war than the Falklands on TV, reading it after seeing the *Gone with the Wind* film on TV.

There is also the difference a second reading makes. My own serial readings of *Gone with the Wind*, first as a teenager, subsequently as an academic studying women's writing of the Civil War, demonstrated to me what other women also testify to; the utterly different text which is produced by each experience. Add to this biographies of Margaret Mitchell and Vivien Leigh, modern reinterpretations of the Civil War such as *North and South*, a novel like Elizabeth Kary's *Let No Man Divide* using the Civil War formula, all the *Gone with the Wind* memorabilia, Scarlett O'Hara wedding dresses, *Gone with the Wind* cookery books, the Reagan–Thatcher *Gone with the Wind* poster.[26] All circulate in and shift readers' memories, and the various meanings of romance texts; just as the Brontës' novels take on different meanings for those who visit the commercialised Howarth Parsonage and buy Brontë liqueur; and Daphne du Maurier's do for those familiar with 'her' Cornwall.

My title was deliberately ambiguous. The romantic reader I have discussed is that non-unified, disparate woman who finds within the genre an address to her own concerns, feelings, needs. Romance is often associated with dreaming: titles of romantic novels like *Hold the Dream*, *Sea of Dreams*, *The Impossible Dream*, the teenage imprint called *Sweet Dreams*.[27] Harlequin romances have an American TV advert showing a middle-aged woman sinking sleepily into bed with her book. Lia Sanders' *The Tender Meaning* (the only black romance I have read) has a dedication 'For Black Girls and Women (who need a dream)'.[28] I think the dreams offered by romance can be claustrophobic, regressive and reactionary, and I find many of the role models offered me as a romance reader depressing and trite. Too often, they seem to suggest I should be more neat and tidy, smile more often at men, and be in a state of constant potential sexuality while sitting in my office or shopping at Sainsbury's. If not that, I should accept that the ways of the world are fixed and predetermined, that class, race, gender, and nation will always out – and are not really negotiable. But dreaming is also about imagining other possibilities, change, difference – sometimes of a collective rather than individual kind. Since the Middle Ages the romance has been crucial in offering visions of the unattainable and ideal, implicating all readers as 'romantic readers'. So in these bleak utilitarian 1980s, I am suspicious of anyone condemning dreams. Feminism and socialism are also about class, family and personal romance – and I see no reason why we should not learn a few lessons from Mills & Boon and Barbara Taylor Bradford, as well as engage in a livelier dialogue with their devotees.

I am not advocating a thoroughly uncritical reader-centred approach. Unlike those reader-response theorists who wish to locate meaning entirely in the reader's mind, I believe that each text determines a set of specific responses, within its own historical, social and narrative constraints, and that it is a reader's (and critic's) task to unlock those. I am not arguing for a celebration of all individual responses, regardless of their relevance to particular works. What interests me is the way that *all* texts produced by particular writers in specific historical circumstances within their genres are used/consumed – in times and places different from those in which they were originally produced – by readers who bring to those texts their own historical and cultural determinations and thus understandings. What emerges from Radway's work on the Harlequin reader and my own on *Gone with the Wind*, is that experience in and practice of reading results in readers who (with varying degrees of sophistication and skill) can select from and discriminate among genres, writers, styles of narration and characterisation, and who can articulate a heterogeneous array of responses to aspects of texts. Psychoanalytic readings have offered wonderful insights into the gendered nature of responses to romances, especially around key issues of sexuality and family romance. But, as Lorraine

Gamman and Margaret Marshment argue in *The Female Gaze*, processes of identification and objectification in narrative fictions operate through class, race and generation as well as gender (also, I would add, nation and region).[29] So the single, universal response posited by a psychoanalytic reading tends to close off different, contradictory and indeed conscious responses to the romance text.

It is politically crucial that feminist critics become aware of those varied responses. As Modleski, Light and Kaplan argue, romance reading *can* offer fantasies of transgression, individual power and autonomy, and indeed pleasurable sexual fantasies to women whose lives offer little of all these. But then the reading of romance may also be confirming Third World women in a knowledge of their own subordination, reminding women of colour that youthful white beauty is the Western norm of feminine sexuality, and warning lesbian women (black and white) of their cultural marginality or invisibility. We have to beware of generalising about readers – who they are, why they read, what their satisfactions are in all texts (not only romance). The worldwide, class/age/race/nationwide appeal of romance does not offer a stable model reader who can be identified. There are many kinds of reader, using romance fiction in different ways, in various contexts, and with specific purposes. The work to be done, following the lead of cultural studies analysts, is an examination of all those readerships and a closer look at the way romantic texts are circulated and therefore acquire meanings among diverse groups and individuals.[30]

Notes

With thanks to Helen Carr for her encouraging support and scrupulous editing.

1 Sally Beauman, *Destiny*, Bantam, NY, 1987.
Jackie Collins, *Hollywood Wives*, Pocket Books, NY, and Pan, London, 1984.
Shirley Conran, *Lace*, Penguin Books, London, 1983, and Pocket Books, NY, 1984.
Colleen McCullough, *The Thorn Birds*, Avon, NY, 1978, and Futura, London, 1980.

2 Section 28 of the Local Government Act (1988), which states that local authorities are prohibited from 'promoting homosexuality' in any form.

3 Barbara Taylor Bradford, *A Woman of Substance*, Grafton, London, and Bantam, NY, 1987.

4 Mills & Boon (UK), Harlequin Enterprises (Canada), and Silhouette (USA), are all owned by the Canada-based communications organisation Torstar Corporation. See Deborah Philips, 'Marketing Moonshine', *Women's Review*, no. 2, December 1985, p. 17.

5 Reay Tannahill, *A Dark and Distant Shore*, Penguin Books, London, and Dell, NY, 1984.

6 Ann Rosalind Jones 'Mills & Boon meets Feminism', in Jean Radford (ed.), *The Progress of Romance*, Routledge & Kegan Paul, London, 1986, pp. 195–220.

7 Susan Howatch, *The Rich are Different*, Pan, London, 1979, and Fawcett, NY, 1985.

8 Barbara Taylor Bradford, *To Be the Best*, Grafton, London, and Doubleday, NY, 1988.

9 Margaret Atwood, *Lady Oracle*, Virago Press, London, and Fawcett, NY, 1982.
Marilyn French, *The Bleeding Heart*, Ballantine, NY, 1981, and Sphere, London, 1987.
Jill Tweedie, *Bliss*, Penguin Books, London, 1985.
Jeanette Winterson (ed.), *Passion Fruit: Romantic Fiction with a Twist*, Pandora Press, London, 1986.

10 Radclyffe Hall, *The Well of Loneliness* (1928), Avon, NY, 1981, and Virago Press, London, 1982.

11 Elizabeth Nonas, *For Keeps*, The Naiad Press, Tallahassee, 1985, p. 133. I am grateful to Carol Uszkurat for pointing me to this and other ideas about lesbian fiction. *Desert of the Heart* is now published in Britain by Pandora Press.

12 Michèle Roberts, 'Write, she said', in Radford (ed.), *The Progress of Romance*, p. 231.

13 Quoted in transcript of interview between Inga Lubbock and Julie Burrell, in J. Burrell, 'The Only Pick-me-up for Incurable Romantics: Mills & Boon', Bristol Polytechnic Humanities Special Study, 1987.

14 Maya Angelou, *I Know Why the Caged Bird Sings*, Virago Press, London, 1984, p. 92.

15 Rosalind Coward, *Female Desire: Women's Sexuality Today*, Paladin, London, 1984, p. 196.

16 Ann Barr Snitow, 'Mass Market Romance: Pornography for Women is Different', *Radical History Review*, no. 20, Spring/Summer 1979, pp. 141–161.

17 See Snitow article for these debates, and also Joanna Russ, 'Some-

body is Trying to Kill Me and I Think It's My Husband: The Modern Gothic', *Journal of Popular Culture*, no. 6, 1973, pp. 666–691.

18 Tania Modleski, *Loving with a Vengeance*, Methuen, London, 1982.

19 Alison Light, '"Returning to Manderley": Romantic Fiction, Female Sexuality and Class', *Feminist Review*, no. 16, Summer 1984, pp. 7–25.
Cora Kaplan, '*The Thorn Birds*: Fiction, Fantasy, Femininity', in *Sea Changes*, Verso, London, 1986, p. 146.

20 Janice Radway, *Reading the Romance: Women, Patriarchy, and Popular Literature*, University of N. Carolina Press, Chapel Hill, 1984.

21 Tony Bennett and Janet Woollacott, *Bond and Beyond: The Political Career of a Popular Hero*, Macmillan, London, 1987, p. 262.

22 See Christine Bridgwood, 'Family Romances: the contemporary popular family saga' in Radford, *The Progress of Romance*, pp. 167–194.

23 Susan Howatch, *Penmarric*, Fawcett, NY, 1978, and Pan, London, 1983.
Zoë Fairbairns, *Stand We at Last* (1982), Virago Press, London, 1988.

24 Margaret Mitchell, *Gone with the Wind* (1936), Avon, and Pan, London, 1974.

25 See Cora Kaplan, op. cit.

26 See John Jakes, *North and South*, Fontana, London, 1983, and *Love and War*, Fontana, London, 1986, televised as *North and South* and *North and South II*, December 1986 and 1987.
Elizabeth Kary, *Let No Man Divide*, Penguin Books, London, 1987.
See also Helen Taylor, '*Gone with the Wind*: The Mammy of Them All', in Radford, *The Progress of Romance*, pp. 113–138
and book about *Gone with the Wind*'s women reader–viewers, *Scarlett's Women*, Virago Press, London (forthcoming).

27 Barbara Taylor Bradford, *Hold the Dream*, Grafton, London, 1986, and Bantam, NY, 1986.

28 Lia Sanders, *The Tender Meaning*, Dell, NY, 1982.

29 Lorraine Gamman and Margaret Marshment (eds), *The Female Gaze: Women as Viewers of Popular Culture*, The Women's Press, London, 1988.

30 See Ien Ang, *Watching Dallas: Soap Opera and the Melodramatic Imagination*, Methuen, London, 1985.
Dorothy Hobson, *Crossroads: The Drama of a Soap Opera*, Methuen, London, 1982.
Bennett and Woollacott, op. cit.

References and Further Reading

Other books and essays on romance and romantic fiction in addition to those mentioned in the footnotes.

Anderson, Rachel, *The Purple Heart Throbs: The Sub-Literature of Love*, Hodder & Stoughton, London, 1974.

Aufderheide, Pat, 'The Sweet Smell of Romance', *New Society*, 4 April 1985.

Batsleer, Janet, 'Pulp in the Pink', *Spare Rib*, no. 109, 1981.

Bromley, Roger, 'National Boundaries: the Social Function of Popular Fiction', *Red Letters*, no. 7, pp. 34–60.

Brownstein, Rachel M., *Becoming a Heroine: Reading About Women in Novels*, Penguin Books, London, 1984.

Brunt, Rosalind, and Rowan, Caroline (eds), *Feminism, Culture and Politics*, Lawrence & Wishart, London, 1982.

Cawelti, John G., *Adventure, Mystery, and Romance: Formula Stories as Art and Popular Culture*, The University of Chicago Press, Chicago, 1976.

Gamman, Lorraine, and Marshment, Margaret (eds), *The Female Gaze: Women as Viewers of Popular Culture*, The Women's Press, London, 1988. Especially Margaret Marshment, 'Substantial Women', pp. 27–43, and Avis Lewallen, '*Lace*: Pornography for Women?', pp. 86–101.

Greer, Germaine, *The Female Eunuch*, Paladin, London, 1971, pp. 171–189.

Griffin, Christine, 'Cultures of Femininity: Romance Revisited', C.C.C.S., 1982.

Hey, Valerie, *The Necessity of Romance*, Kent University Press, 1983.

Jensen, Margaret Ann, *Love's Sweet Return: The Harlequin Story*, Bowling Green University Popular Press, Bowling Green, Ohio 1984.

Kuhn, Annette, *Women's Pictures: Feminism and Cinema*, Routledge & Kegan Paul, London and New York, 1982.

Margolies, David, 'Mills & Boon: Guilt Without Sex', *Red Letters*, no. 14, Winter 1982–1983, pp. 5–13.

Pawling, Christopher (ed.), *Popular Fiction and Social Change*, Macmillan, London, 1984. See especially Introduction and articles by Bridget Fowler on women's magazine fiction, and Rosalind Brunt on Barbara Cartland.

Radford, Jean (ed.), *The Progress of Romance: The Politics of Popular Fiction*, Routledge & Kegan Paul, London, 1986.

Russ, Joanna, 'Somebody is Trying to Kill Me and I Think it's My Husband', *Journal of Popular Culture*, no. 6, 1973, pp. 666–691.

Sarsby, Jacqueline, *Romantic Love and Society: Its Place in the Modern World*, Penguin Books, London, 1983.

Thurston, Carol, *The Romance Revolution: Erotic Novels for Women and the Quest for a New Sexual Identity*, University of Illinois Press, Champaign, 1987.

Women's Review, Issue 21, July 1987, pp. 17–29. (Several articles on romantic fiction, Mills & Boon etc.)

THE SCIENCE FICTIVENESS OF WOMEN'S SCIENCE FICTION

ROZ KAVENEY

The commercial science fiction genre, in which I would personally include much of what is published as fantasy, heroic or horror, as it exists in the United States and Britain has produced a respectable body of explicitly and implicitly feminist fiction, much of it radical in its form as well as in its politics. This is, on the face of it, suprising given how large a proportion of work published within those genres is by contrast viciously militaristic, devoted to intensely stratified models of society, often overtly or at least implicitly racist, and deeply misogynist and patriarchal.[1] Yet in this essay I want to show why the work of writers like Joanna Russ and Ursula Le Guin is nonetheless most helpfully looked at in the broader context of the SF genre, how, given the adolescent male readership at which the genre is largely commercially targeted, they have become as popular as they have within it, and why they have bothered to stay with the genre as it exists in the first place. I shall also look, in passing, at some of the Utopian fictions by women who do not come from the SF background, and at some SF by women which is less explicitly feminist, both from the past, and at the present time.

It would be useful at this point to give a broad outline of the history of SF as it developed as a commercial genre in the United States and subsequently in Britain.[2] Stories derived from the subject matter of, for example, Wells and Verne were a staple and popular part of the magazine fiction of the first two decades of the century at a time when the publishers had not had the idea of category pulps. In the late 1920s and early 1930s publishers noticed the popularity of stories of that kind and created magazines which specialised in them, notably *Amazing Stories* and *Astounding Science Fiction*. Much of the material in these magazines could not really be described as stories at all; they were essentially not very dramatised lectures on the future of technology and technocracy.[3]

The role of women in these, except when serving as object lessons in lectures by the authors on eugenics or the folly of extending the suffrage, was restricted to standing around having things explained to them by the hero and saying 'Gosh. Wow. How terrific.' Such lectures were often mingled with adventure stories in the manner of Edgar Rice Burroughs in which the role of the heroine was restricted to one, being captured by the space pirates: two, twisting her ankle when being rescued from them: three, mopping sweat and/or blood from the hero's brow: and four, being told how brave she was.

The readership of the pulp magazines of the 1930s was primarily male and adolescent, but only primarily so; what is interesting about them at this point is that they took a passionate interest in the content, and occasionally in the form of what they were reading, and communicated fanatically with the magazines, the authors and with each other.[4] Parallel to the commercial magazine culture there grew up a fan culture, which communicated through 'fanzines', about stories, personalities, and above all about ideas. That generation of fans grew up, in a few cases, to become the better-known writers of the 1940s and the 1950s.

Because of that early sense of community, SF as a community has continued to exist alongside SF as a commercial genre. There are two major assumptions that derive from the existence of that community, which are, in the first place, that most people reading and writing commercial SF belong to that community, and in the second place that they are broadly acquainted with at least a sizeable proportion of what has been done and is being done within the form. Writers like Russ and Le Guin started their publishing careers in the SF magazines of the 1950s and 1960s, and regard themselves as being in some measure still part of the field and of the community. Both are intellectually involved with the field; Russ in particular has for a long time been one of the field's most intelligent and stroppy critics. This remains the case in spite of the irritation they have often expressed with large parts of the field.

My second point has a string of further consequences. Because SF is a genre largely consisting of fairly unsubtle adventure stories, it is riddled with stock assumptions as to what, for example, the future is going to be like and look like. One of the standard justifications for the genre's shortcoming for critics like Kingsley Amis has always been that it is a literature of ideas, a fiction in which the idea rather than the individual is the protagonist.[5] This justification is equally often used by all the people who dislike the genre as proof that it is inherently cold, irresponsible and inhumane. In practice, though, what was once an idea has more often become nothing much more than a backdrop. The American critic Gary Wolfe has pointed out the way in which what may have been at some earlier date startling new ideas have become what he calls icons; imagery which the genre takes for granted.[6] Only rarely does anyone think of anything especially interestingly new to do with a spaceship or with a post-atomic wasteland; they have become starting points. Sometimes starting points for novels with vividly portrayed characters interacting complexly with sensuously portrayed backgrounds and complexly imagined models of society, but more often not. These images have become rather pallid because it is so difficult to make them new – Joanna Russ has referred to this as 'the wearing down of genre materials'.[7] This has had two consequences, one clearly beneficial, and one more mixed, for the women's SF of the last two decades. The extent to which many of these stock images have worn down to transparency makes them readily available for the sort of metafictional play which Russ, for example, engages in for much of her fiction. The other more mixed consquence is that in the hands of writers – I will not say less gifted, or less serious, but merely less prepared to examine images and the assumptions that have become bonded to them – I may as well mention Ann McCaffrey – these materials can only to some extent be revivified by rethinking them for a women's audience. Often, though, this attempt fails, and the ensuing thin commercial gruel is regularly cited by the reactionary and misogynist element inside SF as proof that it is a form which women are best off leaving alone. Not that any of them have much room to talk.

Another consequence is that one of the stock subjects of SF is earlier SF. Sometimes referred to more or less overtly, sometimes implicitly, writers tackle themes and ideas introduced by earlier writers, not merely to pile marvels on marvels in the way that, say, crime writers did in the 1930s and 1940s in the attempt to create ever more insoluble locked room mysteries, but to engage morally and intellectually with assumptions taken for granted in earlier stories. Ill-written and morally objectionable as they are the importance of Asimov's *Foundation* stories lies in the way that in them he and his editor John Campbell, his collaborator at least in the thinking behind the stories, debunked the individualistic, militaristic tendencies of the galaxy-wide space opera before and since. They replaced them with a view of politics which took on board a strong element of historical determinism and actually noticed that it is not much good setting up a galactic empire without giving it a firm economic base.

One of the things which feminist SF writers have done is simply to tackle those assumptions in earlier work which happen to matter to them, often those assumptions which degrade and insult women. There is a body of SF ever since Robert Heinlein's *Farnham's Freehold*, which can be categorised as survivalist – and which has clearly influenced the contemporary and deeply reactionary survivalist movement in the United States. It is assumed that the moment atomic war breaks out, or a comet brushes the earth, or your spaceship crashes, you – the assumed you of such stories is of course always male – start reverting to a pioneer mentality, start carving a domain in the wilderness, and get your women breeding.[8] One of the several things that Joanna Russ does in her rather underrated novel *We Who Are About To* is to ask the questions: one, why bother? and two, precisely what, sister, is in all this for me?[9] Her heroine is one of a group of no-hope tourists who crash land on a wilderness planet on which there is absolutely no reason to believe they can possibly survive – they have not the skills or the equipment which might give them even an even chance. When the others decide that they are going to try, rather than, as she intends, making peace with themselves and gently expiring, she explains patiently and politely that she would rather not participate. So they try to force her, and she, as kindly as possible, kills them, one after another. Russ is making a number of points about stock SF assumptions here. If, in a high-tech militarist space opera by, say, Jerry Pournelle, anyone tries to make the male protagonist do something he does not want to and which is against his interests, they get killed. And why should Russ's heroine be any less ruthless in the defence of her autonomy? All sorts of metafictional markers are being put up that our attitude to the heroine's action is meant to be complex, but there are particular resonances for the reader who has read, say, an otherwise totally obscure 1950s story like Randall Garrett's *The Queen Bee*, in which a group of shipwrecked men faced with a similarly stroppy and murderous female solve their breeding problem by lobotomy and polyandry.[10] The sort of dialectical echoing of earlier work I have described already has a further spoiling function; no one could write a story like Garrett's, or return to that story and read it, without being aware of the Russ story and given a bad conscience by it. That is why *We Who Are About To* made and makes so many people so very angry; it reclaimed and colonised a piece of polemical territory.

This tradition of dialectical engagement with earlier texts makes it easier for SF to embody dissent from generally held assumptions about contemporary life. Russ said in 1970 'One would think SF the perfect literary mode in which to explore and explode our assumptions about "innate" values and "natural" social arrangements, in short our ideas about Human Nature Which Never Changes'. Though she also went on to say – and remember the date, prior to most of her own major work – that in SF, 'Speculation about the innate personality differences between men and women, about the family, about sex and in short about gender roles, does not exist at all'. What she and others proceeded to do in their criticism was to establish an agenda in accordance with which all those things were up for discussion. Talking about the SF of the 1950s and its treatment of sexual roles, she also said 'American SF in general ignored women's estate and the problems of sexual structure with which feminism deals. Even such honorable exceptions as Theodore Sturgeon and Damon Knight could only indicate distress at the state of affairs, without providing the political analysis which did not at that time exist'. Yet, just as during the McCarthy period writers like Sturgeon had used SF to express dissent, in spite of the right-wing editors who were publishing his work, so, once a feminist position was intellectually available, it could be embodied in SF just because the established rules of the genre created a space in which expressing an argument was seen by neither writers nor their readership as diverting from literary creation. That readership, young and primarily male, could for a while be assumed to be capable of following the intellectual argument and not regarding the application of reason to something a little more immediate than the establishment of galactic empires as a huge intrusion. Russ's *When It Changed* was one of her first explicitly feminist and misandric stories, and was greeted with enthusiasm and awards.[11] Resentment came later, once it was clear that feminist SF was here to stay.

It has been suggested (by Samuel Delany) that the process of learning to read SF is in part one of learning a habit of inventive reading of texts – which is a part of the reason why a lot of people never acquire the taste.[12] An individual SF text may be obliged to use a commonplace phrase in a context which makes it over – 'He turned on his left side', 'Her world fell apart'. The assumed reader of the genre acquires the habit of noticing and savouring minor cues of language and social detail which sketch in the ways in which an imaginary society works. This habit of agility makes that audience at least theoretically and for some of the time open to accepting imaginary societies whose assumptions differ from their own. Again, this has facilitated the growth of a feminist SF tradition.

In the 1940s and 1950s in the United States, SF was precisely the sort of thing that a good feminine little girl was not supposed to enjoy reading, and so a proportion of those girl-children destined to grow up stroppy did so. Under John W. Campbell's right-wing editorship, largely because he believed himself to be a free spirit who questioned everything, *Astounding Science Fiction* occasionally contained positive images of women as agents, and even where women were shown as subsidiary helpmeets to strong male heroes, they did so in ways showing them to be freer than was allowed for in a standard 1950s model of psychologically adjusted sexual roles. A Robert A. Heinlein heroine riding shotgun on her man is at least not being told she is sick for not being engaged in homemaking.[13] Paradoxically, much of the SF published in and by authors associated with *Galaxy*, a magazine in general of considerably more politically progressive hue, tended, because of the interest of its authors in psychiatry, and thus psychiatric orthodoxy, to be comparatively reactionary in its sexual politics.[14]

The women SF writers of this period tended to be marginalised in one of three ways: one, editors were keen on stories which were 'feminine' in the sense of being saccharine; the work of Zenna Henderson[15] and Judith Merrill[16] does admittedly extend the range of SF material to cover issues like nurture but does so with that sentimentality which the SF of the time tended to confound with emotional truth. Two, women were encouraged to write light jokey fiction like that of Evelyn E. Smith, fiction which keeps a low temperature even in its humour.[17] In some of the work of Evelyn Smith and of Margaret St Clair there is a quiet anger from which Russ probably learned;[18] her own early fiction appeared towards the end of this time and was in more or less that vein.[19]

The third marginalising pressure was that surviving women writers of the 1930s and the 1940s, like Leigh Brackett and C. L. Moore, had had to make their own accommodations to the rules of an earlier date.[20] They used androgynous versions of their names; where they were known to be women, they were also known to be the wives and, more importantly, the best buddies of equally popular writers with whom they often collaborated. And the sort of flowery space opera in which Brackett specialised and in which Moore had made her name, Arabian Nights stuff with a dying Mars full of the echoing whisper of dust in dry canals, was not seen as the cutting edge of the field. Ironically, it had been earlier that Moore had felt able to write about Jirel of Joiry, a medieval swordswoman hacking her way through land-scapes of heavily sexual imagery. What work she produced in the 1950s had to be far more restrained. The tendency to purple prose in both these writers, and Brackett's slight lack of total seriousness were seen as agreeable, but as examples of the second-rateness of women.

An important aspect of the SF of the 1950s turns out in retrospect to have been the SF novels for young adults that André Norton started writing then.[21] She learned from Brackett and Moore a certain touch with exotic locations; and she played up to her audience's emotional needs with her Ugly Duckling child and adolescent protagonists, male and female. Just as the reactionary and militarist ideas of a lot of the current crop of male writers can be laid at the door of the Heinlein juveniles they read when they were young, so too can a lot of the strengths and weaknesses of a lot of the women writers of the 1970s and 1980s be attributed to their reading of André Norton, notably the Ugly Duckling plot, in which an individual with hidden special talents is admitted to the elite of caste societies. Hardly progressive, but alas one of those messages women were likely to learn from some of the SF of the 1950s. In spite of this marginalisation, a number of women came through the 1950s into the more radical days of the 1960s and 1970s still engaged with commercial SF and still prepared to turn to it when they started writing.

Crucially, SF changed radically in the 1960s; a variety of writers and editors became impatient with the complacency and clichés of much of the genre, while still respecting its stock of rich vulgar imagery. What tends to be referred to as the New Wave was a matter of increased literary quality and freedom for literary experiment. A battery of stylistic gimmickries and elaborations were brought up to convey as forcefully as possible a 'Happening World' of chance and sudden change. It became hugely more possible to stretch the genre as a form in which it was possible not only to argue ideas but to reflect through metaphor personal experience. When reactionary critics of the genre like Kingsley Amis stigmatise the 1960s as the point at which it all went wrong, they standardly single out as one of the really awful examples of things that went wrong Pamela Zoline's story *The Heat Death of the Universe*, which links the daily frustrated experience of a hard-pressed wife and mother with the concept of entropy, and is primarily an SF story because it says it is, not because it makes the comment of its scientific reference to real life so crucial.[22] Zoline has written too little, but the moment of her writing of that story is an important signal as to where things could go. Amis is not so far wrong in seeing it as where, from his point of view, the rot set in, and things changed.

Joanna Russ is much more than a confessional writer, but there is an important confessional element in her work, and its explicit arrival signalled her development into a writer of real importance. Her involvement in SF as a writer dates back to the late 1950s, but it was in the late 1960s that she found her real voice. This discovery of her mature style and voice coincided fairly precisely with her coming out as lesbian and her political radicalisation. It is significant that in her non-SF confessional novel about that period, *On Strike Against God*, she sets up as talking heads with whom she can discuss the new issues in her life recognisable portraits of the progressive SF editors, critics and teachers of writing, Damon Knight and Kate Wilhelm, and a more satirical and hostile portrait of the more than slightly macho Norman Spinrad.[23] During this period she established an agenda, at first a very limited agenda, of making the conerns of the genre in which she was writing relevant to her, personally. She had discovered that her distinctive personal voice required the use of a strong female protagonist; her second novel *And Chaos Died* has a slightly wispy, gay male hero and is perhaps the weakest of her novels for that reason.[24] When Russ turned, as she did in some of her best work of this time, to the sword-and-sorcery genre, she did not desire to work in the OTT purple tradition of Moore and Brackett. Instead she produced in her heroine Alyx a protagonist characterised, in her dealings with monsters and mages and barbarian swordsmen, by a materialist common sense and abhorrence of high-flown cant; qualities that are, for Russ, a large part of what a feminist consciousness should be about. Still, in the Alyx stories, which include the SF novel *Picnic on Paradise*, she was not being entirely original.[25] She had chosen as a partner in dialogue the older writer Fritz Leiber, argument with whose themes occurs alike in these early stories and in maturer work like *The Two of Them* and *The Second Inquisition*.[26] Both writers were fascinated by the use of SF as a source of metaphors for confessional writing, and it is clear that during the 1970s they learned from each other, as well as including teasing references to each other's characters in their work.

It was with *When It Changed*, a short story which she contributed to Harlan Ellison's first *Dangerous Visions* anthology, that Russ first became clearly recognised as a force with which to be reckoned. *Dangerous Visions* was conceived of as a manifesto of the New Wave, a forum in which it was possible to say things that could not be said elsewhere in the genre. Comparatively few of its experiments with style and discourse have worn well, but the Russ story is one of those few. Earlier SF treatments of colonies on other planets which have lost one sex to disease had been dominated by heterosexual assumptions; Russ showed a world of women who had found a way of living without men and were not at all grateful for being 'rescued'. As I have said, at first the SF establishment took this on board and then it was gradually realised that Russ meant what she said; in her reviewing and in her stories she dealt with sexist assumptions with an icy ferocity that was a joy to behold. She clinched both her reputation and her status as an outsider within the genre by writing her most important novel *The Female Man*, which uses the stock SF image of the struggle for existence between alternate versions of reality as a way of writing about different ways in which different versions of herself might experience her feminism, might combat worlds dominated by patriarchy.[27] Like a lot of SF which uses the alternate world concept with intelligence, it is a novel about the struggle between texts for authenticity, about how to read, and how to listen to, the stories that the culture tells us about ourselves. It is a novel which stretches traditional forms of the novel, and especially of the SF novel, to breaking point. It is probably the most important single SF novel of the 1970s, in the way it combines its literary experimentation with its radical politics, in its anger and its wit and its poise. The fiction of Joanna Russ takes stock SF material and deconstructs it in terms of asking whose interests a cliché serves and in terms of the authenticity and verisimilitude of the text. There is a paradox implicit in *We Who Are About To*, and that paradox is that elsewhere Russ had written of the difficulty of texts that purported to be documents, whose provenance was part of their verisimilitude; and here she produces a novel that purports to be a suicide note, a transcript of a tape recording that, in the nature of the novel's plot, no one can ever be in a position to transcribe. In all of Russ's work there is a major element of play which should never be underrated: the anger, the showing of claws when her protagonists kill men who stand in the way of their autonomy; these are genuine, but they are also a pose. Russ is an important SF writer, but she is also an important postmodernist.

The other most important woman SF writer of the 1970s and since, more acceptable to the establishment and in many ways more assimilable as an influence, was Ursula Le Guin. Her feminism is less intensely and immediately political than that of Russ. She has been heavily influenced by Taoist thought and its

dualism; her novel *The Left Hand of Darkness* takes its title from an
imaginary proverb to the effect that 'Light is the left hand of
darkness and darkness the right hand of light'.[28] She is a
committed believer in non-violent Gandhian solutions to political problems and to that quietly persuasive tone of voice by
which in that system imbalances and injustices are best resolved.
This stand has caused at least as much irritation to the SF right as
Russ's position, and Le Guin's quiet authority as a progressive
voice hugely outweighs her occasionally irritating 'wet' liberal
side. If you wanted to think of her and Russ as the soft cop and
the hard cop of American feminist SF, you would not be so far
wrong. It is also the case that Le Guin knows her own limitations.
Her problems with the concept of socialist realism, her difficulties with simply using fiction to argue a simple case, her worries
about self-censorship, the 'Stalin in the Soul', make her less
effective when she feels called upon to write straightforwardly
on public issues.[29] Her Vietnam novella *The Word For World is
Forest* ends up being cruder and less satisfactory than her more
indirect work.[30]

In her 1976 lecture 'Science Fiction and Mrs Brown', she called
for an SF that would concern itself primarily with people, for a
value system that was at bottom humane; but she has never
made the mistake of assuming that the best way of portraying
real human values is to be any sort of straightforward realist.[31] In
'psychomyths' like *The Ones Who Walk Away from Omelas*, she uses
the freedom that SF and fantasy give her to dramatise in concrete
and apposite ways various problems of social morality.[32] In her
novel *The Dispossessed*,[33] its pendant short story 'The Day Before
the Revolution', and the linked historical novel about an imaginary country's Romantic revolutionaries, *Malafrena*, she portrays
the mutual interaction of individuals and society with that
vibrant apparent realism that is only really possible when all the
details of the environment have been made up from scratch by
the author.[34] Her characters are at once the three-dimensional
representatives of humanity she called for in the lecture and
stand for something beyond themselves. They act out roles in a
social and moral universe, and the directness and intensity of her
work derives from the fact that she believes that moral universe
to be the most important thing there is. Odo, the dying woman
anarchist in 'The Day Before the Revolution', is a set of manner-

isms and perceptions and memories – we are made to see her alien planet through her eyes and thus are forced to believe that she is in there to see it for us – but she also stands for the author's observation of the old, for the hope that one can attain old age while retaining integrity and dignity; as a portrait of a generation of radicals in our own world as much as in the imaginary capitalism of Urras – and as promulgator of a set of ideas.

By giving that story the title she did, Le Guin cheatingly achieves a sense, a sense no less *real* because we have been tricked into it, of Odo's successful and dominant interaction with her world. If a story with that title is concerned so intensely with an individual, we are half-convinced of that individual's agency within society even before Le Guin has begun to demonstrate it. In *The Dispossessed* she makes use of the knowledge possessed by much of her assumed readership of the consistent fictional universe from her earlier work. This familiar universe gives intensity to our belief that the work the scientist Shevek is doing is important and thereby in the importance of free inquiry even when in the short term it clashes with the demands of what approximates to a just society. She uses the fact that she is writing in a well-known SF form, the linked series of novels and short stories, to set up a moral complexity which avoids a crude opposition of scientist and anarcho-communist society. She is an unscrupulous experimentalist when she wants to be, in the way she uses the standard expectations of fiction in general and SF in particular to manipulate the sympathy of her audience; her artistic integrity has little to do with playing fair in any simple way. She is aware that at a crucial level all fiction is a form of rhetoric, a construct rather than a description of objective truth – though it may *represent* truth – that in art, if not in life, achieved ends justify moderately dishonest rhetorical methods. She works in an art whose nature is deceit, and in SF whose gaudy backdrops and borrowings make that deceit a double trick. It is when one of the two aspects of Le Guin overdominates, when she loses that sense of balance so important to her magicians in the *Earthsea Trilogy*,[35] that her work can become as tediously frivolous as the stories in *The Compass Rose*,[36] or as worthy and earnest as her recent Utopian novel *Always Coming Home*.[37] If Le Guin becomes too involved in either rhetoric for its own sake or a political commitment too urgent for cleverness, she slips from her major status, and becomes ordinary.

Paradoxically, some of the most interesting and complex SF related to feminism came from a writer who for most of her career in the genre continued to use the male pseudonym under which she had broken into the field.[38] This had partly to do with the sexist biases of the market, partly to do with Alice Sheldon's belief that style is androgynous and that she could expose this, more for her private amusement than anything else, by allowing people to write about her work under false assumptions, and partly to do with the habit of obsessive secrecy she had learned while a left-winger doing illegal, clandestine investigations inside the United States for the CIA. James Tiptree was a name she had derived from a jam jar, and for the last years of the 1960s and most of the 1970s she kept up the masquerade successfully, causing a number of critics and commentators to make fools of themselves. She once said,

> Critics talked about my 'narrative drive' as being a male writing style, but narrative drive is simply intensity and a desire not to bore ... Cassandra ... was never accused of a lack of narrative drive. She was just a little before her time, which is often what women's crimes consist of.[39]

What is in retrospect amazing is that people continued to be fooled by the pseudonym even at a point when, in stories like the ironically-titled *The Women Men Don't See*, she was writing fictions which clearly stated that, for many women, men are an alien other.[40] Predictably, a number of writers who had praised James Tiptree's universal grasp of human motivation started, after the pseudonym had become transparent, talking about Alice Sheldon's blinkered and narrow view of the human condition.

The crucial point about her fiction on feminist themes is that it regards sexism and its consequences as a tragedy, as a failure of communication which is not necessary. In *Houston, Houston, Do You Read Me?*, a trio of astronauts are warped through time into an all-female future and soon reveal their true colours through a drunken attempt at rape; they are expeditiously and harmlessly disposed of.[41] But Sheldon sets up a lot of ambiguities here as well; one of the men does not participate in the attempted rape and, further, accepts the necessity of his death. This, even when he knows that the deck has been largely rigged in the first place, that he and his fellows were fed a de-inhibiting drug, partly in the hope that they would do something inexcusable. The story is given much of its tension and strength by the extent to which the author knows that she is fiddling her results for the sake of an exemplary fiction, and is worried by it.

One of the reasons why her best work tends to be her angriest is that her faith in the possibility of solutions is so clearly a matter of faith rather than a rationally arrived at solution. In both her novels, most especially in *Up the Walls of the World*, she shows equal partnerships between the sexes as possible and desirable, but she does so in terms that make it happen only in a context so far removed from common experience as to be deeply unconvincing as a statement about the human condition.[42] Her most negative visions of sexual politics take the form of angry rhetoric; her positive statement offers the easy answers of a fairy tale.

Sheldon's capacity for solid, forgiving portraits, the 'negative capability' through which she painted precise vignettes of the sensory apprehensions and revealing memories of even quite minor characters, sometimes seemed to be trapping her in an impasse. Communication and morality were important to her work from the start – in an early story, Dr Ain tries to persuade humanity against ecodoom in an incoherent lecture before spreading plague as a final answer – but Sheldon's love for her characters and her need to use them to say something beyond the expression of that love began to get in each other's way.[43]

Each of her collections contains at least one story in which an act of sex demonstrates frustrated communication. Genetically-programmed lust for aliens destroys humanity in *I Awoke And Found Me Here*;[44] the evolution of intelligence in an alien species is aborted by the sexual behaviour evolution has also programmed into them in *Love is the Plan, the Plan is Death*;[45] most apocalyptically, the whole of human evolution and endeavour proves to have been a prelude to alien contact, after which metaphysical sexual congress we can all wither away in *A Momentary Taste of Being*.[46] Relationships are seen as always tragic, almost always doomed and as always worth the effort of the attempt. Last year, when her husband became irredeemably incoherent from Alzheimer's disease, Alice Sheldon shot him and herself dead.[47]

These three are far from the only serious women writers working in the SF field. I could go on to talk about Suzy McKee Charnas's dystopian and Utopian diptych *Walk to the End of the World*[48] and *Motherlines*,[49] and the way in which she abandoned the intended trilogy for work which embodied a marginally more conciliatory view of sexual politics like *The Vampire Tapestry*. Lisa Tuttle has applied fairly formulaic horror and SF storylines to particular sets of women's problems which they relate to and metaphorically exemplify.[50] Josephine Saxton uses the genre much of the time to give colour to her confessional writing and additional freedom to her surrealism; the bite and bitchiness of her work would be there without SF, and are when she is not writing it, but she still finds it a useful form to engage with much of the time.[51] On the boundaries of the more commercial end of the genre, Tanith Lee uses stock SF, fantasy and horror tropes to make her work more glamorous and more compelling and her speculations about sexual possibilities more extreme.[52] And there are all the commercial writers who are basically concerned with entertainment but who, like Marion Zimmer Bradley, have taken their developing consciousness, and that of the growing female readership of SF, as much part of the material they work with as a traditional heady brew of oath-taking, desert journeys, sword play and the plighting of troths.[53] Women writing during the years of the revival of the Women's Movement have often come from within the SF community and learned the private but accessible language of the SF genre. It is a language which has often proved useful to their expression of radical and feminist ideas.[54]

Notes

1 See, *inter alia*, the present author's *Science Fiction in the 1970s*, in *Foundation* 22 (NELP).
2 For a useful conspectus of the field, see the historical sections of *The Encyclopaedia of Science Fiction*, Peter Nicholls and John Clute (eds), Granada, London, 1968.
3 See, for example, *Ralph 124C41+*, by the editor of *Amazing Stories*, Hugo Gernsback.
4 See, for general accounts of 1930s male SF fandom, *The Way the Future Was*, by Frederik Pohl, Gollancz, London, 1979, and *The Futurians*, by

Damon Knight, Day, NY, 1977. For accounts of the experience of women SF readers and fans of this and later periods, see the introduction to *The Best of Marion Zimmer Bradley*, DAW, Sacramento, 1988, and the endnote to *The Best of Leigh Brackett*, Doubleday, NY, 1977, as well as various of the interviews in the second volume of *Dream Makers*, by Charles Platt, Frederick Ungar, NY, 1983.

5 Notably in *New Maps of Hell*, Gollancz, London, 1961.

6 Notably in *The Known and the Unknown: The Iconography of Science Fiction*, Kent State University Press, Kent, 1979.

7 In her article of the same name in *College English*, October 1971, and in her irregular review columns throughout the 1970s in *The Magazine of Fantasy and Science Fiction*, as yet uncollected.

8 Robert Heinlein's *Farnham's Freehold*, Putnam's, NY, 1964. The clearest embodiment of this view is contained in *Lucifer's Hammer*, by Larry Niven and Jerry Pournelle, Playboy Press, London, 1977, and Sphere, London, 1978.

9 Dell, NY, 1977, The Women's Press, London, 1987.

10 *Astounding Science Fiction*, December 1958.

11 Included in *Dangerous Visions* edited by Harlan Ellison Doubleday, NY, 1967, and Gollancz, London, 1987.

12 Notably in *The Jewel-Hinged Jaw*, Dragon Press, Pleasantville, 1977.

13 Perhaps the classic text of this kind is Omnilingual by H. Beam Piper (*Astounding Science Fiction*, 1957, and various anthologies such as *Prolog to Analog*, (ed.) J. W. Campbell Jr. since), which throws in a feminist sub-text to a fairly straightforward piece of problem-solving SF. Piper's work, notably the Paratime stories, often features an active and hot-headed male protagonist with a more thoughtful female partner, the two regularly getting each other out of trouble. James Schmitz's work often features such equal sexual partnerships in adventure plots, e.g. *The Witches of Karres*, Gollancz, London, 1988.

14 E.g. The work of William Tenn passim, and *Search the Sky* by Frederik Pohl and C. M. Kornbluth, Ballantine, NY, 1954. The female-dominated dystopia which forms the second section of this latter novel is, to some extent, a tongue-in-cheek comedy of reversal, but far from unalloyedly so. A recent re-issue accordingly tones some of this material down.

15 See, for example, her *Pilgrimage*, Gollancz, London, 1962.

16 See, for example, her *Daughters of Earth*, Gollancz, London, 1968.

17 The short fiction of Evelyn E. Smith is as yet uncollected, and her two novels are only partly typical of her work: some of her better stories occur in various of the anthologies of stories from *Galaxy* edited by H. L. Gold.

18 A selection of St Clair's short fiction is contained in *Change the Sky*, Ace, NY, 1974.

19 Much of it included in *The Zanzibar Cat*, Arkham House, Sauk City, 1983, and in *The Hidden Side of the Moon*, St Martin's, NY, 1987; The Women's Press, London, 1989.

20 See e.g. *Jirel of Joiry* (Pb library 1969), and *The Best of C. L. Moore*, Doubleday, NY, 1975.

21 Norton's work amounts to some fifty titles of varying worth; typical but superior examples are *Catseye* and *Night of Masks*, Gollancz, London, 1962 and 1965. The popular *Witch World* series is written for adults and not wholly typical of her work.

22 Included in her collection *Busy about the Tree of Life*, The Women's Press, London, 1988.

23 Out and Out Press, NY, 1979; The Women's Press, London, 1987.

24 Ace, NY, 1970.

25 These have been collected in various combinations, with and without *Picnic on Paradise*, and with and without an introduction by Samuel R. Delany. *The Adventures of Alyx*, The Women's Press, London, 1985, is the most readily available edition. The collection includes 'The Second Inquisition', which is not really an Alyx story, and excludes 'A Game of Vlet', which is one in all but the failure to name the protagonist and is included in *The Zanzibar Cat*.

26 Berkley, NY, 1978, The Women's Press, London, 1986.

27 Bantam, NY, 1975, Star, Belmont, 1977, and The Women's Press, London, 1985.

28 Walker, NY, 1969; Macdonald, London, 1969.

29 Included in *The Language of the Night*, a collection of Le Guin's essays, edited by Susan Wood, Putnam's, NY, 1979.

30 Originally in *Again Dangerous Visions*, edited by Harlan Ellison Doubleday, NY, 1972, an extended version of the original novella by itself, Putnam, NY, 1976; Gollancz, London, 1977.

31 Included in *Science Fiction at large*, edited by Peter Nichols, Gollancz, London, 1976; Harper & Row, NY, 1977.

32 Included in *The Wind's Twelve Quarters*, Harper & Row, NY, 1975; Gollancz, London, 1976.

33 Harper & Row, NY, Gollancz, London, 1974.

34 Harper & Row, NY, 1979, Gollancz, London, 1980.

35 *A Wizard of Earthsea*, Gollancz, London, 1971, *The Tombs of Atuan*, Gollancz, London, 1972, *The Farthest Shore*, Gollancz, London, 1973.

36 Harper & Row, NY, and Gollancz and Granada, London, 1984.

37 Gollancz, London, 1987. A member of the audience at the ICA seriously dissented from my view of this book as worthy but unreadably dull, arguing that its refusal of story in any conventional sense, and its concentration on ritual and myth, made it a valuable contribution to postmodernist feminist writing, avoiding the pitfalls of stock ideology that traditional story is liable to entail. This

argument is one I am disinclined to accept, but it is clearly a case to answer, and seems to be borne out by Ursula Le Guin's essay in *Women of Vision* edited by Denise Dupon (St Martin's Press, 1989).

38 Sheldon even maintained the masquerade when Tiptree was asked to contribute, as a sympathetic male, to *Khatru*, a 1975 fanzine symposium on feminism and SF.

39 From the interview with Sheldon in *The Dream Makers vol. 2*, Charles Platt (ed.), Berkley, NY, 1983.

40 Included in *Warm Worlds and Otherwise*.
Tiptree's short fiction is included in the following volumes:
Ten Thousand Light Years from Home, Ace, NY, 1973, and Methuen, London, 1975.
Warm Worlds and Otherwise, Ballantine, NY, 1975.
Star Songs of an Old Primate, Ballantine, NY, 1978.
Out of the Everywhere, Ballantine, NY, 1981.
Tales of the Quintana Roo, Arkham, Sauk City, 1987.
The Starry Rift, Tor, NY, 1987 and Sphere, London, 1988.
At least one posthumous volume, *Crown of Stars*, is to follow.

41 Included in *Star Songs of an Old Primate*.

42 Berkley, NY, 1977, and Gollancz, London, 1977.

43 Included in *Ten Thousand Light-Years from Home*.

44 Included in *Ten Thousand Light-Years from Home*.

45 Included in *Warm Worlds and Otherwise*.

46 Included in *Star Songs of an Old Primate*.

47 The fiction of her last years, notably the second novel, *Brightness falls from the Air*, Tor, NY, 1986, and Sphere, London, 1986, can be seen as being more often a meditation on these personal themes than on more public issues, though stories like *Morality Meat* included in *Despatches from the Frontiers of the Female Mind*, Green and Lefanu (eds), The Women's Press, London, 1985, indicate her continuing commitment to an angry feminism.

48 Ballantine, NY, 1974, and Gollancz, London, 1979.

49 Berkley, NY, 1979, and Gollancz, London, 1980.

50 The horror stories of Lisa Tuttle are included in *A Nest of Nightmares*, Sphere, London, 1986; her SF stories in *A Spaceship made of Stone*, The Women's Press, London, 1987.

51 The short science fiction of Josephine Saxton is collected in *The Power of Time*, Chatto, London, 1985, and *The Travails of Jane Saint*, The Women's Press, London, 1986.

52 An author so prolific and varied as to make selection from her work more or less invidious, Lee has a good general selection of her short SF and fantasy, as yet untitled, appearing from Unwin Hyman in the late Spring of 1989.

53 Most of the *Darkover* novels deal with explicitly or implicitly feminist

themes in a context of barbarian swordplay à la Leigh Brackett; Bradley's quasi-fantastic historical novels, *The Mists of Avalon*, Sphere, London, 1984, and *The Firebrand*, Michael Joseph, London, 1987, place the Arthurian legends and the Fall of Troy in deliberately revisionist feminist contexts.

54 There has also been a lot of feminist SF which has tended far more to the Utopian side of the SF tradition, occasionally productively – as in the case of Marge Piercy's *Woman on the Edge of Time*, Knopf, 1976, The Women's Press, London, 1979 – and often not. The trouble with the Utopian tradition is that work written out of it has a far greater tendency to the simplistic and the monotone, simply because sources of conflict are not built in to the form itself. Piercy uses the contemporary dire straits of her heroine and, somewhat less successfully, a rival dystopian future time-line to create conflict; other texts, such as Sally Gearhart's *The Wanderground*, The Women's Press, London, 1985, tend to rely on the reader's imposing a sense of conflict on the text drawn directly from the way her own experience interacts with it. This latter is an honourable solution to a politico/aesthetic problem, in a sense, but one which leaves the text imperfect save in symbiosis with a perfect reader, and this reader would have to share the politics of Gearhart at the moment of writing the book, however subsequent to that moment she was. Utopias are as prone to dating as all other fictions; but most Utopias are far more closed intellectual systems, far less accessible to productively variant readings.

The American market has helped create a 'post-feminist' SF, which either opposes, or takes so totally for granted as to in fact ignore, any practical feminist agenda, and is largely worthless in artistic terms, including those appropriate to genre; the attempts at redressing this balance of some editors, notably those of the British Women's Press, have produced some ideologically sound but, aesthetically considered, deeply naive works. Much of the energy that might have gone into SF in the past has been diverted into heroic fantasy, though writers like Connie Willis, Karen Joy Fowler and Gwyneth Jones are producing worthwhile, and committedly feminist SF.

References and Further Reading

Other relevant essays and books on the practice and criticism of science fiction in addition to those mentioned in the notes, include:

General Studies of the Field

Delany, Samuel R., *The Jewel Hinged Jaw*, Dragon Press, London, 1977.

Nicholls and Clute (eds), *The Encyclopaedia of Science Fiction*, Granada, London, 1979.

Nicholls (ed.), *Science Fiction at Large*, Gollancz, London, 1977.

Foundation (a thrice-yearly magazine published by North-East London Polytechnic).

Platt, Charles (ed.), *The Dream Makers*, vol. 2, Frederick Ungar, NY, 1983. Volume I which was also published by Savoy Press in England has only one interview with a woman, and that was Kate Wilhelm jointly interviewed with her husband.

General Studies of Women's SF

Lefanu, Sarah, *In the Chinks of the World Machine*, The Women's Press, London, 1988.

Le Guin, Ursula, *The Language of the Night*, Putnam's, NY, 1979.

The editorial material in the anthologies *Women of Wonder*, *More Women of Wonder*, and *New Women of Wonder*, Pamela Sargent (ed.), Random House, NY, 1975, 1976, 1978.

Women of Wonder and *New Women of Wonder* also published Penguin Books, London, 1978 and 1979.

WOMEN'S BIOGRAPHY
AND AUTOBIOGRAPHY:
FORMS OF HISTORY,
HISTORIES OF FORM

———◆———

CAROLYN STEEDMAN

In modern literary studies, biography and autobiography are not usually considered together. But that is what I intend to do in this essay – make some observations about the history of these forms, and some suggestions about how a consideration of women's written life-stories might serve to shift the demarcation line between the two. I shall raise these questions by discussing the biography that I have been writing over the last year (and working on for much longer than that) of Margaret McMillan, who was born in New York State in 1860 of Scottish emigré parents, grew up in Inverness, and who died in 1931, an earlier career in socialist and Independent Labour Party (ILP) politics forgotten in the apolitical celebration of her as a saviour of little children.[1]

This essay, then, involves a discussion of literary form, of what literary forms permit and what they prevent in particular historical contexts: that is, the constraints that the form of biography presents me with, writing of a historical figure, now, in the late 1980s; the constraints that the form of autobiography offered to Margaret McMillan, writing her own, very odd, life-story in 1927. In her *Life of Rachel McMillan*, she purported to write the biography of her sister Rachel, and in fact, wrote her own.[2] Particularly, she effected this disguise of herself (if that is what it was; perhaps it was a display, or an interpretation of herself) by appropriating her sister's childhood. Later, I want to return to the figure of the child, and its use in women's life-stories.

Stories, says Lewis Mink, are only truly narrativised when they take on the same meaning for the listener as the teller; and they come to an end when there is no more to be said, when teller and audience both see that this point you have reached, this end, was implicit in the beginning, was there all along.[3] In spoken and written autobiography there is, I think, a simple variant of this narrative rule in operation. The man or woman, leaning up against the public bar, or writing a book, is the embodiment of something completed. That end, the finished place, is the human being, a body in time and space, telling a story that brings the reader to the here and now, to this character in the pages of the book. *Written* autobiography ends in the figure of the writer, and the narrative closure of *biography* is the figure that has been made through the pages of the book.

In narrative terms, these forms of writing – biography and autobiography – must always remain in conflict with the writing of history, which does indeed come to conclusions and reach ends, but which actually moves forward through the understanding that *things are not over*, that the story isn't finished, can't ever be completed, because some new piece of evidence may alter the account. History is a narrative that proceeds by the objectives of exhaustiveness and exception; and its central rhetorical device is this recognition of temporariness and impermanence.

I discuss this difficulty now so that I do not have to *work towards* it as a conclusion, so that I can say simply that one of the problems facing me as a biographer of Margaret McMillan is a conflict between two narrative forms, that of the life-story and that of history. At the same time, the fictionality of all these forms – of biography, autobiography and history – can be suggested, and I will be able to discuss them as forms of writing, that work by emplotment, by the use of figures and allusions, as well as by presentation of their content, which in all three cases is information about lives and times.

'That', as Margaret McMillan once said to a student taking down a lecture from her dictation, 'that will do for the exordium, now for the peroration.' I shall now turn to the problems of writing a biography of Margaret McMillan; problems that are, I think, to do with (a) the current state of feminist biography, and the history of biographical form that it carries about with it; (b) the legacy of a certain kind of women's history; and (c) the subject herself.

If Margaret McMillan is known at all today, it is through a body of educational writing that celebrates her work in early childhood education during and after the First World War. Several hagiographies, which call her variously prophet of childhood, pioneer of nursery education, and a modern Santa Barbara were published between 1930 and 1960, and they serve to neatly sever off her first fifty years, when she was a member of the ILP and socialist journalist and propagandist, from the last twenty (her time as prophetess, seer and saint) after she established an open-air treatment centre and school in the slums of Deptford, in 1910.[4] No one who is familiar with popular history of childhood, in which, as kind people rescue children from factory, mine and physical deterioration, things march to an enlightened present throughout the nineteenth century, or aware of the history of education, which has usually eschewed politics as one of its central organising devices, should be surprised at the effective disappearance of McMillan's first fifty years, within this biographical corpus.

The way seems clear for the historical biographer. A historical biography, one that elevates the political and social setting to the life above its narration, must restore a background to McMillan that deals in terms of culture and class. It must, for instance, make something of her having been born in Westchester County, in New York State, of her father's death in 1865, of the return of a mother and two small daughters to Inverness, to a house of cold, lower-middle-class restriction, an expulsion from a garden of paradise and a garden of childhood, and a prefiguring of the garden in the slum that was the Deptford Centre, half a century later. It must make something of a history of the Highland Clearances, their reverberation and consolidation in both myth and political organisation in the Highland capital during the 1860s and 1870s. A historical biography must place the working life of two lower-middle-class young women, of Margaret and her sister Rachel, in some perspective, must acknowledge that McMillan was unusually well-educated for a girl from her background, being sent to Germany and Switzerzland to train as a finishing governess. It must speculate reasonably on the years she spent governessing in the English shires, speculation that will involve arguing that the fiction she produced for the labour press in the 1890s constitutes some evidence of this period, which is otherwise quite lost to historical view. It must place McMillan's 'conversion' to socialism in the context of the great Dock Strike of 1889, and within the trajectory of British ethical socialism. It must say what being recruited to the ILP in 1893, moving to Bradford to teach a course of adult education in the Labour Institute there, and being elected to three school boards in the city suggest about the possibilities for women's economic and political activity in the 1890s. It must say something important (or at least interesting) about the possible relationships of women to political structures at the end of the last century, exampled in McMillan's involvement in municipal affairs, and about the disenfranchisement of women at this level in an enactment of 1902. It can present her move back to London, in 1903, as a removal from such political structure and political support, and can discuss her courses of adult education, lecturing and writing as an early example of the modern intellectual woman's hustling of a part-time living.

This historical biography can get its fun by delineating a new myth, a myth of Corinne (though, in fact, Ellen Moers got there first, as she so often did) in which the female figure on the socialist platform, the woman speaking there, possesses a charisma and calls forth an adulation that even Keir Hardie could not command.[5] What it certainly has to do is discuss her role as intellectual of the ILP, as translator of a range of physiological and psychological ideas into a coherent theory of childhood and socialism, with redeemed and regenerated working-class childhood the path to revolutionary change. It can show how, through all her fiction, all her journalism, she rewrote and reconstructed her own childhood, and found new places for it within her autobiography, so we might see that significant legacy of British Romanticism, the Wordsworthian child, the marriage between immanence and mortality, a child-figure that measures out a particular aetiology of the self, being used by one woman, in one particular historical context – and for a political purpose, to boot. For of course, what is particularly interesting and important about McMillan's quest for her own lost childhood (a quest that can be seen as the organising principle of the life-story as told in Europe since the early nineteenth century), is that she reorganised and reasserted her own past not just in the words she put on the page, but in the lives of others: the others being poor children, working-class children, the 'children of the dark area'. As theoretical rabbit, this particular biography can pull out of its hat the observation that McMillan's theory of childhood was taken over lock-stock-and-barrel by the ILP, but that neither the executive nor the membership knew, nor cared to know, the roots or the implication of their party policy on childhood: it can ask: what is an idea or a theory when those who hold it do not know its provenance?

Raymond Williams argued that in spite of its seeming simplicity, biography, along with memoir and history, is a difficult and perplexing form, partly because in so rigorously asserting its generic factuality, as opposed to the fictionality of myth, or epic, or drama, the writer can disguise his or her use of epic, drama and romance in the narrative.[6] On this point I shall be quite upfront, and show that I know what I am about. I shall describe McMillan's apostasy of 1929, when this veteran socialist spoke on a Conservative platform for Nancy Astor's nursery school campaign; and I shall write that apostasy as tragedy, if I can. Finally, as its engine of internal deconstruction and as major rhetorical device, the biography has to foreground its major source, which is McMillan's own *Life of Rachel McMillan*, autobiography written in the guise of biography, and show how the living Margaret canonises her dead sister Rachel, so that this *doppelgänger* bears the whole narrative of McMillan's life; so that in the end, my biography may partly serve as an exploration of the romantic variant of the form, in which the biographer seeks a shade of herself in the subject she delineates in the pages of her book.

A historical biography can do all of this, and might even be able, neatly, to raise the question of how literary form influences overt and implied representations of the self. And so what, then, is the problem? Biography is a truly popular form, as a glance at any bestseller list will show; and the biography of women, that has been produced out of publishers' women's studies lists in the last five years or so, has shared this general popularity. Current women's biography owes much of its success, I would speculate, to what makes the form generally popular, and that is first, the confirmation that biography offers, that life-stories *can* be told, that the inchoate experience of living and feeling can be marshalled into a chronology, and that central and unified subjects reach the conclusion of a life, and come into possession of their own story; and second, the way in which biography partakes of the historical romance. By historical romance (which I suppose should more properly be called a romance of history) I mean the hope that that which is gone, that which is irretrievably lost, which is past time, can be brought back, and conjured before the eyes 'as it really was'; and that it can be possessed. Biography takes us closer to its subject matter than does other historical writing, and within the romance of getting closer women must figure with more depth and delight, for as all schoolchildren, set to copy figures from the history books know, the queen is the more interesting figure to trace around than the king, possessing a plethora of lace collars, and farthingales, and ropes of hair. It is by the satisfactory *detail* – which can be sartorial, emotional, domestic – that women are the visible heroines of the historical romance. This delightful weight of detail, littleness, and interiority, is recognised in most literary histories, for whilst it is evident that this culture has bestowed interiority on women at many points and in different ways over the last three hundred years, and that the emerging biographical novel has not been the sole vehicle (we would have, for example, to look at forms as diverse as the *vita*, the written psychoanalytic case study, the 'great heroines' series of 1950s comics and reading primers), it is nevertheless valuable to see Samuel Richardson's *Pamela* (1740) as some kind of ur-text in this regard. All accounts of the development of the novel as a form point to the great divide between Henry Fielding – all surface for his characters, all motivation from without, all classical trope and allusion – and Samuel Richardson, whose fourteen-year-old Pamela is all selfhood, all inside, and whose depth as a point of reference for female interiority has been immense.

So, the reader may reasonably respond that whichever way I tell it, I am on to some kind of winner in writing the biography of a woman. What *are* the problems? Partly, they come from knowledge about existing forms. Put at its simplest, McMillan was a public woman who lived a public space, and the modern

categories of women's history and women's biography make
that remarkably difficult to deal with, unless I proceed by
revealing the detail that lies underneath the public figure – a path
not open to me, as I shall explain.

I shall comment on women's history first of all, for one popular
legacy of the work that has been done in this field over the last
fifteen years, is an altered sense of the historical meaning and
importance of female *insignificance*. The absence of women from
conventional historical accounts, discussion of this absence (and
discussion of the real archival difficulties that lie in the way of
presenting their lives in a historical context) are, at the same
time, a massive assertion of what lies hidden. A sense of that
which is lost, never to be recovered completely, has been one of
the most powerful rhetorical devices of modern women's
history. This sadness of effect is also to be found in much
working-class history, where indeed, a greater number of lives
lie lost. But a comparison between the two shows, I think, that
loss and absence remain exactly that – loss, absence, insignificance – in a way that is not the case in the writing of people's
history. The organising principles of people's history – the
annals of labour class struggle, the battles of trade union history
that might foreshadow a greater and final revolutionary struggle
– all allow the lack of detail a greater *prefigurative* force than
women's history can allow the women whose absence it notes
from the recorded past. Oppression and repression and silence
have a *meaning* within the narrative structure of labour history
that is not the case in women's history. This seems to me to be a
real narrative constraint in writing the biography of a woman
who lived and had her being in a public world; for biography has
to partake of general and current historical understandings of
women's lives, which has given absence a meaning, but a
domestic and a highly detailed one, in a minor key.

I think that this 'meaninglessness' needs to be distinguished
from the literary delineation of 'uneventfulness', which has also
structured much biography of women – and for a longer time
than the insights of women's history have. Lives of famous
women have been presented initially through a domestic detail
that asserts how little really happened to them; then a heroine is
delineated by her eruption from uneventfulness into public life.
In this way, the nineteenth-century heroine of biography in

particular remains an exceptional figure, one whose life-story explains only itself. Partly, this has been to do with the absence of analyses of women's structural relationship to the societies in which they became actors; but the exceptional female figure, or heroine, has also been produced out of the biographer's use of a personal, or individual, frame of time. Early uneventfulness, in which nothing much happens to the heroine, is seen to produce and shape what happens later, within a public space. In this way, the public life is presented as a reverse image of the old, uneventful life, rather than as a set of interactions between the subject and the political and social circumstances she finds herself in. So, as in the tradition of the exemplary religious biography from an earlier period (a variant of the form to which I will return), that which is created in adversity, in isolation, in a life where 'nothing happened', is understood to produce later conduct.

These old assumptions about an individuality formed in struggle and isolation have been reinforced to some extent by a modern psychology of women, the use of which permits a universalisation of domestic conflict. A struggle with a father then might foreshadow a social struggle, against the assumptions of a patriarchal society. Dependency, and the frequent failure of women to make a break from it is then seen as a transhistorical factor, and allows a life-story to be considered in terms of relationships with others and their vicissitudes.

You will see that, as far as Margaret McMillan goes, these conventions place me in real difficulty, for this public woman left no collection of letters, no journal with which to peel away the layers of public form in order to reveal the true woman. I can do something with the huge output of her journalism, particularly with the fiction that uses the figure of the child, and I can certainly historicise the setting to her life. But the life-story I shall tell will not yield any more than have the earlier ones, nor than she did, in her *Life of Rachel McMillan* in 1927. Above all, I cannot attempt to unveil her for the delectation of an audience: I have no secrets to tell about her. Within the form, such secrets are usually sexual, and McMillan appears not to have had a sexual relationship with anyone, ever. She prevents delineation of an interiority; she demands a public life, I think, that might perform the trick – not of dissolving the opposition between inside and outside, for that is not possible – but of letting us see, briefly, momentarily, how we might find new means of interpreting lives that have been lived. It has to take as its central image that arresting rhetorical moment of the woman on the public plat- form, or even more appropriately – and we have a witness to this moment – of the woman in the public square, in the market square, Nottingham, the miners' strike, 1893, and Percy Redfern, the draper's assistant uplifted by her words, 'touched by something vaguely, unattainably fine . . .', remembering them more than half a century later, in his book of 1946.[7]

It was Bakhtin who, in discussing Greek rhetorical auto- biography and biography, takes us to the public square, the place and form of the ancient state, the civic funeral and memorial speeches there delivered, in which biographies 'there was not, nor could there be, anything intimate or private, secret or personal . . . where the individual is open on all sides, he is all surface'.[8] To have found McMillan in a public square is one of the moments that gladdens the heart of the historian, and the writer of the biography can use the analogy to draw the reader's attention to the dead weight of interiority that hangs about the neck of women's biography. But in fact, that prehistory of the form, in which there is no inside, only surface, and both biography and autobiography serve the same political and civic function, does not serve to explain either the difficulties that lie in the way of writing McMillan's life, or the trouble she had in telling her own.

English biography is generally seen as emerging as a literary form in the seventeenth century, as part of a larger body of writings that dealt with spiritual journeys undertaken in indi- vidual lives. The Puritan autobiography is the best known – and most investigated – component of this genre, and was designed to situate a life within the context of God's purpose, and, at the same time, to give an account of its *meaning*, through that very placement within the time and space of a particular spirituality. The important point here is that time and space were specified, in that religious and social milieux came to be described in some detail. The standard histories of autobiography that we possess describe a secular development, out of this religious form, of a specifically historical consciousness, that is, of the understand- ing of the self as formed by a historicised world, by a setting that exists and changes separately from the human actors who find themselves within it.

When spiritual autobiographies of the seventeenth century, and later developments in the form, are labelled interpretative, it means that for their authors, and for a community of readers, the purpose of the life-story lay not so much in its narration, but rather in the meanings it was possible to make out of it. In the same way, the spiritual biography was exemplary in form, its purpose being not just to give an account of a life, but also to make a demonstration of the possible purposes, meanings and uses that might be made of that life-story by others. In her book *Victorian Autobiography*, Linda Peterson describes this hermeneutic tradition as the strongest influence on nineteenth-century autobiography, and describes as well an almost total alienation of women from the form.[9] She implicates in particular conduct book writers like Hannah Moore, who expended many words in the early nineteenth century telling women that the female mind was incapable of making connections between ideas and entities, incapable of drawing out meaning and purpose from the events of a life, incapable of hermeneutic activity (a point that Mary Wollstonecraft had also made, in *A Vindication of the Rights of Woman*, but with less self-congratulation and more regret than Hannah Moore). Peterson describes Harriet Martineau as a rare nineteenth-century female autobiographer, able to perform the interpretative task because she was able to substitute the doctrines of Positivism for Biblical Christianity, as a hermeneutics.

So, the biographical and autobiographical terrain was a male one, and as late as 1938 Virginia Woolf still understood biography to be the form that served above all others to express and affirm a particular kind of masculinity.[10] Nevertheless, the 1920s (the time when McMillan wrote her own *Life of Rachel McMillan*) saw an important appropriation of these forms by women. The following argument is based on the work of Kathryn Dodd, who has discussed this rapid growth of women's life-stories after the First World War by considering Ray Strachey's *The Cause*, that classic text of the struggle for women's suffrage.[11] This was published in 1928, and delineates a history of British feminism and the suffrage movement through a celebration of the achievements of exceptional middle-class women. Dodd sees in *The*

Cause a woman writing a history of women constructed out of numerous biographies and within the framework of Baldwinite constitutionalism. She sees Strachey ignoring actual histories of militancy in favour of a depiction of women succouring and uplifting the needy, notably working women and helpless children. (It was indeed Baldwin's Conservative government that granted the universal franchise that gave women the vote in 1928, not as a capitulation to feminist demands, but as a matter of constitutional inevitability.) Only very broad and general histories of literary form could see the startling appropriation of a hermeneutic form by women in the 1920s as directly connected with the bestowal on them of political meaning and status, though I do think that uses of literary forms in particular periods must always be partly explained by the political and structural relationship of people to the society in which they write.

To some extent then, that kind of political context may explain McMillan's writing of *Life of Rachel McMillan* in 1927 (and indeed, in this odd book, something of the same reworking of the past that Kathryn Dodd has noted in Ray Strachey's *The Cause* is at work, for in *Life of Rachel McMillan* the care and succour of little children, which had in fact been carried out as a matter of political conviction and political policy, becomes the regenerative motor of the world and the history McMillan tells – a progressive cause that lies beyond 'politics').

However, what is more interesting for current purposes is McMillan's writing of a life-story in the guise of her sister's. For about Rachel, there is nothing to tell: she really did possess secrets, but McMillan was not going to reveal them. In keeping them she tells her own story, but minute by minute returns to the fiction that it is Rachel's life she is imparting. I still do not know how I am to read this trope (nor how I am to give it meaning when I write). There were other autobiographical moments in Margaret McMillan's life, for as a leading member of the ILP she was frequently interviewed and asked to contribute articles to the labour press with titles like 'How I Became a Socialist'. Through all of them it is possible to see her working towards the point where Rachel's suffering as a little girl can be offered as the device on which all the political work, all the rescue of other children, in Deptford, in Bradford, rests.

I have already mentioned the particular legacy of romanticism within Western society that has been the establishment of childhood as an emblem of the self lying deep within each individual. I would suggest that in looking at the history of biographical and autobiographical accounts of women's lives we look particularly at the use of their own childhoods, as a means women found to make interiority, smallness and insignificance work as a mode of interpretation. But I am stuck here, between an interpretation that will allow us to see McMillan's use of the notion of childhood as a hermeneutics, as a complex way of revealing and giving meaning to the self, with a use of time that is backward-looking, that looks back to what is already given in the figure of the child – between that, and an interpretation that would see her actual writing of other childhoods, working-class childhoods, as an evasion of the interiority, privacy and littleness that forms of femininity, current at the turn of the century, current now, would have her use to explain herself.

I have told the story so far of the writing of two biographies, their intersection with autobiography and the questions they have raised. I have moved about in the chronology, though I could well have begun with the public man in the public square, and ended with the interior depth of the subject of modern women's biography. But this seemed the best way of drawing attention to the intersection of literary forms with each other, and the political settings that have and do govern depictions of women's lives – and in order to suggest that I want to make the implied meaning of McMillan's own life and writing some kind of denial of interiority – which denial may be a pretence, or a fiction, but one which might do some political or public good by suggesting that the boundaries of these forms, which are more than literary boundaries, might be traversed.

Notes

1 *Childhood, Culture and Class in Britain: Margaret McMillan, 1860–1931* will be published by Virago Press, London, in 1989.
2 Margaret McMillan, *Life of Rachel McMillan*, Dent, London, 1927.
3 Lewis O. Mink, 'Everyman His or Her Own Annalist', *Critical Inquiry*, vol. no. 4, 1981, pp. 777–783.
4 Albert Mansbridge, *Margaret McMillan, Prophet and Pioneer: Her Life and Work*, Dent, London, 1932.

D'Arcy Cresswell, *Margaret McMillan, A Memoir*, Hutchinson, London, 1948.

G. A. N. Lowndes, *Margaret McMillan, The Children's Champion*, Museum Books, NY, 1960.

Elizabeth Bradburn, *Margaret McMillan, Framework and Expansion of Nursery Education*, Denholm Press, Redhill, 1976.

5 The myth of Corinne is a myth of a woman's oratorical powers shown when the eponymous heroine of Mme de Staël's novel holds huge crowds in thrall at the Capitol in Rome with her extemporisations. See Germaine de Staël, *Corinne, or, Italy* (1807), translated and edited by Avriel H. Goldberger, Rutgers University Press, New Brunswick, 1987, pp. 26–31. Ellen Moers discussed the myth of the female orator in *Literary Women*, The Women's Press, London, 1978.

6 Raymond Williams, *Marxism and Literature*, Oxford University Press, Oxford, 1977, pp. 145–148.

7 Percy Redfern, *Journey to Understanding*, Allen & Unwin, London, 1946, pp. 18–19.

8 M. M. Bakhtin, *The Dialogic Omagination: Four Essays* (edited by Michael Holquist), University of Texas Press, Austin, 1981, pp. 130–146.

9 Linda H. Peterson, *Victorian Autobiography: The Tradition of Self Interpretation*, Yale University Press, New Haven, 1986.

10 Virginia Woolf, *Three Guineas* (1938), Hogarth Press, London, 1986, p. 177. I owe this reference to Kathryn Dodd. See Note 11.

11 Kathryn Dodd, 'Historians, Texts and Ray Strachey's *The Cause*', unpublished paper, 1986.

Ray Strachey, *The Cause* (1928), Virago Press, London, 1988.

References and Further Reading

Other relevant essays and books on the practice and criticism of autobiography and biography, in addition to those in the notes, include:

Benstock, Shari (ed.), *The Private Self: Theory and Practice of Women's Autobiographical Writings*, Routledge, London, and University of North Carolina Press, Chapel Hill, 1988.

Brodzki, Bella and Schenck, Celeste (eds), *Life/Lines: Theorizing Women's Autobiography*, Cornell University Press, Ithaca, New York, 1988.

Heilbrun, Carolyn, *Writing a Woman's Life*, Norton, NY, 1988, and The Women's Press, London, 1989.

Jelinek, Estelle (ed.), *Women's Autobiography: Essays in Criticism*, Indiana University Press, Bloomington, 1980.

Marcus, Laura, '"Enough About You, Let's Talk About Me": Recent Autobiographical Writing', *New Formations*, no. 1, Spring, 1987.

Olney, James (ed.), *Autobiography: Essays Theoretical and Critical*, Princeton University Press, Princeton, 1980.

Steedman, Carolyn, *Landscape for a Good Woman*, Virago, London, 1986.

Wilson, Elizabeth, 'Tell It Like It Is: Women and Confessional Writing', in Susannah Radstone (ed.), *Sweet Dreams: Sexuality, Gender and Popular Fiction*, Lawrence & Wishart, London, 1988.

FEMINIST LITERARY STRATEGIES IN THE POSTMODERN CONDITION

CAROLYN BROWN

In the multi-dimensional and slippery space of Post-Modernism anything goes with anything, like a game without rules, Floating images ... maintain no relationship with anything at all, and meaning becomes detachable like the keys on a key-ring. – *Suzy Gablik*[1]

Pastiche: in a world in which stylistic innovation is no longer possible, all that is left is to imitate dead styles, to speak through the masks and with the voices of the styles of the imaginary museum. – *Frederic Jameson*[2]

Unfortunately, 'postmodern' is a term *bon à tout faire*. I have the impression that it is aplied today to anything the user of the term happens to like. Further there seems to be an attempt to make it increasingly retroactive: ... soon the postmodern category will include Homer. – *Umberto Eco*[3]

Postmodernism, the postmodern, post-mo, is suddenly everywhere. From *The Face* to Prince, from *Kiss of the Spider Woman* to Tesco's superstores. All the cultural products claiming our attention are, in some way so we are told, postmodern. A term which has emerged from the obscurity of an academic treatise into general cultural discourse, it was always a rather slippery, uncertain, superficial term, but then uncertainty, provisionality, superficiality is what it signifies. In Baudrillard's hyper-real world of images and surfaces, where does one begin? Where is the position from which 'one' can begin to begin?

I am going to work with the notion that the 'postmodern' condition is roughly equivalent in what is increasingly termed 'post-Fordism', the reshaping of capitalism, with the replacement of mass production–consumption models by diversified and yet global production–consumption.[4] More specifically, I will consider, as Lyotard has suggested in *The Postmodern Condition*, that the postmodern refers to 'changed status of knowledge' brought about, at any rate in part, by information technology, and by the cumulative transformations in representations in the twentieth century. Lyotard takes the word postmodern, an already existing term used by American sociologists and critics, to designate 'the state of culture following the transformations which since the end of the nineteenth century, have altered the game rules for science, literature and the arts'.[5] In Lyotard's account the postmodern is the result of the changes effected by modernism, and by other challenges to nineteenth-century organisations of knowledge, and narratives of legitimation. 'Simplifying to the extreme', Lyotard writes, 'I define postmodern as incredulity towards metanarratives.'[6] The postmodern is a world of plurality of languages, discourse, practices, without nostalgia for unity, for universality, for origin, for a world with guarantees. The 'splintering' of language, the loss of any certain meaning, was a crisis for the modern; as Lyotard writes, 'turn-of-the-century Vienna was weaned on this pessimism'. In the postmodern 'most people have lost the nostalgia for the lost narrative'.[7] If the project of modernism was the investigation of consciousness, sexuality and language, that of postmodernism is to play with identity, desire and simulacra. The notion of the 'lost narrative' is also crucial for considering the question of identity which is both erased and reinscribed in the postmodern condition.

This term, 'the postmodern condition', as a noun, indicates the state of existing within this pluralistic world – and 'postmodern' is the adjective describing those who attempt to write of, to describe, to depict it. For example, that feminism has entered this pluralistic postmodern condition can be seen by the explosion in feminist publishing and the variety of feminist discourses. While there may be scepticism about the original narrative of the Women's Liberation Movement, it is impossible now to ignore the plurality and diversity of narratives of women's existences, the articulation of their hopes and desires in a multiplicity of practices. For feminists, the language of postmodernism has often repeated, although in different terms, their critiques of the Masculine Order of Things. The effect of feminist literary and cultural work has been a multiplication of histories, of narratives, which themselves form part of that postmodern dissolution of history. Feminism now has to exist in the postmodern world, which it has helped to make. The Postmodern has arrived, and the question is not whether to live within it – for we do – but *how* to live within it. And so, how to consider the 'modern' to which we are 'post' is a central task for contemporary feminists, in coming to terms with the changed conditions which exist in the postmodern condition.

The postmodern 'imaginary museum' is a theme-park, not a mausoleum. What is on display in the imaginary museum matters, as does how it is presented within 'the provisional, contradictory postmodern enterprise'.[8] The work of feminist and other Others has transformed the displays in recent years. The interpretation of images, information, narratives, which no longer have what we would consider worthless guarantees of meaning, has become a crucial activity. The theoretical activities grouped under the title post-structuralism, have opened up the conceptualisation of the modern. Andreas Huyssen has argued that 'French theory provides us primarily with an *archeology of modernity*, a theory of modernism at the stage of its exhaustion'.[9] The languages and analyses developed by feminist post-structuralism are attempts to articulate feminist cultural (sexual-textual) politics within the postmodern condition. Huyssen has suggested that the early post-structuralist heralding of the death of the subject is countered by the later post-structuralist theorists, and postmoderns who are 'working towards new theories and practices of speaking, writing and acting subjects'. The minimal self is replaced by 'The question of how codes, texts, images, and other cultural artifacts constitute subjectivity [which] is increasingly being raised as an always historical question'.[10]

The conjuncture of feminism and postmodernism articulates politically the complexity of the postmodern existences and identities. For example, the heated debates surrounding Clause

29, now Section 28 of the Local Government Act 1988, which prohibits the 'promotion' of homosexuality by local authorities, were very much about the issue of identities, of proscribing some, and prescribing others, of the policing of families, in which normality, and the health of society, the nation resides.[11] The strategies around the introduction of Section 28 worked upon many narratives – conscious and unconscious. The significance of Section 28 lay in the way it drew upon, amplified, and legitimised the narratives of homophobia[s], already circulating around and linked in the Tabloid Imaginary with the issues of Aids. It was very much the inarticulation of fears of the postmodern, of the dissolution of the illusion of the nuclear family; an attempt to maintain that the cereal packet norm is real, not a simulacrum. Given that the languages used were somewhat archaic, though nonetheless effective, I looked around in the imaginary museum, for something which would address this concern, through which to raise those questions of genre and gender, identity and politics, modern and postmodern. Preparing this essay in the midst of the debate over Section 28 lent an edge to my consideration of the discussions in recent feminist literary criticism on notions of identity and strategy in respect of modernist texts.

The Lesbian is a wonderful example of the powers of discourse, of the reality of fictionality, named from a mythical community on a small Greek island; constructed in the Western literary imagination in the nineteenth and twentieth century from a few lines of a long-dead poet, and sundry other accounts; reconstructed in those cataloguing medical discourses of the late nineteenth and twentieth century and taken as a point of self-definition, identification and resistance by many women. Walter Benjamin noted the importance for Baudelaire of the figure of the Lesbian as an emblem of modernity.[12] Perhaps it is possible to explore her relevance as an emblem of the postmodern. Although the genre of the lesbian novel is a slightly questionable one, we perhaps can use the anniversary device, beloved of journalists and museum curators, to consider what we might call two classics of the genre. Both *Orlando* and *The Well of Loneliness* were published in England sixty years ago in 1928.[13] There are very different sexual textual strategies operating in these texts, very different theories in these fictions. Broadly,

Orlando offers a fantasy of impossible alternations of gender identity, and *The Well of Loneliness* a classic realist, social problem novel of a 'born invert'. Neither of these texts fits into the category of modernism, but together they offer a modern and relatively accessible point for theorising strategies of difference, for exploring a new subject, articulated around gender and sexual orientation.

The history of the different readings of these texts can illuminate the field in which they operate in our contemporary concerns and illustrate the recent reconstruction of notions of identity and strategy by feminist critics. Critics no longer argue over the fixed sexual identity of Stephen Gordon nor spend their time refuting the idea that she represents a *real* lesbian or even a *real* person. Now they are concerned with the debate over *Orlando* and the role of fantasy, and the multiplicity of the self. The debates over the body and its pleasures went further in the early twentieth century, as always, than the question of a personal identity. They connected vitally with the concept of the nation, so I extend my observations to note the [surprisingly similar] strategies of Woolf and Hall in inscribing the Lesbian into the heart of England. Their ambivalence towards this identity also connects with questions of gendered and sexual identity. Held together in tension, these texts open up those issues of identity, and strategies of response to those discourses of sexuality, gender, and nation, which sixty years later still constitute, although differently, the authoritarian populism of the tabloid press, and governmental action.

On completing *The Well of Loneliness*, Radclyffe Hall wrote to her publisher that she had 'written a long and very serious novel entirely on the subject of sexual inversion'. Hall had no doubt that she wanted to present a positive image of the Lesbian. She continued, 'So far as I know, nothing of the kind has ever been attempted before in fiction. Hitherto the subject has either been treated as pornography, or introduced as an episode . . . or veiled . . . I have written the life of a woman who is a born invert.'[14] *The Well of Loneliness* announced its seriousness with the name of its heroine Stephen, the first Christian Martyr. It appealed to society to accept the unfortunate but superior 'invert'. Hall gave her heroine an idealised English landowning gentleman as a father, and endowed her with those qualities. Alison Hennegan has observed that 'As the man she almost is, Stephen would have been the quintessence of normality ... a worthy, if slightly solemn, upholder of the established social order'.[15] The book charts the existence and the reception of the already constituted Lesbian subject, preferring the line that 'inverts' were born not made – members of a 'Third Sex', which left the other two in place. The text has often been read as autobiographical. Its authenticity was guaranteed by its religious imagery, its purple prose, its acceptance of medical common sense, and its auto-biographical aura – Radclyffe Hall being a well-known 'invert', and the character Stephen being a writer.

The category of the Third Sex enabled some nifty footwork around the issue of, as they say nowadays, 'promoting' homo-sexuality. Those who saw it as an unnatural vice were uncon-vinced. Hall's aim was to educate an unknowing and uncaring lot of 'normals'. It was on their behalf that *The Sunday Express* attacked the book, declaiming that 'sexual inversion and perver-sion are horrors which exist among us today' and that 'inverts' and 'perverts' 'flaunt themselves in public places with increasing effrontery and more insolently, provocative bravado'.[16] A press campaign brought the matter to the attention of the Director of Public Prosecutions. *The Well of Loneliness* and its celebration of martyrdom has not always seemed a positive image. The courts in 1928 thought differently. 'All the characters are presented as attractive people.' Even worse than the pleas for tolerance was that 'the actual physical acts of the women indulging in unnatu-ral vices are described in the most alluring terms ... it is actually put forward that it improves their mental balance and capacity'.[17] The Appeal Court also found it 'a disgusting book, when properly read'.[18] The book was banned. It was not republished in Britain until after the Second World War.

It did better elsewhere, and was translated into eleven lan-guages. In the United States it was widely used in psychology classes. But generations of women have been dismayed by Stephen Gordon, and her 'Well of Loneliness'. Its depiction of the relationship between gender identity, sexual preference, and despair was a high price to pay for visibility. It was an analysis rejected by those who saw Stephen Gordon as a monster. Maya Angelou's account of reading the novel in her youth succinctly summarises the novel's argument. 'They were ... disowned by their families, snubbed by their friends and ostracised from society. This bitter punishment was inflicted upon them because of a physical condition over which they had no control.'[19] Lillian Faderman argued that it had a 'devastating effect on female same-sex love' because of its congenitalist arguments, as well as Stephen's lonely destiny.[20] Even for Hall, Stephen is 'grotesque and splendid, like some primitive thing conceived in a turbulent period of transition'.[21] The descriptions of her do at times resemble those of Frankenstein's monster. This is hardly surprising since she is constructed from the learned discourses whose 'feeble content from the standpoint of elementary rationality, not to mention scientificity earns them a place apart in the history of knowledge'. From the mid nineteenth century, medical discourses on sex had warned that, 'strange pleasures ... would eventually result in nothing short of death: that of individuals, generations, the species itself'. This 'science' promised to 'eliminate defective individuals, degenerate and bastardised populations ... it justified the racisms of the state, which ... were on the horizon'.[22]

The pathologisation of the pervert was the other side of the hystericisation of women. Those women who would not, or could not breed within the family, who claimed illicit pleasures, disrupted the master narratives of racial destiny. The ensemble of strategies fed into a state racism, which was not peculiar to the Nazis. Thus Hall puts into the mouth of Ralph, the cuckolded husband of Stephen's first lover, the remark, 'How's your freak getting on? ... that sort of thing wants putting down at birth, I'd like to institute state lethal chambers!'[23] Hall's evolutionist and eugenicist reverse-discourse enabled connections to be made that perhaps escaped others. Her exiling of Stephen perhaps demonstrates that she had no great faith in either her pleas for liberal tolerance or her tactics of situating Stephen as an exiled English landowner turned gay martyr.

If this novel approached its task of challenging natural assumptions of gender and sexual orientation within English culture head on, Virginia Woolf's *Orlando* has been accused of hiding its 'lesbian subject matter by whimsical devices',[24] and of 'tedious high camp'.[25] It was published in the same year as Woolf was working on the lecture of which *A Room of One's Own* was the published version. Both have been described as being marked by 'repetition, exaggeration, parody, whimsy and multiple viewpoint'.[26] *Orlando* offers a sapphic fantasy in the guise of a biography of a trans-sexual, a man/woman from Elizabethan England to the present, during which time he/she passes from youth to middle age. It is a parodic pastiche of a history of England. *A Room of One's Own* is a theoretical/historical investigation of women and cultural production. Both, as Makiko Minow-Pinkney has carefully demonstrated, move between the demarcations of fictions and theory transgressing their boundaries, not abondoning either mode, but often inverting the kind of truth they claimed. As Hutcheon and others have demonstrated, this has become very much a feature of postmodern writing. Thus, in *A Room of One's Own* Woolf appeals to 'the order of fiction rather than facts, lies rather than truth', in her attempt to construct a female perspective.[27] Minow-Pinkney has pointed out that '*Orlando* has been perhaps the most neglected of Woolf's novels among her critics',[28] and argues that it is its ambivalence of tone (is it frivolous or is it serious?) that renders *Orlando* a difficult text for critics who generally insist on the primacy of seriousnes, rather than of play. Rachel Bowlby observes that '*Orlando* leaves nothing and not even "nothing", the ultimate illusion that all is "illusion" in place, or indeed in time.'[29]

Woolf desired to write *Orlando* in a style, 'very clear and plain so people will understand every word'. 'But', she qualified this desire, 'the balance between truth and fantasy must be careful'.[30] Fantasy is a way of protecting her sources – 'Vita; only with a change from one sex to another'[31] – and enables the celebration of desire – 'I want fun. I want fantasy'[32] – in a book which she wishes to write quickly: 'I shall dash this off in a week'.[33] The entertainment proves time-consuming, a more demanding project than envisaged. Five months later she finishes *Orlando*. Woolf's playfulness about *Orlando*'s category met difficulties; booksellers, confused by its apparent status as biography, as indicated on the title page, and supported by its possession of an index, refused to sell it as fiction. Nevertheless, overcoming at least that joke, *Orlando* sold well, perhaps helped by *The Well of Loneliness* trial at the time. By December 1928, a third edition had been ordered. Woolf made money out of a book for the first time. The book drew no unwelcome attention from the Press.

Perhaps the light-hearted fantasy of *Orlando* enabled it not only to dodge the attention of the Press, but also to break with dominant conceptions of gender/sexuality. It has become a mine of quotes for those concerned with writing on sexual difference, and perhaps only now is the importance of Woolf's move being elaborated upon by feminist writers. The debate on *Orlando* is of more significance than the placing of a novel within a particular canon, although such issues are always symptomatic. It offers a version of feminist considerations on strategies and identities, literary and otherwise, over the last 10–15 years. Lyotard has used the model of Wittgenstein-based 'language games' to inter-pret the shifting diverse discourses of the postmodern condition. For Lyotard a language game is an agonistics, a game of com-petition incorporating ideas of struggle, of power, as well as pleasure.[34] In terms of this 'agonistics', then the postmodern feminist concerns with the subject and language are attempts to change the rules, to alter the positions, to consider more appro-priate strategies. Perhaps Woolf with *Orlando* effected such a shift in the language game of gender and identity that she resembles those 'countless scientists' who

> had their 'move' ignored or repressed ... because it too abruptly destabilized the accepted positions, not only in the university or scientific hierarchy, but in the problematic. The stronger the 'move', the more likely it is to be denied the minimum consensus, precisely because it changes the rules of the game on which consensus had been based.[35]

Thus, while Elaine Showalter's charge in 1977 against the modernist writers, Dorothy Richardson and Virginia Woolf, was that they failed to confront and express their anger, in 1985 Toril Moi's advocacy of Woolf's writing celebrated her irony and wit, recommending her strategies more generally to women writers.[36] Toril Moi argued convincingly that 'Woolf exposes the way in which language refuses to be pinned down to an under-lying essential meaning'.[37] Moi's text seems a little wistful for a macro-politics, but it engaged with, and advocated a language which operated with, and argued for, a different set of strategies. This was more than an individual preference. It is an exposition of the limitations of the concept of the unified self – 'feminist' or otherwise. It is an argument that irony and wit are probably more useful than anger in the sexual textual politics of the postmodern condition. Makiko Minow-Pinkney elaborated even more clearly the doubts over the efficacy of a simple confrontational position. She argued that 'the stridency of the revolt Showalter calls for entails the risk that the patriarchy might simply eliminate women's "anger, fear, and chaos" as insanity, illogicality, disorder, and that what was needed was 'a more subtly resourceful strategy'.[38]

For all four feminist writers, strategies of writing are crucial in undermining those too solid concepts of 'identity', 'experience', 'development', and 'agency'. In Minow-Pinkney's account, Woolf's infamous concept of, desire for, androgyny is not a flight into sameness, into assimilation into masculinity. Rather, it 'becomes radical, opening up the fixed unity into a multiplicity, joy, play of heterogeneity, a fertile difference'.[39] The deconstruction of the fixed, binary positions of gender is carried out under the banner of androgyny, as a naming of difference, or better *différance*, that is, difference without positive terms, a continual deferment of identity. Thus Minow-Pinkney's argument against any simple idea of 'confrontation', whether of woman and man, woman and a patriarchal society, was that it 'offers as an indubitable starting point a subject object polarity that is ... reified and abstract'. She advocated that 'The feminist text must call into question the very identities which support this pattern of binary opposition'.[40]

Woolf's place within the category of 'high modernism' enables Makiko Minow-Pinkney to move on to discuss her work in terms of the postmodern, through the use of Kristevan 'post-structuralist' terms of analysis. Makiko Minow-Pinkney's text works between a reading of both sets of writing (Woolf's and Kristeva's) to address the 'problem of the subject' and 'the project of forging a new kind of subjectivity'.[41] As a part of this project she reverses earlier judgements of *Orlando*, whose transgressive playfulness she argues also characterises all Virginia Woolf's work. Rachel Bowlby, using rather different terminology, argues that Woolf is 'engaged in questioning the very notion of straightforward directions and known destinations ...' and moreover, that 'it is not clear what these lines will be, nor where they will go; nor what a woman may look like, "if and when" she has succeeded in changing the conditions of travel and the present timetable'.[42] In a way, Bowlby's train of metaphors and analogies clearly reveals the play within theoretical discourse, but there is a certain irony and scepticism in Minow-Pinkney's use of Kristevan categories which unsettles any absolute claim to truth, whether of feminist destinations or the nature of 'Woman'.

How then is the identity of 'the Lesbian', which I am suggesting here as an exemplary instance of 'identity', represented in the postmodern? How do the literary constructs which transgress the rules of gender survive? Towards the end of both novels there is an account of the dissolution and multiplication of identity. It is as if the effort of holding together the narrative threads of these 'new' constructions becomes too great, or that some exploration of the fragmentation of 'reality', of the 'subject', becomes neccesary.

Stephen, at the end of *The Well of Loneliness*, abandoned by her lover and her friend, feels herself invaded by an army of inverts. Her destiny presents itself:

> the room seemed to be thronging with people. Who were they, those strangers with miserable eyes? . . . were they all strangers? . . . their pain, her pain, all welded together into one great consuming agony . . . In their madness to become articulate through her, they were tearing her to pieces, getting her under . . . They possessed her.[43]

The novel concluded with an appeal to God, the reader, to be given 'the right to our existence.'[44] The dissolution of identity in this case is arrested only by that appeal – this is a Kristevan *abjection*, not *jouissance*. 'All abjection is in fact a recognition of the fundamental lack of all being, meaning language, and desire . . . Christian mysticism has made this abjection of the self the ultimate proof of humility before God'.[45] This dissolution of boundaries, this possession is thus a lack filled by a plenitude of pain, arrested only by an appeal to the law.

In *Orlando* the experience is less traumatic. Both Minow-Pinkney and Rachel Bowlby have discussed the events following Orlando's trip to London, and specifically Marshall & Snelgrove's department store, and her return in a 'motor car', on 11 October 1928. Orlando's identity is 'chopped up small', it becomes 'an open question in what sense Orlando could have been said to have existed'. Eventually, identity begins to be reasserted, by 'one green screen . . . held on the right'.[46] Minow-Pinkney, following Raymond Williams, stresses that the illusion of identity is resolved, in the conventions of the English pastoral myth, in the country. Bowlby emphasises the cinematic imagery and the illusory nature of this unity. I would like to stress that the process of reconstructing a self takes a little while. As things slowly re-established themselves, Orlando lit a cigarette, puffed, and

> called hesitatingly, as if the person she wanted might not be there, 'Orlando?' For if there are (at a venture) seventy-six different times all ticking in the mind at once, how many people are there not – Heaven help us – all having lodgement at one time or another in the human spirit? Some say two thousand and fifty-two. So that it is the most usual thing in the world for a person to call, directly they are alone, Orlando? (if that is one's name) meaning by that, Come, come! I'm sick to death of this particular self. I want another . . .[47]

Juxtaposed, these two passages open a gap between a potential infinity of selves or at least two thousand and fifty-two and the fixing of an identity. In *The Well of Loneliness* resolution is offered through an appeal to God and the demands of a politics of identity. In *Orlando* it is by habit, and a naming of the subject, an incantation to bring forth oneself and then finally through a constellation of the present, the past becoming phantom, a returned lover, and the clock striking midnight. Perhaps this registers a desire to re-enter 'time' and 'history', through the arbitrariness of the clock, and the date. Neither text offers a final 'fix'. But the attitude towards the multiplication of selves is very different. In *The Well of Loneliness* it is a curse, a violation; in *Orlando* if not cause always for celebration, it is a fairly everyday occurrence – even if needing a cigarette in the country to re-establish the illusion of unity. More important perhaps, Orlando both addresses herself, and has apparently a choice.

Minow-Pinkney has argued that Orlando's exclusion from temporality follows her acquisition of femininity. Her seclusion in the ancestral, familial home is an alienation from history, politics, and society. Orlando dramatises for Minow-Pinkney an

indication of 'the limits of our thinking ... in which sexual
differences are so implacably structured that they do not allow
even a Utopian imagination of a new sexuality'.[48] I'm not sure
that we don't have this 'Utopian imagination' of a plurality of
genders and sexualities – Toril Moi, for example, cites Derrida's
Utopian statement at the end of *Sexual Textual Politics*, 'where the
code of sexual marks would no longer be discriminating'.[49] The
problem is one of not being able to realise this Utopia which
exists in fantasy, or in illegitimate discourses. Thus the play with
sexual differences is the 'fun' and 'fantasy' which Woolf wants
for Orlando, but it is arrested by the limitations of a particular
epoch's construction of, and limitations upon, the feminine
subject.

It may be that this limitation of an epoch is only within
particular languages, discourses, practices. This is indicated, at
least as a possibility, in both novels. Both Minow-Pinkney and
Bowlby discuss this aporia, this 'representational gap' which is
the dramatisation of what cannot be said, what exists beyond
legitimated discourse.[50] Thus, following Orlando's enjoyment of
women's company, the narrator writes:

> So they would draw round the punchbowl ... many were
> the fine tales they told ... for it cannot be denied that when
> women get together – but hist – they are always careful to
> see that the doors are shut and that not a word of it gets into
> print ... All they desire, we were about to say, when the
> gentleman took the words out our mouths. Women have no
> desires, says the gentleman ...[51]

The '– hist –' in this passage performs the same function as the
ellipses which Bowlby finds in much of Woolf's writing; they
indicate 'what is omitted because it cannot be said: because it is
not permitted, and/or because it is not assimilable to the surrounding prose'.[52] Women's desires are silenced by the history
(hist/his-story) of men. Moving out from silenced women's
discourses to 'androgyny' – or playing with masculinity, scarcely
makes this world more accessible to discourse. The biographer of
Orlando's life in eighteenth-century London, where she moves
between polite society and that of the underworld with alternat-
ing and diverse gender identities, gives up, for –

... to give an exact and particular account of Orlando's life at this time becomes more and more out of the question. As we peer and grope in the ill-lit, ill-paved, ill-ventilated court-yards that lay about Gerrard Street and Drury Lane at that time, we seem now to catch sight of her and then again to lose it.[53]

It is significant that these gaps arise in this novel with the feminine Orlando venturing out from the home into the city. It is as if the boundaries constructing femininity, and thus gender, have been ruptured. But whereas femininity in this account can only be passive, or at best silenced, venturing out is also a fairly foggy enterprise. Even in *The Well of Loneliness*, where Hall attempts 'sincerity and truth', all is not clear.[54] Stephen's initials Stephen Mary Oliver Gertrude Gordon – SMOGG indicate that there are silences, deliberate points of obscurity, even in the campaigning biographical novel. The representation of the androgyne, of women, of those outside the 'positive terms' of the dominant gender/sexual orientation conjours up the absence of a fixed, full, self-present, identity. This passage, like Wilde's accounts of Dorian Gray's adventures, represents a movement between that dominant culture, which records, and the hidden 'sub-cultural' world of Orlando's heterogeneous identities and pleasures. But I think we are mistaken if we see this silence as invariably repressive. If we recall here Foucault's considerations on discourse and silence, that,

> Discourse transmits and produces power; it reinforces it, but also undermines and exposes it, renders it fragile and makes it possible to thwart it. In like manner, silence and secrecy are a shelter for power, anchoring its prohibitions, but they also loosen its holds and provide for relatively obscure areas of tolerance.[55]

it becomes possible to argue that there are good reasons for not revealing all, that that is moreover an impossibility, and that to expect any more is to indulge in an illusion of discursive 'free trade'. For there are selves 'too wildly ridiculous to be mentioned in print at all'.[56] However, the psychic and social consequences

of moving between silence, that which is not-said, and discourse, are perhaps demonstrated by Hall's account of Stephen's
abjection, and the fate of *The Well of Loneliness* in its country of
origin, and subsequent effects. Consider also the difficulties of
Orlando's strategies of writing between the said and non-said,
and its subsequent receptions.

The refusal of an ideal of communicational transparency, and
scepticism towards ideas of consensus based on this ideal marks
Lyotard's analysis of the postmodern condition. There must be,
however, a movement between 'silence' – or non-legitimated
discourses and practices, and those which enter into print, into
cultural production. Just as the tension between 'multiplicity'
and 'unity' is worked over and over, so is that between 'silence'
and 'discourse' – or better, 'silenced discourses' and 'legitimated
discourses'. It is an ambivalence, but one which does not allow
for stasis, which does not permit that as a settled state, but is an
oscillation, a continual alternation.

This state marks also the inscription of their Lesbian subjects
with regard to their national identity. As if aware of the attempts
to exile, to silence their characters, both texts refuse an exoticism.
They locate their lesbians in the heart of England, making great
play of their Englishness, their love of the country. *The Well of
Loneliness* opens with a description of 'the country seat of the
Gordons of Bramley', Morton. Morton is situated between
Upton-on-Severn and the Malvern Hills.[57] In exile (in London!)
Stephen suffers from 'the ache that was Morton'.[58] That society is
the subject matter of her first novel, *The Furrow*. In Paris, she
insists '"My home's in England"', . . . for her thoughts had flown
instantly back to Morton'.[59] *Orlando* opens with Orlando in the
familial castle. Indeed a continuing motif of the novel is the
parodic centering of Orlando's estate where 'from the high oak
tree' (on which she writes her major poem *The Old Oak Tree*'
'nineteen English counties could be seen beneath, and on clear
days thirty, or perhaps forty, if the weather was very fine'.[60] This
is later elaborated as 'half of England, with a slice of Wales and
Scotland thrown in'.[61] Much play is made on Orlando's return
from abroad, now a woman, on her claims to that property.
Ownership is part of the matter, in terms of a gender politics, but
as in *The Well of Loneliness* we can see a refusal to be exiled from
concepts of the 'nation'. Yet there is in both texts an ambivalence

to this national identity. *The Furrow*, for example, may well be about being in a rut.

For Lesbians are, of course, as anyone who has played Trivial Pursuits knows, also inhabitants of Lesbos. Leaving aside the present inhabitants of that island, let's take up the reference to the idea of another place, another country, the heterotopic. Both Orlando and SMOGG must be 'elsewhere', in order to become who they are. Orlando's name marks his/her affinity to another country. His transformation into a woman is during the revolution in Constantinople. Her assumption of a feminine identity is amongst gypsies, who in Woolf's mythological world do not fetishise gender difference. Stephen must move to Paris to encounter her community, to begin to inhabit a social role, although here she also must venture outside the polite circles into the underworld of nightclubs and bars in order to meet her community. In *The Well of Loneliness* Stephen discusses the role, or the place of the invert with Valérie Seymour (names are significant in this text). Stephen Mary desires acceptance by society, by the normals, whereas Valérie is sceptical of those who would do it on society's terms, and identifies herself as a 'pagan'. Valérie Seymour is based on the character of Natalie Barney, who fostered a Sapphic community in Paris, but leaving 'real' history aside, let us return to the postmodern from the perspective of the pagan.

For the Romans, *Pagus* denoted a region outside Rome. The signifier 'pagan' through the epoch of Christianity shifts to indicate those who are not Christian, and later, those who are not Jewish or Muslim. It indicated for the West those outside their boundaries. It also comes to denote those sexual and aesthetic dissidents who revise the ideas of the Greeks, particularly those who would espouse a morality, other than that determined by heterosexuality. It has, perhaps with the dislocation of Christianity, ceased to be used so extensively now, but the 'pagan' has been revisited and reworked by Lyotard in the collection of dialogues in *Just Gaming*, where he plays with the ideas of tactics, identity, narratives and gods. 'Gods' have their own narratives, but they also figure in Lyotard's discussion as those who invent narratives, which the humans must play out. Unlike the monotheistic (omnipotent, omnipresent, omnipowerful) God of the Christians, the Greek gods could be outwitted by clever humans. Lyotard suggests that the *pagus* is a place of boundaries. Boundaries are not borders. [T]he relation with the gods ... does not obey a pragmatics of border to border, between two perfectly defined blocks or armies ... confronting each other. On the contrary, it is a place of ceaseless negotiations and ruses.[62]

In Lyotard's text the 'pagan' functions as a heterotopia, an allegory for an ideal postmodern. There is, he says, a pagan ideal, where gods, like humans, 'are heroes of ... almost innumerable narratives', where there is also 'an awareness that the relation between the proper name and the body is not an immutable one ... There is no subject because s/he changes bodies, and by changing bodies, s/he changes ... functions, especially narrative ones'.[63] Thus Oedipus's 'tragedy' is not one of consciousness, but of a failure 'to ruse as a narrator with the story of which he is a hero ... I am ... convinced this must have been a source of comedy to the Greeks'.[64] The concept of identity then becomes a notion which is fluid, non-unified, but which 'exists in a fabric of relations that is now more mobile and complex than ever before ... [for] a person is always located at "nodal points" of specific communication circuits however tiny these may be'.[65] Remaining with the invert, the verb *invertere* translates as to turn over, to turn about, to transpose, to alter, to pervert. These skills are of use in transgressing the boundaries of, for example, genres, of genders, in rusing in others' narratives. The unpleasantness of remaining fixed in the narrative which others construct, or not rusing cleverly enough is perhaps clearly signalled by Stephen Gordon's miserable existence, and the difficulty of rusing, perhaps too well, is illustrated by *Orlando*'s uncertain status.

There are, perhaps, signs in the postmodern constellation that we can begin to think *spatially*, even while we inhabit that impossible and ludicrous space–time of the *post*modern. The future/past Utopia is displaced by imaginary heterotopias, which at least stops the self-contained monologic Grand Narrative of progression/decline, and opens out into polyglossia, into 'other countries'. The Lesbian, through 'another country', constructs, in part, an identity through imagining a different order of things. The rethinking of some Western feminist discourses with a post-structuralist language has not been merely a theoretical questioning of the universalising, individualising language of liberal humanism, nor has it simply been the result of its internally-generated fertility, nor only because of its own contradictions. It has been carried out as well in the wake of the cultural politics of Black British, Afro-American and Third World women. 'Feminist' discourses have moved away from that previously dominant model, which continued to reflect Man back at men, ignoring those outside the partnership. Gayatri Spivak pointed out that this model constituted 'the lie' of 'a truth of global sisterhood', while remaining transfixed by 'the mesmerising model . . . [of] male and female partners of generalisable or universalisable sexuality who are the chief protagonists in that European context'.[66] The fragmentation of the production of discourses, the questioning of the phallocentrism and eurocentrism is part of the postmodern condition. Politics within the postmodern has to be thought differently. The question of politics in the postmodern does not exclude those issues of subordination and oppression, but attempts to consider them in more complex formations, differently. It refuses the archaism of ossified 'oppressions', and asks 'where are we now?'

This excursion into the imaginary museum has been an attempt to consider some of the aspects of the construction of the lesbian, the shifts in feminist strategies, and some of the dilemmas in constructing a self from which to act. The use of the past in pastiche is, at its best, a defamiliarisation; one which disrupts, as *Orlando* begins to do, the national subject, and perhaps less wittingly, as *The Well of Loneliness* also effected. The Lesbian perhaps provides an allegory of identity in the postmodern condition, of the fictionality of identity formed not through an 'authentic history' but through a precession of simulacra. Orlando's multiple selves are resolved unsatisfactorily, as if transitorily, as if the task of ending the story was too 'ridiculous' to attempt, as if any full stop can only be arbitrary, provisional. Stuart Hall has rightly argued that 'Politics, without the arbitrary interposition of power in language, the cut of ideology, the positioning, the crossing of lines, the rupture, is impossible'.[67] But it clearly matters at what point one stops the play of identity, of discourse. What narratives we inhabit, what genres and genders inhabit oneself, are never anyway a matter of infinite choice, but are always already written. The task then is that of 'rusing', of considering the best move within a particular set of circumstances, knowing that the choice of moves is without guarantees of success. For in all the ironic considerations of the structuring of these fictional, lesbian selves, there are moments when I am haunted by the ease with which Hall's novel, despite (because of) its apparent combativeness, disseminated a mythology, which at the very least frightened women, articulated their fears of not being 'normal' – or even disqualified them from being 'abnormal'. Its effects in terms of maintaining the order of gender are quite scary. I am haunted, also, by the obliqueness, the cleverness, the complexity which, I think, masks and reveals a considerable uncertainty within Woolf's novel, and perhaps an ultimate, or transient advocacy of political quietude, despite (because of?) the radical nature of the text. The alternations in *Orlando* between frivolity and seriousness demand a strong reading in order to impose an order, a coherence upon the text. Perhaps that renders it pertinent to the postmodern condition. Maybe it is more fruitful to move from frivolity, pleasures, desires, rather than to hope that by accepting the rules of the orders of discourse one will be allowed sexual/textual existences. But in the 'imaginary museum', between fools and angels, between seriousness and frivolity, discourse and silence, we can perhaps also view, with suitable androgynous embellishments, the ninth of Walter Benjamin's 'Theses on the Philosophy of History', on Klee's *Angelus Novus* which

is how one pictures the angel of history. His face is turned towards the past. Where we perceive a chain of events, he sees one single catastrophe which keeps piling wreckage upon wreckage and hurls it in front of his feet. The angel would like to stay, awaken the dead, and make whole what has been smashed. But a storm is blowing from Paradise; it has got caught in his wings with such violence that the angel can no longer close them. This storm irresistibly propels him into the future to which his back is turned, while the pile of debris before him grows skyward. The storm is what we call progress.[68]

I am haunted too by those institutions, those practices, this country, which make me want to explore these texts which should be, if not redundant, then honourably retired.

Time to leave the museum.

And, has anyone a 'Rough Guide to the Postmodern'?[69]

Notes

1 Suzy Gablik, 'The Aesthetic of Duplicity', *Art & Design*, vol. 3, no. 7/8, 1987, p. 36.

2 Fredric Jameson, 'Postmodernism and Consumer Culture', in *Postmodern Culture*, Hal Foster (ed.), Pluto, London, 1985, p. 115.

3 Umberto Eco, trans. William Weaver, *Reflections on 'The Name of the Rose'*, Secker & Warburg, London, 1984, pp. 65–6.

4 This is an increasingly widespread assumption – see for example the discussion paper of the CPGB, 'Facing Up to the Future', supplement in *Marxism Today*, vol. 32, no. 9, September 1988.

5 Jean-François Lyotard, trans. Geoff Bennington and Brian Massumi, *The Postmodern Condition: A Report on Knowledge*, Manchester University Press, Manchester, 1986, p. xxiii.

6 Ibid., p. xxiv.

7 Ibid., p. 41.

8 Linda Hutcheon, *A Poetics of Postmodernism: History, Theory, Fiction*, Routledge & Kegan Paul, London, 1988, p. 19.

9 Andreas Huyssen, *After the Great Divide: Modernism, Mass Culture, Post-Modernism*, Indiana University Press, Bloomington, 1986, p. 209.

10 Ibid., p. 213.

11 Cf. Simon Watney, *Policing Desire: AIDS, Pornography and the Media*, Comedia, London, 1987.

12 Walter Benjamin, trans. Harry Zohn, *Charles Baudelaire: A Lyric Poet in the Era of High Capitalism*, New Left Books, London, 1973.

13 Barbara Grier, *The Lesbian in Literature*, Naiad Press, Tallahassee, 1981.

14 Cited Lovat Dickson, *Radclyffe Hall at the Well of Loneliness: A Sapphic Chronicle*, Collins, London, 1975, p. 140. (1928 was obviously thought to be a good time to publish lesbian novels because Compton Mackenzie's *Extraordinary Women*, and the collected works of Ronald Firbank, *The Complete Firbank*, were also published.)

15 Alison Hennegan, introduction to *The Well of Loneliness* (1928), Virago, London, 1982, p. xi.

16 Lovat Dickson, op. cit., p. 149.

17 Ibid., p. 165.

18 Ibid., p. 167.
19 Maya Angelou, *I Know Why the Caged Bird Sings*, Virago Press, London, p. 266.
20 Lillian Faderman, *Surpassing the Love of Men: Romantic Friendship & Love Between Women from the Renaissance to the Present*, Junction Books (undated, 1982), p. 323. Reprinted by The Women's Press, London, 1985.
21 Radclyffe Hall, op. cit., p. 49.
22 Michel Foucault, trans. Robert Hurley, *The History of Sexuality. Volume One: An Introduction*, Penguin Books, London, 1981, p. 54.
23 Radclyffe Hall, op. cit., p. 150.
24 Lillian Faderman, op. cit., p. 392.
25 Elaine Showalter, *A Literature of Their Own: British Women Novelists from Brontë to Lessing*, Virago Press, London, 1978, p. 291.
26 Ibid., p. 282.
27 Makiko Minow-Pinkney, *Virginia Woolf & The Problem of the Subject: Feminine Writing in the Major Novels*, Harvester, Brighton, 1987, p. 12.
28 Ibid., p. 121.
29 Rachel Bowlby, *Virginia Woolf: Feminist Destinations*, Basil Blackwell, Oxford, 1988, p. 128.
30 Virginia Woolf, *A Writer's Diary* (1953), Granada, London, 1977, p. 119.
31 Ibid., p. 116.
32 Ibid., p. 136.
33 Ibid., p. 119.
34 Jean-François Lyotard, trans. Geoff Bennington and Brian Massumi, op. cit., p. 10.
35 Ibid., p. 63.
36 Elaine Showalter, op. cit., p. 291.
37 Toril Moi, *Sexual/Textual Politics*, Methuen, London, 1985, p. 9.
38 Makiko Minow-Pinkney, op. cit., p. 12.
39 Ibid., p. 12.
40 Ibid., p. 12.
41 Ibid., p. 196.
42 Rachel Bowlby, op. cit., p. 128.
43 Radclyffe Hall, op. cit., p. 446.
44 Ibid., p. 447.
45 Julia Kristeva, trans. John Fechte, 'Approaching Abjection', *Oxford Literary Review*, vol. 5, 1982, p. 128.
46 Virginia Woolf, *Orlando* (1928), Panther, London, 1977.
47 Ibid., p. 192.
48 Makiko Minow-Pinkney, op. cit., p. 131.
49 Toril Moi, op. cit., p. 76. The full quotation is: 'The relationship [to the other] would not be a-sexual, far from it, but it would be sexual

otherwise: beyond the binary difference that governs the decorum of all codes, beyond the opposition masculine/feminine, beyond homosexuality and heterosexuality which come to the same thing. As I dream of saving the chance that this question offers, I would like to believe in the multiplicity of sexually marked voices. I would like to believe in the masses, this indeterminable number of blended voices, this mobile of non-identified sexual marks whose choreography can carry, divide, multiply the body of each "individual", whether he be classified as "man" or "woman" according to the criteria of usage.'

50 Makiko Minow-Pinkney, op. cit., p. 133.
51 Virginia Woolf, op. cit., p. 137.
52 Rachel Bowlby, op. cit., p. 162.
53 Virginia Woolf, op. cit., p. 138.
54 Radclyffe Hall, op. cit., p. 140.
55 Michel Foucault, trans. Robert Hurley, op. cit., p. 101.
56 Virginia Woolf, op. cit., p. 193.
57 Radclyffe Hall, op. cit., p. 7.
58 Ibid., p. 211.
59 Ibid., p. 248.
60 Virginia Woolf, op. cit., p. 12.
61 Ibid., p. 60.
62 Jean-François Lyotard and Jean-Loup Thébaud, trans. Wlad Godzich, *Just Gaming*, University of Minnesota/Manchester University Press, 1985, p. 43.
63 Ibid., p. 40.
64 Ibid., p. 42.
65 Jean-François Lyotard, trans. Geoff Bonnington and Brian Massumi, op. cit., p. 15.
66 Gayatri Chakravorty Spivak, 'Imperialism and Sexual Difference', *Oxford Literary Review*, vol. 8, no. 1/2, 1986, p. 226.
67 Stuart Hall, 'Minimal Selves', in Lisa Appignanesi (ed.), *The Real Me: Postmodernism and the question of identity*, ICA, London, 1987.
68 Walter Benjamin, trans. Harry Zohn, *Illuminations*, Fontana, London, 1982, p. 260.
69 *Rough Guides* are very useful guides to other countries, which point out pleasures of shopping, nightclubbing, as well as the hazards of race/gender.

References and Further Reading

Other relevant essays and books on the issues raised here, in addition to those in the notes, include:

Baudrillard, Jean, 'The Precession of Simulacra', trans. Paul Foss, Paul Patton and Philip Bleitchmann, in *Simulations*, Semiotext(e), 1983, pp. 1–73.

Connor, Steven, *Postmodernist Culture: Introduction to Theories of the Contemporary*, Basil Blackwell, Oxford (forthcoming).

Eagleton, Terry, 'Capitalism, Modernism and Postmodernism', *New Left Review*, no. 152, 1895, pp. 60–73.

Foster, Hal (ed.), *Postmodern Culture*, Pluto, London, 1985 (esp. Craig Owens, 'The Discourse of Others: Feminists and Postmodernism', pp. 57–82).

Hassan, Ihab, *The Dismemberment of Orpheus: Towards a Postmodern Literature*, Oxford University Press, Oxford, 1982.

Jameson, Frederic, 'Postmodernism, or the Cultural Logic of Late Capitalism', *New Left Review*, no. 146, 1984, pp. 53–93.

Jardine, Alice, *Gynesis: Configurations of Women and Modernity*, Cornell University Press, New York, 1985.

Lee, Janet, 'Care To Join Me in an Upwardly Mobile Tango? Postmodernism and the New Woman' in Lorraine Gamman and Margaret Marshment (eds), *The Female Gaze: Women as Viewers of Popular Culture*, The Women's Press, London, 1988.

Weedon, Chris, *Feminist Practice and Post-Structuralist Theory*, Basil Blackwell, Oxford, 1987.

POETIC LICENCE

────◆────

HELEN CARR

> You are a poem
> Though your poem's nought[1]

wrote Ezra Pound to HD. Feminist critics in the last two decades
have seen such lines as typical of the traditional place assigned
by the male poet to woman in poetry: she is the passive image
rather than energising creator, the object to be written about, not
the subject who writes, the artefact, not the artist. But do women
– or men – always see poetry as such a male-dominated genre
and preserve? In many ways of course it is, and some of the most
illuminating feminist criticism of poetry so far has looked at
women poets' recasting and subversion of male conventions
within the poetic tradition: for example, Margaret Homans's
exploration of how nineteenth-century women poets negotiated
a poetic language in which they as women were subsumed into
Mother Nature, and Angela Leighton's subtle account of Elizabeth Barrett Browning's construction of a fatherly Muse.

Men certainly may predominate in the numbers writing or at
least publishing, but I am less sure whether the gender associations that cling to the concept of poetry, and that make the
writing of it seem a legitimate and appropriate activity for one
gender or the other, are so monolithically male. What about the
idea of poetry as soft and unmanly? The notion of art as
dangerously emotional, moving away from the real world of
business and action, more appropriate to women's concerns?
Has that vanished? Why was it ever there? Surely the modernist
poetics argued by someone like Ezra Pound were at any rate
partly concerned with making poetry safe for men, escaping
from the effeminate gender-bending 1890s, or what Pound saw

as the effete poetry of the 'ladylike' Tennyson or 'mincing' Meredith. He wanted to reconstruct the manly poet who will write poetry which is 'harder, saner . . . "nearer the bone" . . . It will be as much like granite as it can be . . . austere, direct, free from emotional slither'.[2] The sense of poetry as volatile, ready to slip dangerously from control becomes for Pound as for most critics pinned firmly on 'bad' poetry, which is sentimental poetry, and hence associated with the feminine. In fact the elision between the bad, the sentimental and the feminine is so strong that feminist critics tend to concur in condemning such poetry as a product of a distasteful ladylike tradition, what Alicia Suskin Ostriker calls 'the genteel poetry and the genteel ideal of femininity, which stressed the heart and denied the head', without actually asking more deeply about the fears suppressed in such a struggle to repudiate 'emotional slither'.[3]

I want here to raise some questions about women and poetry, about poetry and 'emotional slither', and about the place of poetry writing in our society. Poetry is regarded in our culture in very contradictory ways, and those contradictions seem intimately bound up with gender. It is seen both as a prestigious, élite and esoteric form, and as a private, intimate, intensely subjective one. And whilst considered in the former way women may feel intimidated, in the latter they, and less privileged men, can regard poetry as a place in which they are enfranchised. Women writing poetry won't necessarily see it only in one of these ways: more often both at once, or both at different times. Adrienne Rich in her influential essay 'When We Dead Awaken' talks of her sense of the forbidding weight of male poetic tradition, which she could only evade by constructing a counter-line of exemplary women. I don't want to underestimate that sense of exclusion from the high literary tradition: I just want to suggest that it is only part of a complex of ideas and assumptions, some of which are immensely productive for women. During the last two hundred years, even more perhaps than earlier, masculinity has been the place of the active, the public, the practical, the reason: femininity that of the contemplative, the personal, the dreamer, the emotions. Ever since the Romantics, poetry has had much closer associations with the latter than the former.[4] We need to understand why those associations are there, and how they enter into the practice of poetry. I would want to argue that although these associations are in one sense cultural and historical, they spring from the different way in which language operates in poetry from prose.

The most vivid example I've been given recently of poetry as a demotic, liberating place was at the funeral of the fireman who died in the appalling escalator fire in 1987 at London's busy King's Cross station. One of the dead man's colleagues, I was told, read a poem that he had written in response to the disaster. I was struck by this instance of someone using poetry as a way of responding to deeply disturbing occurrences, as a discourse which could refer to events and states of being which our normal conventions of intercourse make it difficult to speak of, particularly for men. Generally in our culture such poetry is only acceptable in a private or literary context, but the setting of the funeral allows this exception – and this of course was an exceptional funeral, following a tragedy and for a fireman, one of our few folk heroes. Poetry in that context becomes part of a ritual of passage, reordering the disorder of death, but it's a ritual available to a member of the laity, not reserved for either a professional poet or priest.

Many of the poems that were sent into *Women's Review* (and there were a great many) clearly gave their writers a similar sense of freedom, though the context – privately written poems, sent to a small, sympathetic publishing outlet – was more traditional.[5] Poetry was an opportunity for them as women, not a privilege to be wrested from men. I'm not necessarily talking only of overtly autobiographical poems, or of poetry concerned with traumatic events, but of the fact that in our tradition of lyric poetry (by which I mean post-Romantic Anglo-American lyric poetry) writing a poem is a statement that, within those lines at least, the poet is a speaking subject whose subjectivity is being taken seriously. In the Anglo-American and Western European tradition poetry has become associated with the private and the personal. There are no authors here who are political and public forces, like the Romanian Marin Sorescu whose audiences fill football stadiums, or the Chilean Paolo Neruda, loved across every class and group. But although in many ways this is our cultural and political loss, just because poetry is associated with the private and the personal, it is a form which women can feel they have a right to use, even though elsewhere the social conventions they observe and the discourses they use may discount that subjectivity. Our social mores dictate that we are circumspect in revealing emotion. The valued discourses in our culture – science and theory – are those which present themselves as objective and transparent, purged of subjectivity, emotion or ambiguity. In the deviant language of poetry all those murky areas, so culturally aligned with the feminine, can be allowed.

But, you may argue, surely the point is that all language, and specifically traditional poetic language, privileges the masculine position, and that these women in their poetry were struggling with this whether they were aware of it or not? In many ways, I agree. But I also think that we have looked so intensely at that aspect of poetic language that we miss other ways in which poetry can be thought about more positively. Jan Montefiore suggests that the scarcity of women poets in the past is as likely due to their social lack of opportunity as to their sense that the language of Milton or Wordsworth refused them bed-room.[6] I wouldn't want to underestimate the problems women still find themselves up against either in the literary world or in literary language, but that is only part of the story. What I have to say about that story here is not a fully worked through argument. Rather, as with the other pieces in this book, I hope it will suggest directions in which it might be useful for feminist criticism to move.

Directions for Feminist Criticism

Feminist criticism – and here it is no less conservative than any other advanced radical criticism – has not rethought poetic writing in such wide-reaching ways as it has other literary forms. While the concept of literature has been abundantly deconstructed, the old distinction between 'poetry' and mere verse generally remains implicit. Even critics whose theoretical stance makes such an idea problematic have stuck cautiously to the canon. Sub-literary fiction – that is, the kind of fiction that used to be regarded as part of 'mass culture', rather than 'literature', such as popular forms of romance, science fiction, detective novels – has been accepted as an area of criticism; but not sub-literary poetry, which is still belittled, or even not seen as poetry at all. There is, for example, surprisingly little feminist analysis of the lyrics of pop songs.[7] Yet these lyrics form so much a part of the complex of representations in which young women come to understand themselves that it's a curious gap.

I don't want here to attempt such an analysis myself. I want instead to look at the writing of lyric poetry today as a comparatively widespread, even demotic, non-élitist practice, of importance to many women. Many women write poetry, at least sometimes. They may not publish it, or if they attempt to, it may be rejected out of hand; they may cyclostyle it along with the rest of a poetry group, or they may publish in little magazines or slim volumes; they may read their poems at events; some may even win literary awards. For many of them the pleasure comes out of the writing or sharing of poems with a small group, whether or not they publish more widely. When I say I want to think about poetry demotically, I don't mean I'm going to separate off amateur from professional poetry, or even 'bad' from 'good'. I don't want to talk about a tradition of 'women's poetry' because I think even to conceive of one monolithic women's poetic tradition in our multi-racial, multi-cultural, many classed society is impossible.[8] I merely want to speculate tentatively about some ways in which one can think of lyric poetry as process rather than product, and to suggest how that process may operate for women writing poetry today, leaving aside for the moment what is 'successful' poetry.

Recent poetry criticism has found it hard to move beyond the discussion of poetry in terms of close textual criticism. In the last few decades literature teachers from a succession of critical schools have made sure that every literature student learns – or at any rate is taught – to attend to and perhaps find pleasure in highly-wrought and densely-textured writing. Other ways of understanding the forms of pleasure or desire inscribed in poetry have been neglected. When we talk about pleasure in connection with detective novels or romance we accept that it doesn't necessarily come from the linguistic subtleties of the text. It has, perhaps, more to do with the process of arousal and appeasing of desire. And in these postmodernist times, we are increasingly aware that to analyse such generic pleasures adds to our appreciation of how we read more complex texts. To understand what gives pleasure in poetry we must of course take into account its distinctive use of language, but to start with the evaluation of the completed artefact can pre-empt examination of what it is in poetry that we value.

Cora Kaplan talked here about the breakdown of the three-pointed triangle of writing, theory and politics that existed in the 1970s; certainly a gap exists between the way most recent academic feminist criticism has developed and the way in which many poets talk about their work. Many contemporary women poets speak in terms which suggest that their writing is immensely important to them in finding some kind of identity as women outside, as it were, that poetry. Yet the critical tradition which the academics inhabit, going back in some senses to the modernists, but certainly paramount in the New Critics,[9] structuralists and post-structuralists, insists that the poem must be read as an autonomous linguistic artefact.[10] It cannot be understood as the 'expression' of the poet's experience. Most academic feminist critics are now post-structuralists, and they are embarrassed by the comments of practising poets on their own work, particularly if the poets use a vocabulary which includes such words as 'voice', 'experience' and 'inspiration'. Embarrassment is a response often prompted by poetry, particularly 'bad' poetry. We need to understand why: embarrassment is a signal that something has significantly reached us.

I'm not arguing that feminists should abandon the insights of post-structuralism into the mutability and provisionality of meaning and identity. Post-structuralism is the most recent theoretical statement of a scepticism which goes back to the Renaissance at least: and even, according to Umberto Eco, back as far as Parmenides.[11] Now in our post-Christian world the lack of guaranteed meaning is what most of us have to live with. For us, individual identity is what the nineteenth-century French poet Tristan Corbière called a 'mélange adultère de tout' – an adulterated/adulterous mixture of everything.[12] We are each constantly changing, unstable, contradictory: formed, de-formed, re-formed by our personal histories, our social histories, our class and gender positions, our bodies, our hormones, our conscious beliefs and our unconscious drives. We are born into a maze of language through whose contradictions and ambiguities we come to what sense we can of ourselves and our world. As women in the Western world our possibilities and expectations have changed with an extraordinary rapidity: how we recognise who or what we are or might be can be deeply problematic. Yet we are also at a moment of new possibilities. Many of us are far more able than ever before to act as agents in our own destinies. I don't find it possible to return to the idea of an essence that can be called the 'female self', as a critic like Ostriker does. But reading her book, *Stealing the Language: The Emergence of Women's Poetry in America*, it is easy to sympathise with her impatience with the inadequacy of either New Critical or deconstructionist terms to describe what she wants to say about women's poetry in the United States. Her common-sense feminist reading produces a book which details fascinatingly the way women have begun to write about the female body, revise male myths, explore how their female identities can be conceived. Yet her terms ultimately are closed, unlike her observations of change and flux. She writes as if there is one way of being a woman, common to us all, which has been buried and unspoken but which can be gradually recovered and displayed. Yet her very account presents women trying out shifting and evolving possible selves. What she recognises, so usefully, is an intensely strong relationship between these women's sense of the need to rethink and re-feel what it means to be a woman, and their poetic writing.

So how can we talk about the importance of poetry for women? What is the relationship between lyric poetry and subjectivity, between poetic and personal identity? The chasm between the speaker and speech, the poet and poem, the body and language is another of those insights, or one might say anxieties, so present in poetic writing since the Romantics and now central to post-structuralist thought. Language is like a prison uniform, issued to us each and fitting none of us. The complex of history and flesh that we each are can never be represented accurately in a shared discourse. When Maud Ellmann rebukes Eliot for failing to admit that poetry is made not of feelings but words, on the literal level, so to speak, one can't disagree.[13] But I still think some way of understanding the relationship between words and 'feelings' still remains. Ostriker in her book ends up by dismissing the problem – no gap exists for these women, she asserts, between the 'I' of their poems and the 'I' who writes. That statement doesn't seem tenable, but the link between those 'I's still asks for an explanation.

I want to get nearer answering these questions by first step-ping away. I am going to look at how poetry is used in quite a different culture, to evade, as much as anything, some of the constraints of my own critical training. Oral poetry is the main exception to the general critical reluctance to examine verse which might not be necessarily 'good'. Oral poetry is by defi-nition composed by people different from our literate selves, and doesn't raise the same embarrassed confusions, any more than do postcards of bare-breasted Bantu women from the homelands sold to puritan Afrikaaners. Even so, work on oral poetry has been much more aligned with anthropology and linguistics than with literature. But for that reason it has tended to ask quite different questions about poetry, seeing it as a social and discur-sive practice rather than a cultural product. I have spent some time reading and thinking about one culture's oral poetry, that of the Native Americans. At first I was most struck by how different the place of poetry was in their cultures from ours – there was no concept of an autotelic art practised for its own sake and admired in terms of its skill, it is part of social rituals defined in other ways – but I've increasingly felt that the kind of questions prompted there could be immensely liberating for talking about poetry in our culture. What is the social function of this poetry? What is its relation to the central myths and rituals of the society? Who composes or performs it? In what sort of circumstances, and why? What is the relation of the language used in this poetry to other discourses? Our idea of art as autotelic is perhaps a cultural myth, even though the reasons for writing poetry in our culture are not as immediately apparent as in Native American traditions.

Poetry and Cultural Context

Distinguishing between verse and prose is not necessarily easy. The difference is one of degree rather than kind, but all cultures seem to have had special forms of language, set aside from everyday speech, which most exploit the physicality of words, most commonly through rhythm and metre, but also through sound, repetition, parallelism and patterning. In a literate culture the physical arrangement of script or print is important too: indeed, for some twentieth-century poetry, supremely important, as its only overt distinguishing feature may be that it looks different on the page. Because of the artificiality of its language poetry is always a highly cultural rather than a natural form. That may seem a redundantly obvious statement, but the Romantic myth of poetry's origin in the 'savage tribes ... mere expression of passion in the sounds which passion itself necessitates' still sometimes lurks in the Western view of non-Western oral poetry.[14] In many cultures it is associated with the same kind of areas of danger, disturbance and power that Mary Douglas investigates in *Purity and Danger*, her analysis of the way taboos against pollution and rules of purity shape the conceptual order of cultures.

But the practice and the place of poetry varies enormously between and within different cultures. Several disparate forms existed in the different traditions of Native American oral poetry. I will mention three, of which two, as it happens, are male. Most of this Native American poetry was recorded in the late nineteenth and early twentieth centuries by anthropologists who overwhelmingly chose men as their informants. So much more men's poetry than women's was taken down, although that's not an accurate guide to balance in the cultures. But for now gender is not the immediate issue, especially as gender, as opposed to biological sex, has different constraints in different societies. The vision songs of the Plains and Woodland Indians were 'found' when boys at puberty were sent out to fast for a vision, which they would then describe in a song, or perhaps one should rather say, would come to them as a song. This 'vision song' would remain their personal possession. They would sing it as they went into battle, reinvoking the visionary state, rather as if they were taking a psychotropic drug. On the one hand these songs could be described as highly individualised – each man has his own unique song – but on the other, the means by which the vision was gained, and the musical and linguistic form used in the song, was entirely traditional. A few words – generally poeticised or sacred archaic forms – would be repeated numerous times with additional vocatives and particles. When the core words are translated into English they seem like imagist poems (as they were claimed to be when first discovered by American poets), for example:

As my eyes
search
the prairie
I feel the summer in the spring[15]

Quite different are the Navajo chants, used to cure physical and psychic pain. These are traditional, shaped by repetition and parallelism, and accompanied by the telling of a long narrative myth and the making and destruction of the famous Navajo sand-paintings, which illustrate the myth and the chant. They are recited by a chanter, who has acquired his esoteric knowledge through a long apprenticeship. He speaks on behalf of the patient, the whole ceremony lasting between two and nine days. This may sound like a church liturgy, but in fact it is never performed twice the same way. The selection of possible elements is always fitted to the circumstances and problems of that particular patient, so his or her individual plight is placed within a group narrative which always ends with the centring of the individual within harmony and calm. This is a dynamic, not a static harmony: the principal verb in Navajo is 'to go', not 'to be'; life is conceptualised as a 'walk'. 'With beauty before me, I walk./With beauty behind me, I walk./With beauty below me, I walk./With beauty above me, I walk./With beauty all around me, I walk./It is finished in beauty.'[16]

A third form is the poetry of individual shamans, the poet/priest/healers found among many pre-literate groups, particularly in Siberia and the Americas. A chanter is a shaman of sorts, but the more traditional shaman has undergone a personal crisis, experienced as a death and rebirth, a spiritual journey out of the body and back again. This journey can be reinvoked in the singing of the songs brought back from that journey, found there as the young boys found their songs in their vision. The patient in this case is cured by being 'led' by the songs through a similar journey. For example, there was an elderly woman shaman in the Papago nation whose songs were recorded in the 1920s. Known as Owl Woman, she had experienced a period of acute depression following several bereavements as a young woman, which she recounts in her songs as a death in which she visits the spirit-land, is strengthened and returns to life. As I describe it here this may sound a very individual voyage, but again the imagery and the parameters of the experience are traditional in form. Owl Woman's songs about the white mountain in the spirit-land at the edge of the world echo those that appear within Papago myths of origin and those sung by other shamans. Each song is at the same moment conventional and unique.[17]

Drawing parallels from other cultures can be dangerous; but aware as one must be of differences, I think it could be illuminating to compare our poetic practice with what happens here. There are four main points I'd like to draw out. Firstly, in each of these Native American forms there is a complex imbrication of individual desire with a very specific traditional discourse, so that a group narrative or myth or way of symbolising can be appropriated by, or on behalf of, a specific individual for a specific situation. Secondly, the context of this poetry is that of an individual in a state of being which is in some sense abnormal, for example sick or unhappy, or liminal; that is, on the threshold between two accepted states, like the boy at puberty passing from childhood into adult life. Thirdly, all these forms are transformative: they are concerned to change one state of being into another. But although their context may be that of pain, grief, or disorientation that is not what they 'express': their words have much more to do with the pattern of being that they wish to achieve. Although in the sequence of the Papago shamanic songs and in the Navajo chant the symbolic story embodies the process of change, the poetry produces meanings rather than mirroring them. And fourthly, there is the role of the shaman, the voyager and cartographer of the descent into the depths and re-emergence, whose map provides a cure.

Poetic Narrative

To return to the first point: in a literate cosmopolitan society with a proliferation of media, the available myths and discourses are much more various and intermeshed than those of an oral group; but our poetry too is formed of a culturally controlled range of discourses which the individual writer of poetry appropriates or subverts or enters. For us it's perhaps more usually and usefully talked about as intertextuality. All poetry rewrites other texts; perhaps one of the most striking changes in modernist and postmodernist poetry is that these pre-texts are much more overtly used, and increasingly are outside the poetic tradition. The surge of women's poetry specifically rewriting myths and fairy-tales – HD, Anne Sexton, Stevie Smith are only a few of the names one could mention – is one very obvious example of this intertextuality. So is the work of Caribbean poets, both men and women, who are at the moment so actively 'calibanising' European forms by drawing on traditional Afro-Caribbean figures and motifs – Grace Nichols on the Ashanti spider woman, or Fred D'Aguiar on Mama Dot.[18] In the introduction to her book *The Land of Look Behind* the Jamaican/US writer Michelle Cliff talks about her emergence from an education which made her intellectually proficient but which, she says, 'almost render(ed) me speechless about who I am'. She discovered that to write as a Caribbean woman, or man, 'demands of us retracing the African part of ourselves, reclaiming as our own, and as our subject, a history sunk under the sea . . . It means finding the artforms of these our ancestors and speaking in the patois forbidden to us . . . It means . . . mixing in the forms taught us by the oppressor, undermining his language and co-opting his style, and turning it to our purpose'.[19] But intertextuality is often a less obvious process: the reworking of the woman-as-flower image, which Jan Montefiore analyses in poems by Sylvia Plath, Alison Fell and others, or Emily Dickinson's subversion of Isaac Watts's hymns.[20]

Lévi-Strauss says of myth that it is always the transformation of another myth. The same perhaps applies to poetry. It might be objected that this isn't the case in all verse. The point of some of our public poetry is that the poet and the reader give themselves gladly to total absorption in a cultural or group myth. School songs are the most obvious crude example, but it can apply to hymns and many pop songs. But that's really just one way of negotiating the same problem, which is essentially not that of inventing a new narrative, but of making existing narratives your own, whether or not you need or wish to subvert them in that appropriation. The school song is a fusion of mythic elements which come together as a new and formative, some might say, deformative, construction. Even the man Borges describes as rewriting *Don Quixote* word for word is, as he insists, writing a completely new text.[21] Language can't be static; it's this perhaps that the Russian linguist Voloshinov means when he talks, in the context of class and power, of the sign being the site of struggle. When women poets speak of finding a voice and expressing their own experience, they are talking perhaps about this transformation of a narrative, or fusion of narratives, which then work as their own; they make the sign produce new meanings for them.

Barthes argued as long ago as 1957 that 'contemporary myth' was discontinuous.[22] Postmodernists now point out the breakdown of the grand narratives of the Western world: Christianity, progress, humanism. Perhaps their loss has made the kind of provisional and partial narratives that a poem can hold all the more important. Poetry is often not thought of as narrative; but as for Barthes now a phrase can be mythic, even the single image is a narrative, although it may be narrative free of the demands of cause and effect, direction or closure. There is a sense in which all our narratives are decentred, unlike the Native American mythic structures, where the central myths of the society shape the apparently more individual structures. But we all use, and need to use, narratives, as Lévi-Strauss argues, to cope with 'the inchoate and arbitrary' flux of existence. In an article which is one of his most fascinating because in it he makes a rare attempt to come to terms with subjectivity, he tells the story of a Cunan shaman treating a woman through a difficult breach birth. The shaman told her a myth whose progress, a struggle between spirits and animals within her, mimed the journey of the child down the birth canal, including turning it round so its head was in the right direction. It worked: the baby was safely born, though after lurid descriptions of mythic alligators, a sticky-tentacled octopus and the black tiger. Lévi-Strauss goes on to make an analogy with Freudian psychoanalysis: for the successful outcome of such therapy the analysands must find a narrative to provide an organising story of their lives, one which lets them escape the destructive private myths behind their neurotic compulsions. The point for Lévi-Strauss is not whether the elements of the Freudian myth are any more true than that of the Cunan. It is that we need a narrative that makes sense of unspeakable physical or psychic disturbance, reconciling the unconscious and the conscious, if we are to deal with it. Lévi-Strauss is aware of the differences between them, but he is fascinated by the power exerted by a symbolic structuring of experience, in each case through a socially accepted and acceptable narrative appropriated by or for an individual. The narrative orders the subjective experience, but it must do so by mapping that subjectivity on to a wider myth.[23]

We've come to think of the narratives or myths of our society as primarily oppressive and constrictive. But we need narratives: they are where we start. Lyotard, one of those to argue most strongly that the master narratives have gone, has a view of language (which Carolyn Brown uses so productively in her essay) which can illuminate how the fragmented, vestigial narratives of poetry work. He draws on Wittgenstein's idea of 'language-games': language is not as the bearer of absolute meanings, but a collection of different discourses or language-games, each of which has its own rules, which are a kind of pragmatic contract understood, explicitly or implicitly, between the players. But unlike Wittgenstein, Lyotard argues that those games and their rules are always a site to be contested. He sees them as struggle, a competitive game, a series of moves and countermoves, where each move shifts the nature of the game slightly. Once we speak we are players in the game, agents in our lives. We shift ever so little the power relations embodied in language. As Lyotard says, we are all born into stories already awaiting us. But we can negotiate the outcome of the plot.[24] In this period of immense dissatisfaction with the place in our narratives assigned to women, it is not surprising that so much of contemporary women's poetry is occupied with recharting male narratives, playing new moves, struggling to change the rules of the game. In poetry, as in any speech-act, the speaker produces him/herself as an agent. That's perhaps a way of looking at the Lacanian model positively rather than negatively, not at the failure of language ever to encompass a 'true identity' but at how language empowers the speaker to create a pragmatic or strategic identity that can enter the social world. Just to speak is in some sense to control.

Rites of Passage

So to the second point I drew from the Native American tradition: that their verse is associated with disturbed or liminal states. So is much of our lyric tradition, though in more heterogeneous ways. Oral poetry is paradoxically further from ordinary speech and from direct individual communication than much written poetry. In a literate society the development of detailed auto-biographical or individualised content becomes possible in a way only found in the briefest snatches in an oral tradition, so the scene of poetry becomes much more various. Yet living as we do in a society where we are both flooded with possible narratives and yet without any certain structures of meaning, how we cope with desire, death, love, bereavement, outrage, anger, anguish, impotence, despair, anxiety, fear, must perhaps be, for many of us, through fictive forms: films, novels, TV soap opera, romance, pop songs as well as lyric poetry. But lyric poetry remains an important strategy for some in finding an order to the chaos of responses those life-events bring with them; not making private sense of them – that would be psychosis – but finding a fiction which can be shared. For many women in our culture their whole identity is a liminal state. We are not the creatures we grew up expecting to be; lyric poetry is one way of trying out possible selves. 'Piece by piece I seem/to re-enter the world' as Adrienne Rich says.[25]

It's become a cliché now to note that our society is painfully destitute of rites of passages, rituals that accept, order and so mitigate or control the psychic distress or excess we all experience at some time or other. It's an impoverishment, but perhaps, in a multicultural secular society, inevitable. There are no accepted or stable myths that could provide a basis for such rituals. Which is why fictional forms become so valuable: simulacra in place of icons. Ritual places the single sorrow or rite of passage into a shared cycle of being. Take, for example, the poem by Eavan Boland, 'The Journey', which she wrote after her small daughter almost died of meningitis. This isn't mentioned directly in the poem, which instead speaks (whilst saying that's impossible) for all those mothers in the past who have lost their children. She places her poem in the centre of the Western poetic tradition, beginning with a quotation from Virgil's *Aeneid*. As Aeneas follows the Sibyl down to the underworld he passes at the entrance the crying souls of babies: 'never had they had their share of life's sweetness for the dark day had stolen them from their mothers' breasts and plunged them to a death before their time'. But what her poem says has hitherto been unspoken:

> And then the dark fell and 'there has never'
> I said 'been a poem to an antibiotic'
> never a word to compare with the odes on
> the flower of the rare sloe for fever ...

In the poem that follows she falls asleep, dreaming that she is led by Sappho ('it was she, misshapen, musical') into that same underworld, where, however, she is conscious not so much of the dead babies as of their stricken mothers:

> Then to my horror I could see to each
> nipple some had clipped a limpet shape –
> suckling darknesses – while others had their arms
> weighed down making terrible pietàs

The poem's narrative re-enacts her own descent into the shadow of bereavement and return; she sees the silenced women of the past, whose pangs at losing their children have never been adequately chronicled – the only acknowledged pietà, the word reminds us, was Mary's grief for her adult son. The narrative shape of this poem was there for her to take and re-form, standing already as a literary device that symbolises the descent into the abyss, that claims to discover important truths about the world. Her trauma follows an old pattern: yet one unperceived, unspoken – Aeneas only saw the dead infants, not their mothers. Thanks to the antibiotic, she can return. Her isolated anguish becomes part of a historical narrative; her 'horror' turns to compassion and 'love', for those past women and herself.[26]

Much of twentieth-century verse has dealt with such highly charged subject matter self-consciously, as Eavan Boland does here, aware of the structures that form the poem and its subject, aware of the gap between representation and being. The criticism of some feminist poetry has been that it is naively unaware of the problems of language, defiant perhaps about conventional representations of femininity but slipping into other clichés. I think that's sometimes true, but for my purposes here it's irrelevant. I think such poetry can still be a valuable cognitive move for its writers even if not for all of its readers. It is however, I believe, the sort of poetry criticised in those terms which tends to be most popular at poetry readings. Perhaps it is hard to take in the shifting of more than one narrative at once. There's an interesting parallel with some of the indubitably sentimental poetry produced by well-established male poets in Britain at the moment on the New Man as father, which politically, if in no other way, one cannot but applaud, and which gets warmly clapped, for whatever reason, at London's National Poetry Society.

Transformations

The third characteristic of the oral verse, its transformative aim, is both like and unlike our cultural forms. The differences are certainly considerable. We don't expect a poem to 'cure' illness or induce hallucinatory trance in quite this way. Eavan Boland may write a poem to an antibiotic, but she would not use a poem as a substitute for one. Freud may have unsettled our mind/body dichotomy, but it still operates powerfully. The chanter and the shaman clearly have a role that combines priest, psychoanalyst, doctor and poet, and though such a combination of power has great romantic attraction, our poetry is a more marginal and comparatively fragile structure. Yet I've already argued that the transformation of narratives is central to our poetry, and that changing a narrative changes how we experience ourselves. We see this in contemporary poetry in postmodernist terms – a plethora of images that we catch and recombine. Julia Kristeva sees similar transformations in modernist poetry (changing from one sign system to another is how she puts it) and Isobel Armstrong has suggested that the transformation through poetic language of the 'categories' of subject and object is at the heart of Romantic poetry. To some extent lyric poetry takes on, in a more tentative way, the role of religion in 'making sense', not by giving an explanation or answer, but by simply finding a way by which contradictions and confusions can be set down and found a shape, by finding words which draw the inchoate into signification.[27] Michelle Cliff's first piece of writing, she says, other than a dissertation, was entitled 'Notes on Speechlessness' and

was indeed just that, notes, 'jagged, non-linear, almost short-
hand', though even that had a pre-text, the story of the wild boy
of Aveyron, whose inarticulate wildness she could there make
speak for her, and provide a first stage in her exploration.[28]

The significance of the narratives of fictive forms isn't that they
provide causally argued explanations like the narratives of
science or politics, or absolute and comprehensive claims to truth
like religion. Their narratives are not necessarily logically, not
even in the case of poetry syntactically, coherent: the narrative of
a poem may be closer to that of a dream (and of course it has often
been suggested that the principles by which Freud said dreams
are ordered, displacement and condensation, are versions of
metonymy and metaphor). Poetic images, like those of dreams,
can stand in for the otherwise unspeakable, for conflicts which
may be repressed below the level of consciousness, psychic or
social, or in the realm of the pre-linguistic, or pre-conceptual. In
Emily Dickinson's poetry, Cora Kaplan argues, she explores
imagistically her divided psyche, 'Ourself, behind ourself con-
cealed' prefiguring any systematic psychoanalytic theory of the
multiform personality.[29] But the process is more than that. In a
poem like, for instance, 'Because I could not wait for Death', its
poetic form immediately signals that the poem need not work in
the terms of everyday narrative: we accept that its story need
have no more consequentiality than a dream, but we know, as in
a dream, that it is of consequence.

Some psychoanalysts suggest that 'areas of creativity' provide
a space between fantasy and reality where psychic dramas can be
worked through.[30] Poems don't reach a rational stasis: they
move, in both senses, through symbolic patterning. They don't
necessarily resolve or unify, but they are productive processes.
According to Toril Moi, Julia Kristeva seems to be suggesting
something like that in her later work: after analysis, the analy-
sand will reach, not a static cure, but the possibility of being a
'work in progress', constantly producing him/herself through
imaginative speaking or writing, without being trapped by inner
conflict either as a fixed self or in a meaningless void.[31] Kristeva,
whose work is so alert to the inseparability of the psychic, the
social, the somatic and the linguistic, moves away from the
ultimately bourgeois notion of texts as 'objects', autonomous or
otherwise. She sees them as processes, whether written or as

read, just as each one of us has to be understood as a subject-in-process. In her earlier writing what she stressed was the subversive force of 'poetic language', by which she meant avant-garde modernist writing, whether poetry or prose, to call in question the certainties of the dominant discourse. 'Poetic language' with its disruptions of usual patterns of signification and syntax, through its discontinuities, gaps and ruptures, through its exploitation of the materiality of language, destabilises meanings and speaks what before had no place in the symbolic structure which is our shared discourse. Poetic language alters, or any rate fractures, ideology because its physicality is in touch with the preconscious and the unconscious.

This can to some extent be said of all poetry. Lyric poetry perhaps should be seen as a form of play, both in the deconstructionist sense of experimenting with the multiform possibilities of signification, and in the Kleinian sense of a symbolic acting out of psychic conflicts. To understand poetry, we would need to understand the interaction of those two forms of play. I don't think we yet do, though Freud's suggestion that jokes, punning and wordplay throw up unconscious associations is often cited as a possible entry into the problem. Playing with the sounds and the patterns of words allows the unconscious to evade the censors of rational discourse. Language as a system may be shared and arbitrary, but as a practice it is each of us libidinally charged: our desires are its energising force. Language registers our psychic drives (called in French so much more evocatively 'pulsions' so they can be seen as waves pushing against the normative constraints of language; as Kristeva puts it, 'waves of attack against stases').[32] Poetry is perhaps as Kristeva argues where in language those 'pulsions' can be registered most powerfully; but always, since it is through language, by fusing the psychic and the social.

This relationship between the psychic and the social is clearly very different in different historical matrices. In the Native American oral poetry there was no suggestion of reformulating social structures, only of evoking the mythic map which lies behind both the social and psychic order; the rhythms and sounds of oral verse work with its mythic images to achieve affective states in harmony with that imaginary cosmos. There's no doubt that most poetry in the 1970s and 1980s isn't trying to do either that or what modernist poetry was doing. For modernist writers it was imperative to use language explosively. They felt society and social practices as a carapace, or worse, a room like the one in Poe's story whose walls inexorably close in.[33] They struggled, as it were, against an immensely powerful dominant language that systemised subjectivity like a railway timetable. The situation for us is different. The explosion has happened, though most people would see modernist poetry as tracing the seismic shocks rather than causing them. What that explosion was we are not sure – it's variously explained as Freud, the First World War, Auschwitz, the loss of Empire, the crisis of reason, the growth of the multinational, the spawning of media – but we know it has taken place. Late capitalism has dispersed the familiar prison warders of nineteenth-century bourgeois culture. We have to make sense of our world before we know how to react. It's not that discourses of class, race, gender don't still oppress, but they do so differently, and at the moment we don't really know how. We are trying to pick up pieces of these shattered narratives and see what sense of them we can make, and what sense they make of us. I think at the moment many of us are deeply confused about where and how power operates in our society, in what way our social system continues the order of the past and how it has changed it, about what it means to be a person, let alone a woman. This is at any rate what I see behind the postmodern quest to remake compulsively our relation to the past. Perhaps that's the process celebrated in Amy Clampitt's poem about the car lot, 'Salvage', where

> the bag-laden
> hermit woman . . .
>
> stoutly
> follows her routine,
> mining the mountainsides
> of our daily refuse
> for artefacts: subversive
> re-establishing
> with each arcane
> trash-basket dig
> the pleasures of the ruined.[34]

Finally, in looking at the transformative intention of the oral poetry, I want to draw attention again to the difference between the initiating context of distress or disorientation and the ordered poem. Because of the artifice of any poetic language the divide between the impulses and conscious ideas and the eventual words is more striking than in a prose form. It is this divide that is perhaps described by the Greeks when they speak of inspriation, or in the post-structuralist insistence that the subjectivity found in a poem is its creation not its creator. Even in the two examples I gave when the oral poet was composer as well as speaker of the verse, the important moment is not the creation of the song but its recital. Poets are most importantly their poems' first readers.

The Shamanic Text

I want to look finally at the role of the shaman, who is by definition a poet whose creativity speaks for more than him/ herself, who is read, so to speak, by many. I suggested before that the shaman in an oral culture is priest, psychiatrist, poet and doctor all at once. (There are those who claim that the heart of Christianity is shamanic, with Christ's descent into hell and resurrection as its paradigmatic journey, which I find more attractive, but perhaps no less reductive, than the Frazer fertility myth.) Psychoanalysts have claimed that they fulfil better the role of shamans, making the journey to the recesses of their own unconscious and by their esoteric knowledge leading others through those Stygian paths. But I think in poetry too we look to a shamanic figuring, reading poetry that makes sense at least within the poem of where we are. Some poetry is pleasurable and empowering for the person who wrote it. That's a good thing; but some is also pleasurable and empowering for others. And perhaps this is where aesthetic value begins. I don't think we will ever return to claims for the absolute value of works of art. We've realised that many of the terms in which we evaluated them have been Eurocentric, bourgeois, patriarchal. Brecht suggests we should talk of 'weaker (simple) and stronger (complex) pleasures.... The last-named ... are more intricate, richer in communication, more contradictory and more productive of results'. The theatre must represnt, he says, 'people's lives together in society' but the pleasure felt in watching that skilfully done 'must be converted into the higher pleasure felt when the rules emerging from this life in society are treated as imperfect and provisional'. Poetry that draws in the complexities of our psychic and social lives in all their intricate contradictoriness, providing a narrative while exposing its provisionality, is poetry that gives, in Brecht's terms, the stronger pleasure.[35] I'd like to think that this defintion could be reconciled with our more usual formalistic criterion of pleasurable poetry as that which exploits most richly the resources of language.

Conclusion

Lyric poetry, I am arguing, is a process which enables writers to position themselves as agents, to claim a value for their subjectivity, to make sense, not logically but psychically, of themselves in the world, to renegotiate the relation between preconscious and consciousness, unconscious and conscious, psychic and social. Perhaps in the postmodern condition women poets, because they have to be so aware of the need to read the narratives and rewrite them, to find psychic maps, could claim to be the poets most typical of our age. Certainly I would want to argue they are at a moment of creative plenty. (I am tempted to say, with almost the whole of Western culture available for rewriting at the change of a pronoun, though of course it's not as simple as that.) Stephen Heath suggests that 'in the overall system of sexuality that is tightened to perfection in the nine-teenth century and that still today determines so powerfully in so many ways the facts of our lives, male sexuality is repetition, female sexuality is query (darkness, riddle, enigma, problem, etc.)'.[36] As I suggested at the beginning, femininity is still in many ways the place of the private, the feeling, the dream. Our relation as women to those constructs of femininity and female sexuality isn't simple, but I think as Heath says they still enter into our positioning of ourselves in the world. And that position, margin rather than centre, mobile rather than fixed, questioning rather than certain, has been the place of poetry.

Poetry since the early nineteenth century has given a high value to a decentred and questioning subjectivity. Some critics on the left have condemned that tradition as one of the excesses of bourgeois individualism, while feminist critics have seen it as high male egoism. But I think that it's important not to forget the radical potential of that romantic legacy, which made possible the kind of oppositional strategies within bourgeois capitalism that Raymond Williams has argued have formed so much of the artistic tradition of the last two hundred years. The Romantic poetic position is sometimes read ahistorically: they were asserting the right of those without social power to speak: they claimed to be legislators, but that they knew they were unacknowledged.[37] Women in our Western cultures are still marginal to the central social formations, and often not even sure, as our position has changed so rapidly, about the place we have on those margins. So the tangential tolerance of poetry, its tradition as a site of resistance to the dominant social and economic forces, makes it a peculiarly helpful place for women to test out and explore their relation to the general culture.

The modernists were of course no less resistant than the Romantics but they wanted to insist on the centrality of art. Hence the unease over the connotations of effeminacy that hung around the notion of poetry. When Pound condemns emotional slither, he's still aware that poetry has to be, in psychoanalytical parlance, language charged with affect. But he needs to see that affect or emotion as fixed and determinate. ('By hardness I mean a quality in poetry which is nearly always a virtue – I can think of no instance when it is not.') Bad writing is rotten, slushy, muzzy, bloated, loose; good writing is clean, 'sane and active ebullience', leading to 'clarity and vigour'; beauty is 'hygiene'.[38] The crusading bluster of his bludgeoning critical style and that emphasis on cleanliness is certainly impossible now to divorce from his anti-Semitism.[39] I can't develop that here, but I'd like just to point to his fear that he is impinging on the taboo, the soiled, what Kristeva calls the abject and Mary Douglas ritual uncleanliness, contagion or pollution. In oral cultures poetry is often integral to those periods or ceremonies which deal with the taboo, at once sacred and defiled, empowering and dangerous. I think something of the same hangs round our poetic practice. In our society we have strong taboos against the expression of overt passion (in the broadest sense) and lyric poetry is one place where those psychic energies are allowed to find a place. But our anxiety about the process is very great. As in the oral culture, it is a special discourse, limited to certain contexts. We demand order, control, the sanction of art, to protect us. Perhaps rightly so. The other side of what Rimbaud called poetry's power to change the world is madness.

One project of feminist criticism must be to examine that male anxiety aroused by poetry's place of 'query ... darkness ... enigma'. But it must also be to continue to explore the importance of poetry for women in all its complexity and contradictoriness and in all its forms. As Virginia Woolf wrote: 'The streets of London have their map; but our passions are uncharted'.[40] Maps are not identical with towns any more than poetry is with passion. But they each make further exploration possible.[41]

Notes

1 Quoted in Susan Gubar '"The Blank Page" and Female Creativity', Elizabeth Abel (ed.), *Writing and Sexual Difference*, Harvester, Brighton, 1982, p. 75.

2 Ezra Pound, *Literary Essays*, Faber & Faber, London, 1954, pp. 276, 425 & 12. The long quotation is from 'A Retrospect' published in 1918 but incorporating earlier work. Although so different in other ways, he reacts here as do the aggressively manly imperialists and public school men, like Newbolt. Quite different, of course, from E. M. Forster – indeed what they are anxious to spurn – who, in *Howards End* (1910), shows the world of the arts as feminine, that of business masculine, though he points out those terms are not to be narrowly tied to biological sex.

3 Alicia Suskin Ostriker, *Stealing the Language: the Emergence of Women's Poetry in America*, The Women's Press, London, 1987, p. 15.

4 In a way the relationship of women to poetry could be seen as a synecdoche of their relation to literary studies as a whole. Although men dominate the teaching and administration of English studies in universities and polytechnics, far more women study literature at 'A level' and in higher education than men. Our cultural norms make it a more appropriate place for them than it is for men: Lisa Jardine has suggested this is a problem even for radical male critics, whose 'tough', 'rigorous' language is always striving anxiously to reassert the masculinity of their profession. '"Girl Talk" (For Boys on the Left)', *Oxford Literary Review*, vol. 8, no. 1–2, 1986.

5 *Women's Review*, of which I was a co-editor, was a British monthly

women's arts and culture magazine published between October 1985 and July 1987.

6 Jan Montefiore, *Feminism and Poetry: Language, Experience, Identity in Women's Writing*, Pandora Press, London, 1987, p. 31.

7 There are exceptions of course: for example, Suzanne Moore's perceptive analysis of Prince's 'Signs of the Time' ('Getting a Bit of the Other: the Pimps of Postmodernism', in Rowena Chapman and Jonathan Rutherford (eds), *Male Order: Unwrapping Masculinity*, Lawrence & Wishart, London, 1988, pp. 165–6), though perhaps it is significant that she comments on the kind of play of ambiguity and paradox which traditional poetry criticism is best at handling. See also her 'Here's Looking at You, Kid', in Lorraine Gamman and Margaret Marshment (eds), *The Female Gaze: Women as Viewers of Popular Culture*, The Women's Press, London, 1988.

8 I'm not saying there are no traditions of women's poetry. There is a tradition of American feminist poetry; I've heard interesting arguments for the self-conscious tradition of Victorian English women's poetry; there is a Maori tradition of women's songs of loss. None are universal.

9 For readers who have not been through this particular mill, I should explain that New Critics are not new, but a school of criticism, or perhaps approach to criticism, first identified by John Crow Ransom in 1941, which emphasised close reading and attention to the form of the literary object rather than its history. For structuralism and post-structuralism see the first chapter.

10 Post-structuralists such as Maud Ellmann in *The Poetics of Impersonality*, Harvester, Brighton, 1987, and Anthony Easthope in *Poetic Discourse*, Methuen New Accents, Methuen, London, 1983, would argue that the modernists and the New Critics really smuggled the personal in through the back door, but that's not what I'm concerned with here.

11 Umberto Eco, trans. William Weaver, 'The Crisis of the Crisis of Reason', in *Travels in Hyperreality*, Picador, London, 1986, p. 127.

12 Michael Hamburger, *The Truth of Poetry*, Penguin Books, London, 1972, p. 54.

13 Maud Ellmann, op. cit., p. 42.

14 Samuel Taylor Coleridge, 'On Poesy or Art', in *Miscellanies, Aesthetic and Literary*, George Bell, London, 1892, p. 42.

15 Frances Densmore, *Chippewa Music II*, Bureau of American Ethnology, Bulletin 51, 1913, p. 254. The work I have done on Native American poetry has been largely on the way Euro-Americans have misread it for their own purposes – something the colonial situation has made inevitable – so I'm aware there is an irony in my attempt to use it. I don't want to claim here I am giving a 'true' version. I'm simplifying

and selecting, but I hope I am being as honest as I can and treating this tradition with respect.

16 Washington Matthews, *The Night Chant, a Navaho Ceremony*, Museum of American Natural History, vol. VI, 1902, p. 145.

17 Frances Densmore, *Papago Music*, Bureau of American Ethnology, Bulletin 90, Washington, 1929.

18 Grace Nichols, *i is a long memoried woman*, Karnak House, London, 1983, p. 65, and Fred D'Aguiar, *Mama Dot*, Chatto & Windus, London, 1987.

19 Michelle Cliff, *The Land of Look Behind*, Firebrand Books, Ithaca, NY, 1985, p. 14.

20 Jan Montefiore, op. cit., pp. 16–20.

21 Jorge Luis Borges, 'Pierre Menard, Author of the Quixote', in *Labyrinths*, Penguin Books, London, 1971, pp. 62–71.

22 Roland Barthes, trans. Stephen Heath, 'Change the Object Itself', in *Image-Music-Text*, Fontana, London, 1977, p. 166.

23 Claude Lévi-Strauss, trans. Claire Jacobson and Brooke Grundfest Schoepf, 'The Effectiveness of Symbols', in *Structural Anthropology*, Penguin Books, London, 1968, pp. 186–231.

24 Jean-François Lyotard, trans. Geoff Bennington & Brian Massumi, *The Postmodern Condition: a Report on Knowledge*, Manchester University Press, Manchester, 1984, and with Jean-Loup Thébaud, trans. Wlad Godzich, *Just Gaming*, Manchester University Press, Manchester, 1985.

25 Adrienne Rich, in *The Fact of a Doorframe*, Norton, NY, & London, 1984, p. 55.

26 Eavan Boland, 'The Journey', in *The Journey and other poems,* Carcanet, Manchester, 1986, pp. 39–42.

27 Julia Kristeva, trans. Margaret Waller, *Revolution in Poetic Language*, Columbia University Press, NY, 1984, and Isobel Armstrong, 'Language as Living Form', in *Nineteenth-Century Poetry*, Harvester, Brighton, 1982.

28 Michelle Cliffe, op. cit., p. 12.

29 *The Complete Poems of Emily Dickinson*, (ed.) Thomas H. Johnson, Faber & Faber, London, 1970, p. 333, and Cora Kaplan, 'The Indefinite Disclosed', in Mary Jacobus (ed.), *Writing Women, Women Writing*, Croom Helm, London, 1979, and reprinted in Cora Kaplan, *Seachanges*, Verso, London, 1987. She doesn't quote that particular line in that article, but did so when making the same point in a talk on 'Women and the Gothic' I heard her give some years ago.

30 See Joyce McDougall, *Theatres of the Mind*, Free Association Press, London, 1987, p. 10

31 Toril Moi (ed.), *The Kristeva Reader*, Basil Blackwell, Oxford, 1987, p. 14.

32 Julia Kristeva, op. cit., p. 28. She adds that these stases are 'themselves constituted by the repetition of these charges'.

33 Edgar Allan Poe, 'The Pit and the Pendulum', in *The Portable Poe*, Viking Penguin, London, 1945, pp. 154–72.

34 Amy Clampitt, *The Kingfisher*, Faber & Faber, 1986, pp. 93–4.

35 Bertolt Brecht, trans. John Willett, 'A Short Organum for the Theatre', in *Brecht on Theatre*, Methuen, London, and Hill & Wang, NY, 1964, pp. 181 and 205.

36 Stephen Heath, in Alice Jardine (ed.), *Men in Feminism*, Methuen, London & NY, 1987, p. 13.

37 For an illuminating defence of the complexity of the Romantic view of the self and self-consciousness see Isobel Armstrong, op. cit.

38 Ezra Pound, op. cit., pp. 21 and 47.

39 See Adorno et al. for an analysis of fascism, in *The Authoritarian Personality*, Harper & Row, NY, and Hamish Hamilton, London, 1950, and compare this language here with his very similar descriptions of usury in *The Cantos*.

40 Virginia Woolf, *Jacob's Room*, Penguin Books, London, p. 90.

41 This essay was not one of the original ICA talks. Since I didn't have the benefit of discussing this with the audience I am particularly grateful to Isobel Armstrong, Philippa Brewster, Maura Dooley, Bridget Smith, Eric Triggs and Tony Carr for reading and commenting on it.

References and Further Reading

Besides the works mentioned in the notes, the following, some of which were mentioned in the text, deal with the issues raised here.

Abel, Elizabeth (ed.), *Writing and Sexual Difference*, Harvester, Brighton, 1982.

Douglas, Mary, *Purity and Danger*, Routledge & Kegan Paul, London, 1966.

Finnegan, Ruth, *Oral Poetry: Its nature, significance and social context*, Cambridge University Press, Cambridge, 1977.

Gilbert, Sandra, and Gubar, Susan (eds), *The Madwoman in the Attic: The Woman Writer and the Nineteenth-Century Literary Imagination*, Yale University Press, New Haven, 1979.

Gilbert, Sandra, and Gubar, Susan (eds), *Shakespeare's Sisters: Feminist Essays on Women Poets*, Indiana University Press, Bloomington, 1979.

Homans, Margaret, *Woman Writers and Poetic Identity*, Princeton University Press, Princeton, 1980.

Leighton, Angela, *Elizabeth Barrett Browning*, Harvester Key Women Writers.

Rich, Adrienne, 'When We Dead Awaken', in *On Lies, Secrets and Silence*, Virago Press, London, 1980.

(There is no one good introduction to Native American poetry: however, *Smoothing the Ground: Essays on Native American Literature*, (ed.) Brian Swann, University of California Press, Berkeley 1983, is a useful collection of essays whose notes provide extensive bibliographic references.)

PART III

---◆---

The Empire Strikes Back

PRIVATE SPACES TO PUBLIC PLACES: CONTEMPORARY ASIAN WOMEN WRITERS

NASEEM KHAN

It was wet and cold. Inside the house, Sparrow Woman bustled round tidying up her neat home.

"Let me in, please," pleaded Crow. "It's cold and dark out here."

Sparrow Woman went on bustling round; "Just a minute, Crow," she said.

"Please, Sparrow," he begged, his wet feathers sticking to his shivering frame. "Please let me in."

"Soon, Crow, soon." And at last she opened the door. Crow hobbled in, wet through, ice cold.

"Poor Crow," said Sparrow Woman, "How cold you are. Why don't you go and sit on the plate I've just been cooking my chapatis on. It's nice and warm. . ."

So he did, gratefully. And he got burned to death.[1]

This bloodthirsty fable for Indian children has, on the face of it, a lot to say about the ideal, supposedly female virtues – home-loving, protective of the family hearth, small-minded, cold-blooded. On the side of law and order, forethought and plan-ning, she is the backbone of the conservative, traditional, time-less world. No rackety Crow welcomed here, over her neat threshold. Certainly not. To perdition with him, like all social deviants and misfits. And the prissy, pious Sparrow lives virtu-ously on.

This may be the preferred image of women promoted by society. Reality, however, and the evidence of the writing by Asian women in both the subcontinent and Britain, puts quite a different gloss on things. Look beyond books produced recently by women whose thinking has been affected by international feminism, and a different person emerges. The heroines of Kamala Das, for instance – hardly part of the literary establishment – do not conform to the stereotype of mythic female virtue, the biddable, sweet-voiced Sita, the self-sacrificing wife of the god-hero Rama. Manasi, in her bestselling *Alphabet of Lust*, is a self-seeking striver, exploiting men in her political rise (including a sad and passive husband) in an aggressive macho manner. Shakun, in Suniti Aphaie's story 'The Dolls' (translated from Marathi for *Truth Tales*), has an equally honest attitude to sex in her relationship with Kishorebhai, the buyer of her dolls. Even the popular novels translated from Hindi and other regional languages that once swamped railway station bookstalls (until the ubiquitous Mills & Boon drove them out) contain less predictable, punchier and essentially more dangerous women than the anodyne stereotype suggests.

The further one looks, however, the more unreal the stereotype becomes. Statistics call the lie on it. Far from being helpless and dependent, women are – in 35 per cent of cases – the major supporters for their families. 63.6 million women in India work. The lot of the working woman – rather than being protected in safe 'nice' areas (like hairdressers and secretaries of the West) – is particularly hard. Statistics show them almost always at the bottom of the heap, paid less and liable – with the mechanisation of previously labour-intensive fields – to get sacked sooner. The percentage of women working in the mines and in textiles has dropped dramatically with mechanisation. On the land, the new agricultural development has resulted in the marginalisation of women's voices. On the one hand, the use of pesticides has, for instance, resulted in the decline of women's grass-cutting as an important source of income. On the other, the encouragement of rural co-operatives has given the voice predominantly to men.

This, it might seem, takes us far from the area of women's writing. In fact, it gives a sharper and more urgent context to the writing, and the struggle which it represents. It also acts as a warning against accepting clichés as the final word. Indian women (or Asian women) have been popularly seen in the West as beautiful gilded birds. There is more to them than that – they are fighters and redoubtable women, fighting to emancipate themselves from the restrictions of myth and history.

The way in which oppression has been expressed has, interestingly, changed over the decades. Consider, for instance, the work of Kamala Markandeya and, specifically, her novel *Nectar in a Sieve* in which the hardship that faces her heroine Rukmani is accepted, Job-like, as part of a divine plan. The hardships are dire. A tannery opens near their South Indian village and sets in train events that undermine the tranquil traditional family structure. She and her husband work as landless labourers and finally lose their livelihood; her sons are destroyed; her daughter is repudiated by her own husband, since she turns out to be barren. This is taken as unfortunate but understandable, since a peasant society needs sons. Finally, after all her privations, her husband now dead, Rukmani finds peace back in her village. A bitter life, it has nevertheless been irradiated by the love between the husband and wife. Although Kamala Markandeya is clear that Rukmani's life is a harsh one, her story is more about the way in which the traditional values bestow strength and spiritual depth. The tannery destroys the old harmonies. But it cannot destroy the old spirit. The theme of the conflict between tradition and progress is one Kamala Markandeya carried on beyond this 1953 novel. It can be found, for instance, in the later *Pleasure City* too.

Compare *Nectar in a Sieve*, however, with more recent work and you can see a rather different consciousness at work. Padma Perera's stories, for instance, are not at all unappreciative of the supportiveness and cohesiveness to be found in the traditional extended family. Her stories in *Birthday-Deathday* take a fresh delight in the eccentricities of family characters. But she does not glorify oppression by seeing it as a means to a spiritually greater end.

The central figure of 'Pilgrimage' ironically ends up in the spiritual retreat of an ashram, but the point of the story is not religious quest. It concerns the passion a young man conceives for his youthful stepmother. Driven by guilt he leaves home and makes his fortune. He returns only when he learns of his father's death. Finding that his stepmother has decided to go and live her life out in an ashram, he dutifully escorts her there on the train.

He finds her more elusive than ever, though in a somewhat different way. 'Once she might have sought to fill this quiet with meaningless questions about his well-being, his job. Mouthing all the parrot politeness for which our women are trained from birth: learn to yield, learn to placate. . . . Without saying a word, she was telling him what it was like to be a woman.'[2]

But even that is a romanticisation. Realities are harsher. Taxed by him with having married someone so very much older, she at last finds a voice.

> "What can *you* know?" With the sudden overwhelming authority of anger, she wrested the words from him, all the old placating gentleness gone. "You live in your world of ideas, what can you know of hunger and poverty and the pain of being a woman? My father was ill. There was no money for either medicine or food."
>
> "You mean my father bought you?"[3]

Padma Perera anticipates the reader's objections to what is, after all, a somewhat hackneyed situation: her hero is stunned – 'he had consigned this sort of situation to the drivel of third-rate films'. But the stepmother (never given a name in the story) escapes the trite scenario in which she's been confined. She escapes the need always to be defined in terms of family duties and relationships. Finally – without fuss – she is allowed to become her own woman.

Protective systems like the family can also be neurotic defensive ones. In another of these stories, 'Weather Report', Ramesh, settled in the United States, advertises for and acquires a wife. 'Pretty, fair, convent-educated virgin under 23,' it said, 'Without spectacles, caste no bar, required for handsome rising electronic engineer, 5'9", residing in USA. High character, no habits. Widows and innocent divorcees please excuse.'[4] Arrived in the United States, the story's narrator finds herself shut up by her husband, protected from the alien culture that might corrupt her and debase the value of the truly Indian wife he has found to match his stature. But she is a strong woman who will not put up with containment. She runs off. The stepmother of 'Pilgrimage' makes her own life (albeit belatedly). The older women in other Perera stories are zestful, sturdy and independent-minded.

The most violent story of female exploitation is arguably Bapsi Sidhwa's *The Bride*. It is based on a true story. Zaitoon, a Punjabi woman, marries a man from the tribal mountain areas, expecting to find a life of noble, romantic primitiveness. She is instead horrified by the poverty, backwardness, privation, and by the utter subjugation of women in this quintessentially macho society. She attempts to escape and makes an epic trek over the exposed mountains to the bridge that marks the end of tribal jurisdiction. There she finds her husband and his male relatives waiting to avenge the shame she's brought down on them and hack off her head. There are no holds barred in this first novel. No golden age here or harmony with nature. Ms Sidhwa is quite frankly horrified by all that nature. Although she loads the scales to such an extent against her heroine as to lay her open to a charge of masochism, her heroine Zaitoon does win through. It is a traditional rattling good yarn. Apart from an early fascination with romantic fantasy Zaitoon never connives at her own oppression.

The graver oppression is the type that affects self-esteem, distorts expectations and sets an agenda for a woman even before she is born. Duty creeps in everywhere. Shashi Deshpande's central character in *That Long Silence* tells herself ruefully that she has not been well brought up; her sister-in-law, Prema, reprimands her for not realising she is failing her husband Mohan:

'So when Prema had said, "Mohan, you have a button missing," I had not realised that I was expected to feel ashamed, to take the shirt immediately and sew on the missing button. To me, it had seemed a conversation between Prema and Mohan, nothing to do with me at all.' Jaya's background has not prepared her for the sparrow-wife conformity of her more orthodox in-laws. Brought up as an adored only daughter, college-educated and with literary aspirations, she has problems in comprehending the ways in which wives, it is generally considered, ought to behave. 'So I had been silent, even when Subha [Mohan's niece] a spoilt and pert girl, had added, "Poor Monanna, looks like he'll have to fix his own button."

"Certainly not!" Prema had retorted. "Here, Mohan, give it to me."

It had not occurred to me that this too had been intended

as a reproach, even though Prema had made it explicit by raking me from head to toe with an elder-sister-of-your-husband's-look'.[6]

'These women of Mohan's family were right', concludes Shashi Deshpande's Jaya: 'I would pattern myself after them. That way lay – well, if not happiness, at least the consciousness of doing right, freedom from guilt.'[7] Guilt – that old acquaintance of women everywhere – will come in again later.

Potent though its presence is in the modern novel, guilt is not the driving force. More powerful is the growing awareness of constriction, the determination not to accept. Why – since *Nectar in a Sieve*, say – has there been such an undoubted change in consciousness? There are, for a start, historical reasons. In several books awareness goes hand in hand with a sense of disillusion, with the sniff of corruption in the body politic. *That Long Silence* directly connects the two. Jaya and her husband are Indian yuppies, the new business-rich. In the book they've made a tactical withdrawal from their fancy Churchgate flat while the scandal involving Mohan's business methods hopefully dies down. 'I . . . I've just accepted a few favours from people I know,' [he says evasively] 'Things are not too bad.'[8] Leena Dhingra's promising first book, *Amritvela*, has her narrator returning to India after some years and, through the safety of re-encountered family love, perceiving other things – hypocrisy, arrogance, class tyranny, superficiality. Where, she asks, is the principled India for which her parents had fought that was intended, like the Labour Party, to be a moral crusade? The disparity between dreams and reality destabilises on a broader front, calls into question other old certainties. Who makes history, who sets the values? It's a question beneath Amrita Pritam's poem (translated from the Punjabi):

Resigned

It's been happening a long time.
Time bribed
And bought
Pages of history, without its knowing.
Changed some lines,
Rubbed off others

Whenever it wanted.
History felt mad and depressed
But forgave the historians.
But today it's sad.
A hand unfolds its cover,
Tears off a few pages
And tapes fake ones in their place.
History looks
Quietly comes out of the pages
And stands under a tree
Smoking a cigarette.[8]

Internal history has had an effect on the way in which women see themselves. So have external events. The international Women's Movement has found articulate contributors in the subcontinent. The flow of ideas has been a rich one. Several writers for a start have footholds in two continents. Bapsi Sidhwa, Kamala Markandeya and Suniti Namjoshi all live in or have strong connections with the United States. Shashi Deshpande, at an ICA meeting, admitted she felt she had more in common with Western women writers. Discovering them had been, she said, like suddenly finding her literary lineage. In India itself, women's groups, organisations and conferences have set themselves the task of setting the agenda for feminism. In Pakistan the popular uproar about the imposition of religious Shariat law – a step backwards for women – is striking evidence of the presence of women determined to define their own lives. All this is part of the matrix from which the writing springs.

Are there, though, distinctive signs that denote a new genre? One of the aims of the ICA talks, from which these essays come, was to explore the way in which women's consciousness had made over traditional forms and created new genres: Keri Hulme's use of Maori forms for instance, or the return, in Caribbean work, to the oral springs.

Asian arts in general have followed a similar shift in orientation. Radical theatre has consciously gone out to rediscover – after years of being impressed by the West – a specifically Asian form. In have come the lively diversity of folk techniques (with their very different theories of theatricality), the rediscovered canon of old texts, the vigour of regional languages and cultures.

The new theatre can – in theory – go anywhere, do anything, is cavalier with history and audacious with form.

Literature however – or more particularly, writing in English – has felt the existence of more impediments. The oral language tradition has always been a thriving one and, even from the poetess Mirabai centuries ago, open to women. The vernacular offers the challenge of forms that differ hugely, from topical satire to the formal dictates of traditional ballad form with its refined imagery and allusions. Writing in English cannot but present questions for language carries its own internal rules, is shaped by a particular sensibility.

Sujata Bhatt writes in her long poem 'Search for My Tongue', in which she weaves English in with Gujarati:

> There was a little girl
> Who carried a black clay pitcher on her head,
> who sold water at the train station.
> She filled her brass cup with water,
> stretched out her arm to me,
> reached up to the window, up
> to me leaning out of the window from the train,
> but I can't think of her in English.

That image of straining – of one woman reaching out, in vain, to touch the other – is a poignant one for an incompatability that must be part of the life of the woman who writes in English.

> You ask me what I mean
> by saying I have lost my tongue,
> I ask you, what would you do
> if you had two tongues in your mouth
> and lost the first one, the mother tongue,
> And could not really know the other,
> The foreign tongue.[9]

That coexistence of two worlds can, as British Asian writers particularly find, be abrasive. It can create confusion. Some of the Asian Women's Writers Workshop, who recently produced their first anthology *Right of Way*, 'found' [they said] 'it difficult to appreciate translations of Urdu or Bengali poetry. Anglicised responses to the style being flowery or sentimental demanded discussion and contextualisation. Short stories which were rooted in the literary traditions of the sub-continent were considered to have abrupt endings; further discussion revealed that the marked ambiguity of the endings was common to our literary traditions. . . . As a group we have yet to define our literary criteria.'

The dichotomy of language and culture need not be seen, as some do, as a source of anguish. It can also, however, lend an urgency to the task of finding one's way between the different stones. And it is possible to use those stones to construct a new shape; necessary, arguably, if one is to survive. There are some signs of a distinctive approach. The frequency of the use of the first person singular is, for instance, striking. Shashi Deshpande uses it, and Kamala Markandeya; many of Padma Perera's stories employ it, Bapsi Sidhwa's latest *Ice-Candy Man*. Suniti Namjoshi's witty latter-day fables use it, making the link immediately clear between it and the old storytelling tradition. She learned to be a writer, said Bapsi Sidhwa, listening to stories from her mother and her ayah. The use of the first person singular reinforces that link. It bestows a direct sense on the narrative. One is at the characters' shoulder; there is no distance, no barriers. The warmth of involvement is notable. (Adil Jussawalla, however, would disagree. His anthology *New Writing in India* – which regrettably contains only three women writers in a total of forty – claims subjective writing 'is the writing of a bourgeoisie at a dead end'.)[10]

It is also interesting to trace similarities of imagery in Asian women's writing. One particular theme – of physical impediment – jumps out of a number of works. Its roots are ambiguous ones and go back to mythological times. Most resonant is the story of Gandarhi, part of the *Mahabharata*.[11] There are many self-sacrificing women in Hinduism – women who follow their husbands through tribulation and exile, women who plead with the gods to take on punishment or death intended for their husbands. But Gandarhi has special significance. In order to be at one with her blind husband, she binds up her own eyes permanently so that she neither can see. Being blind, however, is a dubious state. Like Gandarhi, Jaya in *That Long Silence* blinds herself: 'I was an ideal wife too. I bandaged my eyes tightly. I didn't want to know anything. It was enough for me that we moved to Bombay, that we could send Rahul and Rati to good schools, that I could have the things we needed ... decent clothes, a fridge, a gas connection, travelling first class.'[12]

Deliberate blindness is one method in modern times of survival. Deliberate dumbness is another. The weapon of silence is an angry one – even in India where, like fasting, it can carry spiritual merit. It can damage the wielder. It was the final resort of Mohan's mother against a violent and arbitrary husband: 'Women in those days were tough', says her son, admiringly: 'He saw strength in the woman sitting silently in front of the fire, but I saw despair', says Mohan's wife, Jaya. 'I saw a despair so great that it would not voice itself. I saw a struggle so bitter that silence was the only weapon. Silence and surrender.'[13] Silence is a powerful weapon. Padma Perera's intransigent granny in 'Mauna' starts her weekly silence as a way of getting her own back. And she continues it, despite mammoth inconvenience, until the day she dies.

And so, says Deshpande, is that other ostensible female virtue – reliability – a powerful weapon. Far from serving their men, as the world believes, women are in fact controlling them. 'Don't try to act the martyr', Jaya is told by the only honest man in the book. 'You really enjoy it. Making others dependent on you. It increases your sense of power. And that's what you really want, all you bloody looking-after-others, caring-for-others women.'[14]

Blindness, silence and self-inflicted disability are not special to works from the Asian sub-continent. They are themes that are strongly present in a book that's an integral part of the Asian British experience. Ravi Randhawa's *A Wicked Old Woman* is an angry fractured book about angry fractured people. Its central character, Kulwant, has deliberately chosen retreat, rejecting the agenda life offers her, its options drastically curtailed and limited by both racism and sexism. A young woman (or youngish – her sons are married), she takes on the persona of as revolting an old woman as she can: stick, Oxfam clothes, NHS specs and a pathetic, hobbling, shuffling walk, hand held out quaveringly for help – of course, totally unneeded.

Deliberate disability – like a brand of self-maiming – is rife in her circle of woman friends. Shanti, whose daughter Rani has run away from home, refuses – literally – to open her eyes: she feels and fumbles her way through life. Rani, when finally found, is in a coma: paralysed by the trauma through which she's lived and refusing to acknowledge her Asianness, having killed the man who'd assaulted her. She lies in her hospital bed, eyes open but sense gone. There is a long road to tread, but finally, as a result of female mutual support, the various disabilities are healed. Kulwant's disguise is discarded and she returns to the active mainstream of life.

Learning to take the initiative and to act for oneself (not for husband, father, family) is a lesson to be learnt across the board. It's central too in Suniti Namjoshi's delightful fantasy world, in which in *Conversations of Cow*, the narrator has a confusing friendship with a sharp-tongued lesbian cow, and also in Nina Sibal's ambitious first book, *Yatra*. The two books are very different: while the first is ironical, self-mocking and small, *Yatra* is a large would-be political novel in which the fortunes of the main characters – especially the dark-skinned woman Krishna – embody and symbolise the fortunes of India. Nina Sibal claimed on BBC radio that Indian women's writing had been narrow in scope, based on personal relationships. She picked for herself a vast canvas, a time-scale that ran over a century and a cast of hundreds. Executed with vigour, though not always discrimination, it aimed also to appropriate the 'good' points of male writing – its scope, energy, intellectuality. *Yatra*, meaning a journey, is the odyssey undertaken by Krishna. It is also the journey of past quasi-mythical women of her family. By the end, Krishna (named for the blue god, and the owner of a skin that darkens mystically as her identification with her father's country becomes more profound) has turned from passive wife to active campaigner. Her apotheosis has come about through having taken on the mantle of her ancestors' history – their pain and their triumphs.

Bold as she is, Nina Sibal does her fellow writers a disservice in seeing their work as that of miniaturists. A concern with moral issues and questions of definition – neither of them small-scale – runs through the novels and stories of writers both on the subcontinent and in Britain. The dilemma for the latter is far more painful, and the choices more polarised. Which customs to follow? Which side to belong to? Leena Dhingra travels back to Delhi and quietly lets the alienating effect of India creep over her heroine. Ravi Randhawa's heroine, anxious to commit herself utterly to her Asian roots, demands an arranged marriage straight from school, to the bewilderment of her parents. The hazards of a racist society, and rules that are not of one's own making confound, if not create, the confusions of identity. The novel itself, in this shifting and uncertain world, can act as a means of achieving self-definition as well as a reflection of its absence. Different writers search for it in different ways. Nina Sibal employs a sprawling prose, epic in its proportions, vast in its ambitions and sometimes purple in its hue. Leena Dhingra is lucid and understated. Randhawa's jagged juxtaposed fragments find no echo in Anita Desai's crafted prose (substantial work that needs consideration on its own). Beneath the variety, however, is a common concern with finding a place in a world where Sita has lost her pre-eminence. What is the new place of women, what are the limits of our power? Where is that line of balance that runs between a tradition that is supportive and one that is destructive: To Adil Jussawalla, the concern of these writers with such questions may seem only 'subjective' and therefore a dead end. In fact it is patently a growing point: a move from the interior preoccupations of private spaces, to the wider complex canvas of history and the present, public places of the world outside. Suniti Namjoshi sums it up with customary wryness in one of her *Feminist Fables* called 'The Female Swan':

And then there was the duckling who aspired to be a swan. She worked very hard, studied the history and literature of swans, the growth of their swanhood, their hopes and ideals, and their time-honoured customs. In the end, even the swans acknowledged that this duck had rendered them a signal service. They threw a banquet (no ducks invited) and gave her a paper, which clearly stated that thereafter she would be an Honorary Swan. She was highly gratified, as were some of the ducks, who began to feel that there was hope for them. Others just laughed. 'A duck is a duck,' they said, 'and ought not aspire to be a swan. A duck, by definition, is inferior to swans.' This seemed so evident that they forgot the matter and paddled off.

But there were still others who were angered by this. 'Those ducks do not think,' they said. 'But as for the learned one, she has betrayed us to the cause of swans. She is no longer a duck. She is a swan.' This too seemed evident. They turned to Andersen.

'Well,' he said, 'there are a great many ducks and a great many duck-ponds.' But that didn't help, so he tried again. 'The thing is,' he said, 'you are beginning to question the nature of ducks and the values of swans.'

'Yes,' they said. 'But where will it end?'

'I don't know,' said Andersen. 'You are learning to fashion your own fables.'[15]

Notes

1 The traditional sparrow-crow folk story is the archetypal one of waster v. prudent found also in the ant and the grasshopper, though in the former case there is a gender difference. Sparrow builds her neat house of wax and survives. Crow, whose house is of dung, comes to a bad end.
2 Padma Perera, *Birthday-Deathday*, The Women's Press, London, 1985, p. 87.
3 Ibid., p. 88.
4 Ibid., p. 148.
5 Shashi Deshpande, *That Long Silence*, Virago Press, London, 1988, pp. 83–4.
6 Ibid., p. 84.
7 Ibid., p. 11.
8 Translated from the Punjabi by Mahendra Kulasrestha, *New Writing in India*, (ed.) Adil Jussawalla, Penguin Books, London, 1974, p. 280.
9 Sujata Bhatt, *Brunizem*, Carcanet, Manchester, 1988, p. 65.
10 Adil Jussawalla, op. cit., p. 34.
11 There's a vivid (shortened) prose version of this epic *Mahabharata*, by R. K. Narayan, Heinemann, London, 1978.
12 Shashi Deshpande, *That Long Silence*, Virago Press, London, 1988, pp. 61–2.
13 Ibid., p. 36.
14 Ibid., p. 84.
15 Suniti Namjoshi, *Feminist Fables*, Sheba, London, 1981, p. 18.

References and Further Reading

This includes the novels and stories mentioned in the text (excluding those referenced in the notes) and some further examples of Indian women's writing:

Asian Women's Writers Workshop, *Right of Way*, The Women's Press, London, 1988.

Cobham, Rhonda, and Collins, Merle (eds), *Watchers and Seekers: An Original Anthology of Creative Writing by Black Women living in Britain*, The Women's Press, London, 1987.

Das, Kamala, *Alphabet of Lust*, Orient, Hyderabad, 1976.

Desai, Anita, *Clear Light of Day*, Heinemann, London, 1980.

Desai, Anita, *Fire on the Mountain*, Heinemann, London, 1977.

Desai, Anita, *Games at Twilight*, Heinemann, London, 1978.

Desai, Anita, *Voices in the City*, Orient, Hyderabad, 1965.

Dhingra, Leena, *Amritvela*, The Women's Press, London, 1988.

Grewal, Shabnam; Kay, Jackie; Lander, Liliane; Lewis, Gail, and Parmar, Pratibha (eds), *Charting the Journey*, Sheba, London, 1988.

Kali for Women, *Truth Tales: Stories from India*, The Women's Press, London, 1986.

Karodia, Farida, *Daughters of the Twilight*, The Women's Press, London, 1986.

Markandeya, Kamala, *Nectar in a Sieve*, New American Library, NY, 1954.

Markandeya, Kamala, *Pleasure City*, Chatto, London, 1982.

Namjoshi, Suniti, *Conversations of Cow*, The Women's Press, London, 1985.

Randhawa, Ravinder, *A Wicked Old Woman*, The Women's Press, London, 1987.

Saghal, Nayantara, 'A Situation in New Delhi', *London Magazine*, 1977.

Sibal, Nina, *Yatra*, The Women's Press, London, 1987.

Sidhwa, Bapsi, *The Bride*, John Murray, London, 1983.

Sidhwa, Bapsi, *Ice-Candy Man*, Heinemann, London, 1988.

THEMES AND TRENDS IN
CARIBBEAN WRITING TODAY

———◆———

MERLE COLLINS

I am going to talk about writing and political themes in the writing of selected Caribbean women. I won't be attempting a survey, but will talk about specific experiences and about my own experience.[1] There is often an artificial debate about whether writing should be just writing, or whether it should be committed writing. Very often when people ask 'Do you see yourself as a committed writer?' I wonder, 'What is that really?' It's a non-question in a sense because I think it is impossible to write what I would consider a literary piece that starts somewhere up there in the air and is not related to what people are actually experiencing. You react in one way or another to the experiences that you live through. As a writer, you can't ignore their effect on you.

For example, when you look at your television screens and see people in South Africa running, singing, chanting, you don't expect the chant to be something about 'Oh how beautiful is the sunshine, oh how beautiful is the sky'. If you talk about flowers, or whatever image you choose, whatever it is, the images still relate to the feeling, relate to the struggle, relate to the blood, relate to what is happening around you. It's in that sense that I say it's a type of non-question. Writing is the result of one's experiences. And the writing of the Caribbean women today echoes the experiences of the women, young and old, within the Caribbean, echoes the experiences of the people in the Caribbean generally, the experiences of a so-called developing region, and of the effects of colonialism and imperialism.

In Jamaica, for example, one of the things that Louise Bennett's poetry did for the period in which she was writing was essentially to make a political statement about language. In a work such as her poem 'Capital Site', the interesting thing for me is that although it's important to know the context, especially to know its political context, you can still enjoy and appreciate the writing without knowing exactly what went on.[2] But knowledge of the political context enhances your appreciation. Let's take an example: during the period of the 1950s there was much talk about Federation for the Caribbean, or rather for the British-controlled Caribbean. Britain was at that time considering giving independence to the colonies (a subject which has its own history of struggle though the whole question of *giving* independence is slightly ludicrous) – and thinking that in the circumstances a federation would be the best arrangement for administrative reasons.

Yet precisely because of the colonial history, these islands are very divided. The Grenadian formal education system, for example, because of its colonial nature, has tended to focus on the British reality, not on what is happening in Barbados or Jamaica or in St. Kitts, or, for that matter, on Grenada itself. Similarly, education in St. Kitts, Trinidad, etc. had this colonial bias. We looked to British poetry, British history. We even learnt British nursery rhymes. By the time you left school, or high school, you might be familiar with the Brontë countryside. You might know Shakespeare, but your knowledge of Caribbean history or Caribbean literature could be minimal. There were leading individual political activists who recognised the importance of federation, but a regional unity was not really part of a cultural attitude. There was great insularity.

With the discussions on Federation, several islands were concerned about not being hampered in their development by those considered more backward. And one of the divisions was over the issue of the capital site. Where should the capital of this Federation be? One group was apparently promoting the idea of Grenada as a capital site. The local newspaper, *The West Indian*, ran several articles lauding this idea, and requesting Grenadians to show themselves worthy of this great honour. Then a Barbados newspaper began to run articles challenging this idea. There was a conference and later a commission on the issue of the federal capital; selected persons from Britain went to each island to visit and try to assess which was the best capital site; eventually they came up with the idea of Barbados. Whereupon Trinidad and Jamaica co-ordinated to oppose the idea.

Out of all of this confusion Trinidad emerged as the capital and there came Louise Bennett's poem 'Capital Site'. Her brilliant idea was this: why not just have a 'plane, give it the name 'Capital Site', let it touch down and stay on each island for a day or so, and in the end we will all have a capital site? When we read that poem, without access to information about the issue, we can enjoy the poem for itself, for its use of language, its use of satire. But the knowledge of the history, of the political history which is its framework makes the work much more exciting and much more interesting.

Another poem by Louise Bennett, entitled 'Pass fi White', tackled the whole issue of shadism, what I call shadism, in the Caribbean.[3] Because of the colonial history, it was very important what shade a person was, very black, or not quite so black, light-skinned, or very light-skinned; the closer you were, in fact, to massa's colour, then the more important you were. In this context, Louise Bennett wrote this poem about someone's daughter having gone to North America, and then being able to do very well over there because she had 'passed'. It wasn't a question of attaining any kind of academic qualification, but of passing for white, which was in the colonial context itself a very important kind of examination. Again, the understanding of the poem is enhanced by an appreciation of the socio-political context.

Louise Bennett also broke new ground by her use of the Jamaican language to explore the socio-political reality. In the early literature of the century by people writing about the region, local languages were used for humour, or to indicate the ignorance of the protagonist. This emphasis on using the language for humorous themes, to the detriment of more serious issues, is also there in some early Caribbean writing. But this attitude was challenged with changing political ideas, and with the developing political consciousness following the 1930s, which for the Caribbean was one of political ferment. In his work *The West Indian Novel and Its Background*, in a chapter entitled 'The Language of the Master', Kenneth Ramchand quotes Edward Long, a British historian:

The Negroes seem very fond of reduplications to express a greater or less quantity of anything; as: walky-walky, talky-talky, washy-washy, happy-happy, tie-tie. . . . In their conversations they confound all the moods, tenses, cases and conjunctions without mercy; for example, I surprise . . . me glad to see you . . . how you do . . . me tank you; me ver well.[4]

Edward Long's conlusion is that these 'Negroes' don't know how to use the English language. And it is as a result of a developing political consciousness among Black people that different things are happening in language today. Today there is ongoing research on Caribbean languages which reflect a re-appreciation of our history, a re-appreciation of ourselves, so that we don't seek to define ourselves using Europe as a base, as though our own story is rooted in European history and cultural norms. Recent research substantiates the opinion that the historical basis of Caribbean languages is in fact mainly the African ancestry, since the majority of the Caribbean population is African. Of course this is not to ignore the fact that Asian languages are also of importance notably in Trinidad and Guyana, where approximately half the population is Asian. But with this majority African inheritance, you have in the language the use of structures which come historically from various African languages. Researchers in this field include Morgan Dalphinis, who has written *Caribbean and African Languages*, and researched the whole question of the way in which Caribbean languages have come out of the tradition of African languages; there is also Hubert Devonish, who deals with the issue of language and power.[5]

There are words which Caribbean people have been conditioned by the history of African subordination to think of as 'lower class', or simply not proper English, which are in some cases Wolof words, words which in fact belong to the Wolof language of Senegal. There are words like 'konkey', which is a food, an inheritance from 'kenke', which in the Fantsi language, of Ghana, is used for the same food. The Jamaicans call this food 'doukunu', the same word used in Gaa, another Ghanian language. So that our language becomes exciting when it is properly researched, and can be traced back to our ancestors. But our educators were colonial powers, themselves ignorant of our culture, and having the superiority which made all of that seem to them unimportant and unworthy, with the result that we, the colonised, were taught to devalue ourselves and deny our history. It comes out of that whole experience of slavery, that whole history of subjection in the region to colonial cultures and imperial interests. It is within this context that we have to identify as an important political move Louise Bennett's use of the Jamaican language to explore socio-political issues.

In looking at what is being done by women writers in the Caribbean, let us take a look at the work of the Trinidadian Merle Hodge, who wrote *Crick Crack, Monkey*.[6] Dealing with Trinidadian socio-political realities, Merle talks about a young girl growing up, for whom receiving an education was very important. Education has a preponderant importance in the Caribbean context because it is often the only vehicle for social advance. That is a very complex thing because what it means in practice is that education can be alienating in terms of the divisions between classes. Merle Hodge directly tackles class issues by exploring the attitudes to education, the interaction between Tee's two aunts, one working-class, the other middle-class, and Tee's own increasing reluctant acceptance of the life-style of the middle-class aunt whose aspirations echo those of the society and are reflected in the type of education she is receiving.

Many years after writing this novel, Merle Hodge worked in Grenada during the period 1979 to 1983 and was involved in putting out a new reader, the Marryshow readers. One of the concerns of this work was to look at the question of presenting students with new images, of moving away from concentration on the white, middle-class images which are imported from Europe or the United States. It confronted the fact that even when there are Black images, still these tend to be middle-class, or at least concerned not with a majority Caribbean reality. So that children read about Mummy who is in the kitchen with her apron and Daddy who comes in at a certain time, has his meal ready for him, etc., etc. Besides the fact that there are lots of single-parent families with no Daddy coming in at regular intervals, Mummy herself, if she lives in the countryside as do many Mummies, is very often out in the garden cutting or picking something, or cracking cocoa or doing some other work.

When this kind of Mummy does not appear positively in books, it means that something is wrong with your life. In her work, therefore, Merle confronted the need to move away from negative representation of the reality for so many young Caribbean people.

Now to move on quickly, since there is still quite a lot to say, to Zee Edgell from Belize. Belize has been known to refer to itself (or perhaps I should say Belizean politicians have been known to refer to Belize) as a Latin-Caribbean country. At the period focused on by Zee Edgell in her novel *Beka Lamb*, Belize was British Honduras. Belize calls itself Latin Caribbean because geographically it is in Central America, close to Spanish-speaking countries, and had much more of a recent association with Spanish colonial history than those other Caribbean countries whose recent colonial history is one of British domination. Also, Spanish is still very much spoken in Belize.

Writing out of that experience, Zee Edgell has themes which are very similar to the themes that Louise Bennett and Merle Hodge and I myself write about. But of course the voice is Belizean, reflecting that reality. Her novel, *Beka Lamb*, too, can be enjoyed without close reference to Belizean politics and history, but knoweldge of that framework increases the appreciation of the work. Zee Edgell begins her novel:

> On a warm November day Beka Lamb won an essay contest at St. Cecilia's Academy, situated not far from the front gate of His Majesty's Prison on Milpa's Lane. It seemed to her family that overnight Beka changed from what her mother called a 'flat-rate Belize creole' into a person with 'high mind'.[7]

One could almost say that education is like a noose around the necks of the young women in this novel. One young woman, Toycie, has her entire life completely spoiled when she becomes pregant because it means that her chance of a formal education is gone. All her aunt's efforts on Toycie's behalf are down the drain and her guardian is very upset. Toycie has to leave school, and there are no real opportunities for adult education. Toycie's one opportunity to move out of the poverty into something better is therefore snatched away.

Zee Edgell deals very practically with this issue. At the beginning of the novel, when Beka wins the essay contest, immediately her family recognises her possibilities, feels that she can no longer be considered a 'flat-rate Belize creole'; she is no low-class person any more. And they discuss the fact that in the past Beka would never have won the contest, an indication that things have really changed. In times past, Beka wouldn't even be at a convent school reserved for the élite. But now she is not only there but has won an essay contest held to celebrate the seventy-fifth anniversary of the Sisters of Mercy in Belize. This theme of the convent and the importance of the church in education is one that I also deal with in *Angel*.[8] After the legal termination of chattel slavery, education was given over largely into the hands of the church, and church schools were established. And because there was a very strong Catholic presence, especially in those areas which also had a history of French or Spanish domination, the convents emerged to assume tremendous importance, first of all for the training of the local élite. In the early days there were also very few scholarships, given to enable those deemed brightest from among the working class to have an opportunity for secondary education. There was great competition for these places at high schools throughout the region, and the theme features in the work of many Caribbean writers. There were more scholarships as time passed, but competition was still keen.

Zee Edgell outlines the pressures that were on her protagonist, Beka, and on her friend, Toycie, to do well at school. In addition to the pressures that confronted the young men in this situation, there were for the young women the additional pressure associated with the constant reminders to avoid pregnancy. The issue is very effectively and poignantly dealt with in this novel.

There are constant references in the novel to formal Belizean politics. Guatemala is near to Belize; they share a border, and Guatemala laid claim to some of Belizean territory, so that Belizeans have lived with constant discussion of the dnager of absorption by Guatemala, because of a border conflict inherited from colonial times. Zee Edgell makes references also to the People's Independence Party (PIP), its role in the country's political life, and the attitudes of the people to the party. The party is trying to facilitate moves such as what Beka's grandmother calls from the washtub at the house bottom to a classroom overlooking the sea. The PIP of the novel is roughly equivalent to the People's United Party (PUP), led by George Price, which was engaged in similar struggles in Belize at the beginning of the 1950s.

I mentioned earlier that an element which is also present in my own novel *Angel* is the role played by a convent education in shaping a particular view of life. Zee Edgell approaches this theme also. It has to do with an entire way of perceiving the world, and of presenting yourself to that world – attitudes to both spoken language and body language. The language of education generally is the language of the colonial 'master' and particularly during the period that Merle Hodge, Zee Edgell and I wrote about, the attitude to the colonial language of power was reinforced by an education which contributed to the concomittant continuing devaluation of both the spoken local langage and the body language which included considerable movement of the hands, etc. In schools throughout the region, convent or otherwise, attitudes towards the teaching of language reflected the colonial attitude which said not that you spoke a *different* language at home and on the streets, but that essentially one was good and the other was bad. The whole issue of language and power and the need to learn English within this context is not one that was usually approached.

So clearly when children, and in particular working-class children, get home, they are conscious of this distinction, conscious of the fact that the language of parents, of relatives, of themselves, is bad. School is therefore a vehicle which facilitates movement to a supposedly superior class.

In the development of my own writing, I had to make a conscious choice eventually about the language in which I wanted to write, and decided on the use of both the Grenadian language and the English. Because this is in fact our reality. At school, what was referred to as West Indian literature for me was at first a Friday afternoon pastime. When it was introduced in a serious way on the GCE syllabus, there was V. S. Naipaul's *A House for Mr. Biswas*.[9] When *A House for Mr. Biswas* got on to the O level syllabus, we students regarded it as a fantastic achievement because it meant that now Naipaul was sharing places with those whom we thought of as the real writers – Shakespeare, Keats, James, Hogg, etc. All of this was part of the self-negation;

because we were not introduced to many Caribbean writers, we did not value our own. Our all-important O level papers were, after all, being corrected in Britain. Now there is the Caribbean Examinations Council (CXC) and the GCE, or the new GCSE, is gradually being phased out, but is still adhered to by some as symbolic of the excellence of British education. This merely indicates what an excellent rule of colonial control was served by the institutions of British education.

In my own fifth form I remember studying *A House for Mr. Biswas*, Macbeth and Hardy. And I enjoyed literature. Because of this, and because my experience at school was largely of British literature, when I first started writing secret poems at school, I patterned myself after my then favourite writer – Hardy. Anyone who has heard me speak on these issues before has also heard me quote Hardy, because I cannot forget what an important place this British writer had in my life at a time when I knew no other Caribbean writer sufficiently to value him or her. I would be on my way home, thinking, listening to the sounds around me, looking at the sea, and feeling what I thought then was poetic, and the poem that would come to me was

> I leant upon a coppice gate
> When Frost was spectre-grey
> And Winter's dregs made desolate
> The weakening eye of day. [10]

I liked the words, I liked the movement of the poem. And that was the kind of reality I was familiar with in a poetic, what one might term a 'literary', sense. The literature that I studied and loved made important in print the experiences of Hardy and Keats and Wordsworth, so that, confronted with the beauty and sadness and pain and joy of my own surroundings, I turned to my British books for guidance as to expression of my feelings. I was steeped in the 'Ode to Autumn', the 'Ode to a Nightingale' and so on, without being introduced also to serious study of a writing that rooted me in my own reality. So you can understand the kind of ambivalence out of which came my first attempts at writing. I used to write secretly these beautiful sonnets. Of course they weren't so beautiful, and I destroyed them.

Then, later on, the first thing – the first poem, that is – that I left on paper was one that is now published in *Because the Dawn Breaks*, a poem called 'Nabel-String', written when I was living outside of Grenada and thinking of the reality back there.[11] It was written basically in Grenadian, in the so-called dialect. It is interesting for me that it was the first poem I had the confidence not to destroy, partly also because it was written for public recital/performance. It was like finding a voice for the first time. I believe I wrote that poem and kept it because I was living outside of Grenada, and in a sense beginning for the first time to think with pride, with a measure of belonging, of that reality, of that language. But in Grenada itself when that reality was closer to me I was at first writing different kinds of things entirely, trying to concentrate on both the content and the form of what was presented in my text-books. Perhaps it also has something to do with being better able to assess and evaluate events and experiences from a distance.

There is the whole issue of oral presentation, which is very important for me, in prose as much as in poetry. The socio-political context within which my writing really emerged in a stronger more political way, was the revolutionary period, particularly for me between 1981 and 1983, in Grenada. The political situation gave me the urge to write. The first poem written within Grenada during this period, 'Callaloo', was performed within a women's group.[12] They decided when they heard it to work on it for presentation at a bigger event.

It was out of that kind of experience that my first writing of poetry within Grenada developed. Later on, the response of larger audiences to my ideas and expressions gave me the confidence to continue writing. I did not really think of writing with a view to publication until after 1983, after the events in Grenada, after the implosion, you might call it, which caused the collapse of the party and government, after the American invasion. Before that, writing meant having a vocal and participatory audience, having people respond verbally to the work. So it was really with the loss of that audience that I began to think at all of publication.

Which brings me to the final thing that I want to mention; it is almost a question of why we write at all. Why do we write? Who is our audience? For example, it's good to be sitting here in London, telling you about my ideas, putting some of the writing by Caribbean women into a political context. But I feel also it is extremely important first to write for and to our communities and to be able to have this kind of discussion within our communities, whether here in Britain, or in the Caribbean, or wherever you have the communities to which the writing directly refers. I don't want to be writing just so that we can discuss the whole issue of art, so that we can talk theoretically about attitudes towards language. You wonder what difference it makes, and to me it is very important that it makes a difference – makes a difference in terms of the way people view themselves, in terms of the way people will interpret their history. I hope that it will make a difference to their self-image. I remember speaking to a grand-aunt who had read *Angel*. She told me she enjoyed it, that seeing the language written down gave her some ideas for things she wished to write. Someone else who was participating in that convesation said, 'Gosh, but we don't talk so bad', which started us off on a whole discussion of what is talking bad and not talking bad. We talked about the power of languages, why it is that when you speak American you don't speak bad English, you speak good American, and the particular place of African-American language within that scenario. All of the ideas expressed weren't mine. I introduced the topic, one idea touched off another, and even the person who had commented about not talking 'so bad' came up with some really radical ideas on the language issue. And at the end of it all my aunt said, 'It's true, but I suppose you really have to study this thing to see that.' And that set off all kinds of thoughts for me about this whole question of who I am writing for. Because I would like to think that people are going to read, to enjoy, to laugh at sections and also get the feel of the point about self-worth. That is why it is important that that kind of thing is taken up by the schools, by the community centres, etc., so that people can discuss those issues at that level and in a sense appreciate what many writers are trying to do in terms of self-perception, in terms of the way women perceive their role in society, and in terms of the way we perceive our story as a Caribbean people.

Notes

1 Merle Collins' talk is given here as an edited transcript. One of the subjects she raises in it is the importance of the oral form in her

own work, so that this is a particularly appropriate method for presentation of her views. It is a very personal account, spoken from her own experience, written here as she expressed the ideas she wished to share and reflecting her feelings about this writing in March 1988.

2 Louise Bennett, *Jamaica Labrish*, Sangster's Bookstores, Jamaica, 1966, p. 166.
3 Louise Bennett, *Selected Poems*, Sangster's Bookstores, Jamaica, 1982, p. 101.
4 Kenneth Ramchand, *The West Indian Novel and Its Background*, Heinemann, London, 1983, p. 85.
5 Morgan Dalphinis, *Caribbean and African Languages*, Karia Press, London, 1985.
   Hubert Devonish, *Language and Liberation: Creole Language Politics in the Caribbean*, Karia Press, London, 1986.
6 Merle Hodge, *Crick Crack, Monkey* (1970), Heinemann, London, 1981.
7 Zee Edgell, *Beka Lamb*, Heinemann, London, 1982, p. 1.
8 Merle Collins, *Angel*, The Women's Press, London, 1987.
9 V. S. Naipaul, *A House for Mr Biswas* (1961), Penguin Books, London, 1969.
10 Thomas Hardy, 'The Darkling Thrush', in James Gibson (ed.), *The Complete Poems of Thomas Hardy*, Macmillan, London, 1976, p. 150.
11 Merle Collins, *Because the Dawn Breaks: poems dedicated to the Grenadian people*, Karia Press, London, 1985, pp. 1–6.
12 Ibid., pp. 23–6.

PART IV

---◆---

Generic Strategies

FUTURES IN FEMINIST FICTION

SARA MAITLAND

Before starting this essay I have had to think extensively about how I feel about allowing myself, or anyone else for that matter, within the context of the Women's Movement, to act as 'prophet', as visionary, or to pluck a term from a much more feminised historical tradition, as seer – see-er – or sibyl. I am very hesitant indeed to cast the writer, the artist, simultaneously as The Prophet, The Wise One. This is particularly hard for those of us who repudiate emphatically any concept of the writer as 'inspired' (breathed-into is the literal translation here) or transcendent, god-kissed, ahistoricised heroine. I at least was outraged with Alice Walker when in *The Color Purple* her acknowledgements included her thanks to 'the characters who came': they didn't come, she made them up and should, I think, take responsibility for that.[1] Simply in my experience, making things, characters, up, is mostly hard work and frankly frequently tedious, and I increasingly believe it is dangerous, at least politically, to imply otherwise. So for me at least any discussion of 'futures in feminist fiction' cannot honestly incorporate Cassandra-like wailings. Cassandra, incidentally, as a punishment for refusing the sexual advances of Apollo, the god of (among other things) poetry, music and inspiration, was doomed to the thankless role of always foretelling the future with total accuracy and never having anyone believe it. Christa Wolf in her quite extraordinary novel – if novel it is – named after this rather complex lady explores exactly what this might mean in terms of contemporary visioning by contemporary visionaries.[2] It is not a job that I wish to undertake. I am absolutely not going to forecast what will happen, because what happens to writing, I believe, is dependent on what happens within society and within the political structures which enables the publications, which enables the consumption, which enables the readership and that forms the consciousness and the subconsciousness and – at least in part dare I say – the unconsciousness of writers.

Before I launch into what I think *can* be said in this area, I want to add one thing; recently I spent twenty-four hours with a group to which I belong and we came up with a verbal conundrum, which seems relevant here. This is a group based primarily on political alliances and we were discussing the increasing feeling of despair that we are all suffering from: over and over again we were all using the word 'disillusioned'. Then someone pointed out that if what one had held in the past was an 'illusion' then it was very healthy, even important, to be 'disillusioned', relieved of illusion – or delusion. If on the other hand what one had held before was 'vision' – 'silent upon a peak in Darien' – then what the present political climate was doing was 'disvisioning': and it was important that we realise that there was no word – at least within this culture and language for 'disvisioning'. No word to describe the experience of having had a real vision, a true vision of possibility and then having that taken away from you. That word, that event, is one that necessarily must be denied by bourgeois culture. I was brought up with a wicked myth – that you cannot put the Truth down, that it will win in the end; I think we have to fight that very carefully; alas, indeed it is highly possible to put the truth down, to destroy even the dream of it, and in fact the truth has been put down. Can it be that all visions, or prophesies, or whatever, that are not in the process of being realised are thereby proven as illusions/delusions? We have to face the real possibility that through social circumstance we may now be in the process not of being *disillusioned*, but of being *disvisioned*: an act of violence, not therapy. And I cannot look at the future of my own job, or anyone else's job, without at least acknowledging this possibility.

This is not an irrelevant question in the context of this series of discussions. The futures of feminist fictions depend on whether there is any real content, any envisioning or transforming content, in the act of making public the products of the imagination. The great romantic mythology insists that there is: that Utopias and dystopias, and at a different level role models and accurate descriptions at the imaginative level are in some way fertile, creative – not simply a result of creativity but creative in themselves. A more modernist view of the imagination, however, would suggest that they are no such thing: that cultural artefacts are simply the products of the society which generates them; that politically they are 'structures of consolation', 'myths' in the old sense of that word; and that personally they are individualistic therapies for both producer and consumer. Are all fictions indeed what Angela Carter describes in her very interesting article in Michelene Wandor's book *On Gender and Writing*, too many modern novels as being: 'etiquette books' to teach young women how to behave in social echelons that they may wish to aspire to?[3] We do have to ask whether imaginative works are vehicles of social revolution, or time out from the struggle. How I might foretell (or foresee or predicate or prophesy) the future of feminist fictions depends at this point enormously on what I, or you, think fiction is and what it might be.

Nonetheless the concept of prophecy is not entirely unuseful. The tradition through which we in the West have mainly learned our use of the very word prophecy is the ancient Hebrew tradition, wildly distorted by the Christianising of that tradition. The early Christian church, for its own reasons, needed to see all the Old Testament prophetic literature as both foretelling the adventure of their Jesus, and typologically precursing it. It is therefore extremely hard to decode this literature now, especially as it has so profoundly informed our ideas of what is beautiful in literary terms (which is why a great number of English language feminist fiction writers, including myself, depend so heavily on biblical rhythms, and overtones, as much as on biblical themes and characters). But modern biblical scholarship has made it clear that Hebraic prophecy was not about visionary insights into the future so much as about highly critical and accurate analysis of the present, and the probable or possible consequences of such personal and political 'signs of the times'. Thus within the prophetic tradition there is always a dialectical balance between the fact that 'beautiful on the mountains are the feet of them that bring good news' and the warnings against the 'false prophets who cry "peace, peace" and there is no peace'.

What this means to me is that to speculate on the futures of feminist fiction it is crucial to look, critically, at the presents of feminist fiction, and at the political and cultural (if there is a difference) circumstances that have produced it. And I have to start by acknowledging a crucial – and frequently denied – failure in feminist fiction. In doing this within this present and specific context I want to stress that, as I understand it, straight – or literary, or mainstream – fictions are as much genre fictions as those usually demeaningly so named. There's the romantic novel, the SF novel, the Booker Prize Novel, the crime novel, the social-realist novel, the South-American-influenced-magic-realism-novel, the historical novel, the East-European-influenced-politically-significant-novel [not too many of these], the French-influenced-structuralist-novel-of-ideas, the Bildungs-roman, the comic novel, the melodrama, etc., etc., etc. Genre and sub-genre and sub-sub-genre in infinite divisions, each as the semioticians and structuralists have explained to us, convincingly, with their own codes and tropes, all of which have been used by feminists and in many cases used extremely well, and many of which we have learned to read and decode. And very nice too, there is nothing derogatory in this list or fact. But what there is *not* in this sense is The Feminist Novel. And this is sad and perhaps surprising. We have, I think, to admit a failure: the failure of feminist fictions. More than ten years ago I was involved with four other women in a writers' group which shaped me, indeed defined me as a fiction writer, and specifically as a feminist writer; it was the group that produced a book of short stories called *Tales I Tell My Mother*, which was published almost exactly eleven years ago, in 1978.[4] Since all five women in the group have since continued as professional writers it may be worth naming them: Zoë Fairbairns, Valerie Miner, Michèle Roberts, Michelene Wandor and myself. This group was quite an early and explicit attempt to write something called 'feminist fiction': the book the group produced is not only structured as a collective fiction rather than as a simple anthology or collection, it is written in the hope, or rather the belief that there is such a thing as a feminist fiction in the structural, formal, generic sense; that, as it were, the platonic ideal of such a genre were there in the sky waiting to be revealed in all its pristine glory. That hope and conviction, often in rather brash ways, punctuates almost every page and especially the short essays on feminism and fiction that are scattered through the pages and which we saw as structurally, formally, integral to the book. The book is buoyant with the conviction – touching and naive as it may seem now – that we were moving forward the possibilities of fiction in a new and radical way; and that we were not doing this on our own – that there was a ground swell and we were joining it, which would, and pretty soon, create the whole new formal situation in which feminist fictions writers would work. And as a matter of fact I do believe that as a formal, as a structural, enterprise, *Tales I Tell My Mother* stands up as one of the most ambitious and interesting fictions of this round of the Women's Movement. However, what in fact most of the members of that collective did next was to go on to write novels. I would like to say sincerely that between us we have written a good number of very interesting and reasonably effective novels, but they are not – and neither, by and large, are the other novels of the Women's Movement – particularly innovative structurally. They have certainly not generated anything that could be seen as a new genre, despite the various different attempts to package them as such – and I don't mean that word disparagingly at all. Most would-be literary novels written by feminists fall structurally, or at very least in terms of plot, into a very old pattern: Girl meets love object (now renamed either 'girl' or – the new and dazzling hero of the highbrow romance – Independence). Girl meets Independence, Girl loves Independence, Girl loses Independence through a lover's quarrel of some sort or another (usually not through her own fault but through the machinations of some sinister villain: her mother – now replacing the wicked step-mother because we're post-Freudians – some man or other, or that mysterious hooded stranger called The Wicked System), Girl searches for Independence, Girl finds Independence and rides off into the sunset with Independence astride her saddlebow. This, for all it is dressed up with complexities and culture is exactly the pattern of, for instance, my own last novel *Virgin Territory*;[5] nor do I think it a bad novel I would like to say. In terms of subject matter and character development, as well as the intellectual questions that it raises, and the focusing of the writing sentence by sentence itself, it is at least ten light years better than anything I wrote in *Tales I Tell My Mother*. Feminist fiction has been immensely successful in terms of pushing the boundaries of traditional genres out enough to include our interests and our concerns. Nor should this altogether surprise

us; the British novel has always, whatever the literary They want
:o tell us, been very much the preserve of women – both as
writers and readers. The novel has played an important part
throughout its history in the feminisation and domesticisation of
prose writing. It was already formally amenable to the insertion
of a new generation of women's concerns: as can be seen in the
extraordinary flowering of what can now be seen as pre-feminist
or even proto-feminist women novelists of the 1960s who helped
form the climate and mood which enabled feminism to articulate
itself in the 1970s.

Nonetheless I think we must face up quite seriously to the fact
that despite some valiant efforts, we have failed to do what we
believed we would inevitably do which was forge a genre which
was *ipso facto* feminist. I am often asked what that form would be,
or what elements it might contain – the problem is that having
failed to produce it, it is impossible to answer the question. But
there are some compass bearings which I might indicate. The
first is around the feminist principle of collectivism: one of the
reasons why I wanted to be in a writers' collective back then is
because I believed in the idea of the collective. Valerie Miner
pursued this idea in her novel *Movement*[6] and Michelene Wandor
and I took it further in *Arky Types*[7] which was published last year.
I think that *Arky Types* is a key text in this discussion (one of the
nice things about co-writing a book is that you can boast of it
freely, since you are praising not yourself but the other) – it is an
epistolary novel; a genre rather out of fashion now, but it
shouldn't be; the personal letter as much as any literary form
mediates between the individual and the social. By inventing
letters the author is obliged to give up a certain power and
subjectivity. By using more than the singular writer all the
writers involved in a collective text are forced to give up their
traditional privileges, of control, of assertion, of dominance. We
need more serious experiments in what collective writing could
produce.

And along with that goes certain ideas about closure and
endings which are for me best articulated by Barthes in *The
Pleasure of the Text* when he talks about the satisfaction of a closed
ending – when you know what is ordained so to speak – in
contrast to the 'Bliss' experienced by an open-ended text.[8]
(Could I instance Shakespeare's *Twelfth Night*: on paper this is a

classic comedy text, but in fact it is extraordinarily radical; one of the heroines is rewarded, *rather than punished*, for a 'wrong' sexual-object choice. Gender and its meaning is entirely opened out by the ending of this play; it is nearly impossible to leave a half way decent production of it without wanting to explore that confusedness, to take it further.) Form requires (*desires*) conclusion, requires tidiness, requires the good ending, and the novel particularly thrives on that requirement; but a radical, philosophical claim of feminism is about being-in-engagement and we have not explored enough ways of writing that animating sense into our fictional texts.

I do not here want to more than indicate these two areas which seem to be worthy of more attention. I am simply saying that there was some sense of both these things in the earlier feminist fictions which seem to have been defeated by the weight of genre expectation crushing down on both writers and readers the gravity of the desire for satisfaction. I am not arguing that this was, or was not a good thing, but when we look to what might be the future of feminist fiction we have to realise that this failure to create a genre, a literary discourse of our own (and I use both these terms in absolute preference to the concept of a language of our own) leaves us dependent on what happens to fiction more generally when we think of the directions we might be moving in. And the future of fiction more generally depends inevitably in what happens culturally and politically at large, as this will both inform the Women's Liberation Movement and inform the fictional genres within which we both read and write.

Now the problem is, it seems to me, that that context looks extremely grim, certainly in the short term. I would like to give you a few concrete examples of what I mean. I think the social context that is creating, and will be created by Section 28, for example, may prove immensely damaging to the development of feminist fiction. It is wellnigh impossible to imagine a feminist fictional world in which there are by cultural demand no lesbians: lesbianism has become, rightly I believe, an almost sacred icon of feminist fictional strategy. If it becomes culturally or economically impossible for publishers to include this sort of material in anything they publish one of two things must happen (they can both happen simultaneously of course): there will either be a conscious self-censorship by feminist writers, or a

growth of samizdat texts. Actually we should recognise that
neither of these events would necessarily be wholly bad for
feminist fiction: in the former case, the need to express all the
values now strategically and imaginatively short-handed into
lesbianism might drive writers into an imaginative innovation
whose products we cannot easily guess at. The fact that it would
be an appalling loss for all of us, particularly for lesbians, and
especially for young lesbians, in terms of self-recognition and
self-development, should not blind us to the fact that if I had a
lover who was a writer I would rather receive *Orlando* or *Paris,
France* from her sweet hands than *The Well of Loneliness*: it is not
necessarily the case that repression makes worse fiction,
although it may well make very unhappy people.[9] In the latter
case, the samizdat text has by its very forbiddenness a radical
impact in the simple act of reading it far greater than the winning
of 1,133 Booker Prizes. That said, I still feel that it would be an
extremely sad context in which to have to write fiction, and that
the future of our fictions could not be other than profoundly
affected by it. I suspect, knowing myself too well, that by and
large it would lead to the gentrification of feminist fiction, and
hence – since we are and have always been a movement, for quite
demonstrable historic reasons, deeply dependent on our printed
texts – to the still further gentrification of feminism itself.

To offer another example, I do not see how the present British
government's education policies – as expressed both in the
Education Reform Act of 1988 and the savage cuts being imposed
on all Education Authorities, especially if continued through the
next decade, can do other than reduce the level of literacy – both
actual and functional – among young women not yet in school.
We have to face the fact that there is a possibility that there will
simply be a diminishing, or even non-existent, audience for
our wonderful, radical, genre-coded fictions. Again, possible
responses to this development in terms of fiction are complex.
Some feminists might abandon writing altogether as a means of
communication. For the rest there would certainly be a polari-
sation. Some would choose to write knowingly and consciously
only for an élite (a class élite) readership. (To some extent of
course this happens already – and causes real and vital debate in
countries where literacy cannot be taken for granted in the way
that it is here – but at least in the imagination even the most

'literary' women have been able to conceive that their readership could grow, that new women could be added into it, rather than see literary skills, and access, diminish.) Other writers would temper their writing specifically for a growing group of sub-literate readers. What sort of text these last might produce is a fascinating question, but it would I think inevitably be radically different from either the increasingly literary, sophisticated, and genre-determined fictions that we are now moving towards, or the fictions now being produced targeted at the younger woman's market.

Finally, I believe with considerable depression that we have to face, as a movement born out of the success of liberal capitalism, and as a movement that was complicit in the failure of genuinely revolutionary change almost at our own birth, that we are now in very grave danger of entering a phase of what is classically described as true barbarism. And again this could have a number of different results: it could lead to didactic fictions, as we fight the last great battle – the Feminist heroine at Ragnarok or Armageddon. It could also lead, as Emma Tennant suggested recently, to an increased ability to write and read magical and surreal fictions (if the socially real is so bizarre the imagination is freed: indeed that seems to be happening, and if the combination of political repression, political engagement, semi-censorship and total lunacy that has been current too long in South America is anything to judge by might well be a positive literary force in a sick kind of way). However, it seems to me that it is just as likely, since we have failed to establish a genre that is genuinely autonomous of the cultural mainstream, to lead both to decadent texts and to nihilist texts. Which, at the worst, could finally wrench the Women's Liberation Movement away from its primary roots as both a social movement and an ethical movement – and deliver it signed and sealed as it were into the hands of defensive liberalism as an individualistic and aesthetic tool of reaction. I am unable to escape in my mind from the very beautiful image in one of the most genre-coded texts I know – a children's futurist fairy story novel by Ursula Le Guin called *The Farthest Shore*, where the collapse of the world order makes it impossible for anyone to sing the songs and dance the dances through to the end.[10] Every one starts with good will but the rivers of imagination and the channels of form have simply run dry, and there are no stories possible any more.

So is there an alternative, a different way of shaping the future, of fending off, so to speak, the barbarian invasion? First there is the serious possibility that we could, and even should, simply do without novels at all. If we can learn to survive without the National Health Service, and without primary schools, perhaps we can survive without novels. Or rather, we can choose to abandon them, as a failed strategy, with cries of 'Back to the drawing board' – or ironing board or school board. With our energies freed from the long pursuit, we might be able to think of some entirely new imaginative and cultural engagement which would better express and enable our social aspiration. The novel has long been accused of being a middle-class and bourgeois form – perhaps we could just admit that this was a correct analysis and not write or read any ever again. This is not a frivolous suggestion.

However, I do believe – I have to believe – that there is somehow, somewhere something which could be called not futuristic, but visionary fiction – that is a fiction which can make visionaries of us all, that can re-vision us. It would have to be a fiction that worked by articulating the channels of hope, and to do that it would have to be a truthful fiction. The first truth it needs to articulate is against a great indulgence of the Women's Movement; an indulgence that I must say I profit from as a writer – that novels are somehow magical, that fictions can do it for us. But I don't think they're magical – I think they're hard work and I think they are real. At this point only imagination can re-vision us, by showing us where we are. But this re-visioning is not going to happen unless we take with the utmost seriousness the threats to us as writers, the threats to us as readers. We must acknowledge that these threats are born out of a cultural failure in feminism, which must reflect a political failure within feminism. Then this must be countered by a better theory of cultural production and of the uses and meanings of language; but also by a determined and probably sacrificial attempt to write texts which do in fact reflect *our socially complex* (visionarily aristotelian and yet complicit in our own failure) *present tense, and our modes and methods of aspiration* (of desire) *towards change* (towards transformation) [the switch in modes of discourse here is fully deliberate and the feminist writer of our futures may well need the technology that could provide the multiple/simultaneous text] *towards our multiple futures.*

Notes

1 Alice Walker, *The Color Purple*, The Women's Press, London, 1983.
2 Christa Wolf, *Cassandra, A Novel and Four Essays*, Virago Press, London, and Farrer Strauss, NY, 1984.
3 Michelene Wandor (ed.), *On Gender and Writing*, Pandora Press, London, 1983.
4 Zoë Fairbairns, Sara Maitland, Valerie Miner, Michèle Roberts, Michelene Wandor, *Tales I Tell My Mother*, Journeyman Press, London, 1978.
5 Sara Maitland, *Virgin Territory*, Michael Joseph, London, 1983.
6 Valerie Miner, *Movement*, Methuen, London, 1987.
7 Sara Maitland and Michelene Wandor, *Arky Types*, Methuen, London, 1987.
8 Roland Barthes, trans. Richard Miller, *The Pleasure of the Text*, Hill & Wang, Radclyffe, 1975.
9 Virginia Woolf, *Orlando* (1928), Panther, 1977.
    Gertrude Stein, *Paris, France*, Liveright, NY, 1970; Brilliance Books, London, 1982.
    Radclyffe Hall, *The Well of Loneliness* (1928), Virago, London, 1986.
10 Ursula Le Guin, *The Farthest Shore* (Part 3 of *The Earthsea Trilogy*), Puffin, London, 1974.

FEMINISM, WRITING, POSTMODERNISM

———◆———

LESLIE DICK

At the very first meeting in this series, Cora Kaplan proposed an ideal space for the production of feminist texts, a kind of triangular space, with on the one side, feminism as a social movement, and on the next, feminist criticism (whether inside or outside the academy), and on the third, the feminist writer.[1] Thus the writing would be informed by the social movement *and* by the critical theory, and both the movement and the theory would respond to the writing, making a context for the reception of the text. My immediate response was: this is completely idealistic, when has this *ever* happened? It seemed like a fantasy of a politicised avant-garde – so very far from present reality. Then I remembered the 1970s, and work like Mary Kelly's *Post Partum Document*, which seemed to be an example of what Cora Kaplan was describing.[2]

Post Partum Document unquestionably took the form of an avant-garde art work, coming out of the aesthetically and politically transgressive practice of conceptual art. In *Post Partum Document*, Mary Kelly made use of content and materials (the stained nappy-liners were most notorious) which were seen to be outrageously inappropriate to the walls of the art gallery. At the same time, the work was profoundly rooted in the social and political experience of motherhood within the patriarchy. Yet, *Post Partum Document* also succeeded in being an autonomous theoretical work, an intervention from the place of the mother, within current debates on psychoanalysis and feminism. The triangle – art/politics/theory – holds.

There are a few examples of this kind of work, but I couldn't immediately think of any novels, at least in English. And since what I was trying to do in the novel I wrote, *Without Falling*, was to work through, in fiction, some of the issues raised in feminist psychoanalytic and literary theory, I was very interested in the whole idea of the relationship between the social movement, critical theory, and artistic practice.[3] All of which raises many questions – about Thatcherism, the fragmentation of the Women's Liberation Movement, the retreat of theory into the academy, the terrible top-heaviness of the literary scene itself, the appalling lack of progressive literary magazines, the age-old antagonism between artists and academics, writers and critics, and so on.

I'm not going to discuss these here – partly because, more urgently, I want to talk about what's possible in writing, what happens next, and I want to talk about postmodernism. I will, however, tell a publishing anecdote, which points to some of the ironies of the great divide between theory and writing. When I was trying to find a publisher for my book I would go to bookstores, and to the ICA, and I would see what all the women I knew were reading, which was *theory*, and I'd say to myself, surely if women want to read Jane Gallop and Julia Kristeva and Toril Moi, they'll want to read my book. I fondly imagined there was what's called a *market* for a novel like mine. When Serpent's Tail, which is a new, small, adventurous, left wing publishing house, decided to publish my book, they adamantly refused to have either the word 'feminism' or the word 'psychoanalysis' anywhere near the book's cover or publicity. They thought it would 'put people off'. The triangle had collapsed. My publishers preferred to market my book as 'postmodernist'.

I would like to discuss the question of postmodernism and modernism, partly because it's an issue that has come up in some of the earlier papers, and partly because thinking about genre, and repetition compulsion, and high art, and pulp fiction, inevitably brings theories of postmodernism to mind. It was in following tangents, tracing connections between theories of postmodernism and theories of genre, that I was able to think about my own work in relation to genre writing, and to think about possibilities for a contemporary feminist avant-garde.

One of the vexing things about postmodernism is the problem of definition, and I would like to begin by using the work of

Barbara Kruger to serve as an example of what I mean by postmodernism.[4]

First, postmodernist work challenges the (modernist) polarity between 'high' and 'low' culture, art and kitsch. Barbara Kruger's work is presented both in the art gallery, *and* (always) on posters, postcards, billboards, T-shirts, matchboxes, etc. Further, she uses the visual language of commercial art, especially glossy magazine and billboard advertising techniques, to make her aesthetic effects.

Secondly, postmodernist work uses strategies of plunder and purloinment, plagiarism, replication and simulation, not merely to construct a more complex and enriching art work (the modernist project), but to challenge the category of what an art object is, to call the whole artistic project into question. Barbara Kruger uses recycled photographic images, which she 'steals' – they are all old photographs because they have to be out of copyright – and places them in juxtaposition with abrupt slogan-like texts, addressing the spectator and disrupting any settled expectations he or she might have. Repeating the same format (huge black and white photo, same typeface, narrow red frame), she presents an object that sits uncomfortably somewhere between a *Vogue* layout, a 1950s advertisement, and the explicitly political work of an artist like John Heartfield. The repetitious, mechanical and plagiarising practices all show her debt to the work of Andy Warhol, while her use of image and text is very much in the conceptualist tradition (like Mary Kelly or Victor Burgin).

Thirdly, an anti-purist, mixed media or hybrid approach is key to the production of this work. What's being challenged is the uniqueness and purity of the 'high' art work, and the special relationship of the reader to that work. Modernist 'high art' eschews politics; within the mythology of modernism, political content equals propaganda, and propaganda is the lowest of the low. Barbara Kruger reinserts a political critique into the art gallery, simultaneously calling into question the fervid disavowal of political meaning by both advertising and 'high' art.

I am aware that using visual art as the example for an account of postmodernism may be an idiosyncratic way of approaching the question of postmodernism and modernism in literature, but it's the clearest way I know how to think about it.

To turn to modernism, momentarily: there's no question that

the great classic modernist texts like *The Wasteland* and *Ulysses* make radical use of parody, quotation and allusion, as literary strategies. Joyce took the great Homeric myth, cornerstone of British nineteenth-century culture, and plonked it down on a rainy day in Dublin. Eliot quoted and transposed, in order to parody original texts, subvert expectations, and satirise the contemporary city. So quotation, allusion and parody are not solely qualities of postmodernist work; it's important to remember that modernist writing is playful, self-reflexive, and so on. Indeed, on some level *all* literature relies on reference to other texts to take shape and make sense. Genre writing explicitly works by referring to previous examples of itself, and either sustaining or subverting the narrative and formal elements that make up the genre. In genre writing especially, rules are made to be broken.

The high modernist novel, however, is by definition *not* a genre novel. The purity and uniqueness of the work of art was a sacred tenet of those theorising modernism (although few poets or novelists would claim that kind of aesthetic isolation), and genre novels were dismissed as kitsch, 'lowbrow', and unworthy of serious consideration. As a result, it's something of a radical critical strategy to insist on the relevance of genre, to read *Moby Dick* as an adventure story, *Crime and Punishment* as a thriller, *Jane Eyre* as a 'penniless servant ends up marrying the master of the house' Mills & Boon-style moral romance. Suddenly all the high seriousness of modernist criticism starts to fall away, and it begins to seem much more like pleasure...

It's clear there are very important links between genre writing and the culture of postmodernism. It's partly that genre is 'low', and therefore postmodernist (camp) sensibility loves it. While genre writing casually discards the idea of originality as the final measure of value in art, postmodernists see originality as an interface between ideas of property and the market place (where copyright protects and plagiarism is against the law) and the idea of the individual (the unique, coherent, creative mind, generating unique, coherent creations).

Genre writing is also about *subcultures*. When you think of Philip K. Dick, undoubtedly a great postmodernist, he was working within a context of the highly developed subculture of science fiction. And Kathy Acker, whom I consider to be the exemplary postmodernist writer now, is firmly placed with her feet grounded in youth subculture, rock'n'roll, and her head full of *books*, serious books. These subcultures take the form of cliques, clubs, fanzines, and other modes of interaction, distribution, and access between the artist and her audience. When Kathy Acker reads from her novels on stage at a rock concert between two bands, the limitations of the novel as a form are being challenged in an entirely new way. (Not unlike Barbara Kruger's matchboxes.)

To look at these issues a bit more closely, I would like to examine the ways in which Kathy Acker's writing fits into my schema of postmodernism. Her work effaces the distinction between high and low art, it explodes literary hierarchies, so that, in her books, you can't tell if you're primarily reading a work of pornography, or soap opera, pulp fiction, or high modernism. Plagiarism is fundamental to her writing practice: other books are raided, ripped off and recycled, imitated, parodied, rewritten and manipulated in as many ways as she can come up with. The mixed media aspect is clear in *Don Quixote*, for example, which veers through political satire to doomed love story, to drama, to history lesson, etc., and *Blood and Guts in High School*, which is interspersed with drawings, Maps of Dreams, etc.[5]

But Kathy Acker's work is extremely unusual – postmodernist practice in writing tends to be harder to find than in visual art, and possibly one reason for this is that *modernism* in writing wasn't nearly so extreme as it was in painting. By far the most extreme modernist writer was Gertrude Stein, and it's no accident that Stein is probably the most important stylistic influence on a writer like Kathy Acker. In her project of being the Picasso of literature, Stein, the ultramodernist, pushed writing as far as it could go; now Acker takes the work of Stein and pushes language, writing, literature, even further.

To return to a consideration of genre for a moment: from the point of view of the reader, the 'addict', genre is about repetition, that is, formula and variation. From the point of view of the writer, a specific genre can be an 'enabling device', a formal structure that allows and controls and prevents meaning, a syntax. Literary strategies help enable the writer to overcome internal blocks and censorships; specific genres displace raw (emotional) material into highly structured forms, thereby making it possible for the writer to deal, for example, with death, or violence, or desire. Genres also work to help her keep all this material, this plethora of words and ideas and emotions, in some kind of control.

But genres are not just forms, they are also institutions. Between, on the one hand, *marketing*, and on the other, audience *addiction*, genres have a tendency to rigidify, to sediment and fossilise. There are two possible responses a writer can make to this: one, to revive the institution; two, to isolate and extract forms from the institution, without getting involved in the institution. These are two very different strategies. The first is what we have mainly been discussing during this series of talks: it's about making the detective story, for example, come to life, say something new, through giving it a feminist content, or a woman protagonist. Whereas the second is, for example, *lifting* a detective story motif, or plot, or character type, *out* of the genre, because you can see how it would be useful to you for a completely different project – and your book doesn't thereby become a detective story.

Sometimes genre elements are lifted and recontextualised in order to accomplish the revival of the institution, one genre feeding another, so to speak, as for example the Western was revived by adding detective story elements. Angela Carter's infusion of gothic, vampire motifs into the fairy tale in *The Bloody Chamber* demonstrates how this kind of raiding practice can both lay bare the mechanics of writing and give the fairy tale back its ancient emotional power.[6] Reviving the institution is, as I see it, pouring your lifeblood into the genre, probably because you love it; you, the genre-addict-as-writer, love detective stories, or tales of vampires. The second strategy, on the other hand, is more like scavenging, ripping the genre off. It's making use of some of the elements of the genre, while discarding the implicit values of the genre as institution. It's destructive, and disrespectul of the genre, which it treats like an abandoned car – steal the windshield wipers, the wheels, the wings, and eventually even the engine.

I'd like now to say something about my novel, *Without Falling*, which is not a genre novel; if anything it works as a kind of deconstruction of various genres, but it has some specific things in common with genre writing. Generally speaking, the classic bourgeois novel, from Samuel Richardson on, consists of a detailed phenomenological account of how people relate to each other within a social context. And in a sense, the modernist novel merely focused the details differently: *The Waves* is still about people and their relationships within society; it's still about intersubjective relations. Genre novels are *not* about this. They're about mystery or excitement. They're about fantasy or Utopia. They repeat *processes*, processes like: 'let's imagine another world' (SF), 'let's solve the problem of death' (murder mysteries), 'let's follow the rocky road to true love' (romance), etc. These processes are repeated over and over, and to a great extent it's the processes that the reader engages with, rather than the characters in the book. That's virtually a classic definition of genre fiction: it has 'cardboard characters'. And a definition of the modernist novel might be: the elaborate and careful manipulation of language in order to detail ever more precisely the intricacies and complexities of subjectivity and relationship. It's very different.

In an earlier paper, Carolyn Brown said that the project of modernism was the investigation of consciousness, sexuality and language – all of which were seen to be problematic. I think this is a fine description of the work of writers like Virginia Woolf, James Joyce, and (even) D. H. Lawrence (once described by Angela Carter as an honorary 'sister'). As a writer, I would wish to work within that specific field of endeavour.

At the same time, I'm not interested in *character*. I'm interested in psychoanalysis, which is a theory of subjectivity. So I'm interested in psychological *processes and predicaments*, and (almost like the genre writer) I want the reader to engage with those processes, critically, rather than to identify with my characters. I want to sustain for the reader a position of pleasurable distance, contemplating the special effects, smiling even while reading about the most harrowing things. I want both: for the reader to be right inside the charcter *and* to be looking on. I would like to maintain this distance by artifice in writing, so the reader never forgets she is reading (like the genre addict admiring the workings of the machine), and by interrupting expectation with outbreaks of laughter. I want all the deep insight of modernism and the harsh cynicism and emptiness of postmodernism. I want the intense pull of narrative, without an overt plot. I would like to make the reader laugh and cry and feel sick; I want a bodily response. And nothing pleases me more than the women who say they read the book in a rush, or in one sitting, the way one reads a romance or a great detective story.

In a sense, *Without Falling* traverses a number of genres, some of which don't tend to be thought of as genres, and I'd like to run through them very briefly in conclusion. Firstly, this novel is a romance, or an anti-romance. The heroine is a woman in search of love. The book is about mistaken love, and the emotional sado-masochism of sexual relationships. By attempting an analysis of these mechanisms and processes, it *undoes* the romance.

Secondly, *Without Falling* refers to the eighteenth-century gothic and the nineteenth-century melodrama, partly in terms of the painful extremities of emotion contained within it, the violent extremes the heroine persists in pursuing, but mainly through the centrality of the body in the text. Inspired by Hélène Cixous' *cri de coeur*, I wanted to write from the body, to write the woman's body, specifically.[7]

In many ways, this book falls within the (as yet unacknowledged) genre of the modernist novel, using fragmented narrative, shifts in point of view, first, second, and third person, internal monologue, and varieties of text (letters, journals, dramatic dialogue). To get an analytic distance on this emotional body, it strives for a precise use of language to denote, control and present it. Furthermore, it is a classic first novel, in that it is compulsive, driven, and it enacts an oedipal drama, being both an appeal to and an attack on its own symbolic mother (feminism) and its symbolic father (theory) – an oedipal drama at the level of the novel itself.

Probably most influential has been my reading of the psychoanalytic case histories of Freud, of which the case history of Dora is for me the most poignant.[8] Freud's double use of narrative, in retelling his patient's tale, and in presenting to the reader his own detective work of interpretation, is exemplary. What's particularly striking (and infuriating to some readers) about *Without Falling* is how flat the male characters are; like the so-called cardboard characters of the genre novel, they are simply presented as pawns in the heroine's game. This freedom to ignore conventions of three-dimensionality is partly a result of being more interested in psychological processes than in character, but also, for example, in the Dora case history, people like Herr K. really are only significant as figures in her story – what's important about them is what they mean to *her*. In many ways, *Without Falling* is a study in narcissism, its strengths and weaknesses, and the heroine's predicament is one in which she has the greatest difficulty in recognising the existence of the Other, especially when she is in love with him.

Finally, *Without Falling* is a challenge to the genre of the feminist novel, if we can think of that as genre, the novel of positive role models and peppermint tea. It's a book that came out of endless reading of books by women (for five years after leaving college I read only books by women), and a great deal of reading of feminist literary and psychoanalytic theory. I wrote it as a feminist novel, however dark its insights into the contradictory predicament of femininity might be. I am Lacanian enough to feel that the feminine position is impossible, and yet it is what we inhabit, it is the language we speak. I wanted to address those contradictions, which I felt was undoubtedly a feminist project, a project of inventing (or reinventing) the theoretical novel.

To return to where we began, and re-examine my perception of Cora Kaplan's ideal triangle as a fantasy of a politicised avant-garde. For feminist writers now, one question would be: if postmodernism formulates the terms of a contemporary avant-garde, what might be the possibilities for genre writing within it? Yet it's possible to stand this question on its head, through looking at a book like J. G. Ballard's *The Atrocity Exhibition*, a classic example of avant-garde SF, a book that demonstrates how genre subcultures can create a space for the production of transgressive and oppositional avant-garde writing.[9]

Avant-garde art has traditionally been thought of, and dismissed, as élitist, for a tiny minority audience, but possibly this is no more the case than in genre writing, which is always *for* a self-selected minority group of aficionados. (Maybe the exception to this is the genre of the airport novel, which is for anybody, which is to say it is classically defined as the book for people who don't read books.) If the avant-garde can be thought of as just another subculture, the next question might be: can we imagine a feminist avant-garde, a feminist postmodernism – that would reinstate the ideal triangle, with a postmodern politics on one side, and a postmodern feminist theory on another? I would argue that those already exist, that's the space we are working within *now*. Maybe we can think of postmodernism as producing a space for what has been described as 'crossover, hybridisation, and inter-zoning' between these different subcultures, different genres, and different oppositional and transgressive artistic practices, a space for raiding, scavenging, subverting and reviving the forms and narratives of writing we love.[10]

Notes

1 This talk was given as the last in the series on genre and women's writing at the ICA in London in early 1988, and as such was, to a certain extent, written in response to some of the previous contributions. I have retained the informality of the original piece, in which I was asked to speak on the topic of genre and women's writing now, specifically in relation to my own writing practice. The talk took the form of a somewhat tangential collection of thoughts on feminism, postmodernism, and the avant-garde.

2 See Mary Kelly, *Post Partum Document*, Routledge & Kegan Paul, London, 1983. A question arose in discussion: how transgressive *are* nappy-liners? What about Duchamp's urinal? To which I replied: The nappy-liners were extremely transgressive, in a feminist sense, in that this is material (baby/mother/shit stuff) that is totally suppressed within high art culture. The urinal and the nappy-liner are no more symmetrical and interchangeable at the level of cultural meanings than masculine/feminine is within the patriarchy. (Which is to say, men piss in urinals, women clean them.) Both the tabloid and the quality press found the nappy-liners deeply outrageous and offensive, generating debate along the lines of the debate around Carl André's bricks, including talk of taxpayers' money, etc. The nappy-liners (which crucially were stained, marked with the residues of baby shit) are still referred to whenever there's an avant-garde art scandal in the Press. They've become part of popular mythology.

3 Leslie Dick, *Without Falling*, Serpent's Tail, London, 1987, and City Lights, San Francisco, 1988.

4 See Barbara Kruger, *We won't play nature to your culture*, ICA catalogue, London, 1983. In this essay I refer only to Barbara Kruger's work of the early 1980s, as illustrated in this catalogue.

5 Kathy Acker, *Don Quixote*, Paladin, London, 1986.
— *Blood and Guts in High School*, Grove, NY, and Picador, London, 1984.

6 Angela Carter, *The Bloody Chamber*, Gollancz, London, 1979.
7 See Hélène Cixous, 'The Laugh of the Medusa', in Elaine Marks and
    Isabelle de Courtrivon (eds), *New French Feminisms*, University of
    Massachusetts Press, Amherst, 1980, and Harvester, Brighton, 1981.
8 See Sigmund Freud, 'Fragment of an Analysis of a Case of Hysteria',
    Standard Edition VII (1905e), Hogarth Press, London, 1953, and
    Penguin Freud Library, vol. 8, Penguin Books, London, 1977.
9 J. G. Ballard, *The Atrocity Exhibition*, Triad, Gainesville, Panther,
    London, 1979.
10 Peter Wollen, 'Semiotic Counter-Strategies: Retrospect 1982', in
    Readings and Writings, Verso, London, 1982, p. 214.

NOTES ON CONTRIBUTORS

CAROLYN BROWN is a lecturer at Thames Polytechnic and for the Open University in English Literature. She is at present writing a book on *Women, the City and Postmodernism*.

HELEN CARR is a freelance writer, and was one of the founders and co-editors of *Women's Review*. She has taught at the University of Essex, for the University of London Extra-Mural Department and Thames Polytechnic. She wrote the booklet to accompany the Thames Television series on *Women Writers*. From 1990 she will be a co-editor with Isobel Armstrong of a new women's arts and cultural journal to be published by Oxford University Press.

MERLE COLLINS was born and brought up in Grenada. With Rhonda Cobham she edited *Watchers and Seekers: An Original Anthology of Creative Writing by Black Women living in Britain*, The Women's Press, 1987. Her novel *Angel* was also published by The Women's Press last year. She has also published a collection of poems, *Because the Dawn Breaks: poems dedicated to the Grenadian people*, Karia, 1985.

ROSALIND COWARD is a writer and journalist. Her publications include *Patriarchal Precedents: Sexuality and Social Relations*, Routledge & Kegan Paul, 1983, and *Female Desire: Women's Sexuality Today*, Paladin, 1984. With Linda Semple she edits the Pandora Women Crime Writers series.

LESLIE DICK's first novel *Without Falling* was published by Serpent's Tail in London in 1987 and by City Lights in San Francisco in 1988. Her story 'Envy' is included in *The Seven Deadly Sins*, (ed.) Alison Fell, published by Serpent's Tail in 1988. She also writes about books, painting, and performance art, occasionally. She is currently working on a second novel.

CORA KAPLAN is Professor of English at Rutgers University, USA, and compiler of *The Salt, the Bitter and the Good: Three Centuries of English and American Poets*, Paddington Press,

London and NY, 1975, and of *Sea Changes: Essays on Culture and Feminism*, Verso, 1986.

ROZ KAVENEY is a freelance journalist and publishers' reader. She writes on science fiction for the academic science fiction journal, *Foundation*, and on fiction and general literary topics for the *TLS*, *The Sunday Times* and the *New Statesman*.

NASEEM KHAN is a writer and journalist. She wrote the weekly arts-in-society column in the *New Statesman* for three years and is author of *The Arts Britain Ignores*, Community Relations Commission, 1976, and *Ocean of Milk: a Guide to Indian Dance* (forthcoming). She also started MAAS (Minority Arts Advisory Service), co-ordinated the alternative Festival of India and was *Time Out*'s Theatre Editor

ALISON LIGHT is a lecturer in English at Brighton Polytechnic. Her most recent work includes a study of romance fiction and Daphne du Maurier's *Rebecca* (Feminist Review no. 16), which is part of a book to be published by Routledge entitled *The Haunted House: the Englishwoman's Novel and the Conservative Imagination*.

SARA MAITLAND's first novel, *Daughter of Jerusalem* (1978), won the Somerset Maugham Award. Since then her books include the novel *Virgin Territory*, Michael Joseph, 1984, a study of the drag artiste Vesta Tilley, Virago Press, 1986, and *Telling Tales*. Journeyman Press, 1983, a collection of short stories. Most recently she has published *Arky Types*, co-written with Michelene Wandor, Methuen, 1987, *A Book of Spells* (a collection of short stories now available in paperback from Methuen), and edited *Very Heaven: Women's Lives in the 1960s*, Virago Press, and is working on a third novel about women, dinosaurs, gardening and adolescence.

LINDA SEMPLE is a bookseller and writer. With Rosalind Coward she edits the Pandora Women Crime Writers series. She is at present writing a book on women crime writers, to be published by Pandora.

CAROLYN STEEDMAN is the author of *The Tidy House*, Virago Press, 1982, *Policing the Victorian Community*, Routledge & Kegan Paul, 1984, *Landscape for a Good Woman*, Virago Press, 1986, *The Radical Soldier's Tale*, Routledge, 1988. She edited *Language, Gender and Childhood*, Routledge and Kegan Paul, 1984, with Valerie Walkerdine and Cathy Urwin. She is Senior

Lecturer in Arts Education at the University of Warwick, and an editor of *History Workshop Journal*.

HELEN TAYLOR is Senior Lecturer in Literary Studies at Bristol Polytechnic and has published widely on women's writing. She is author of *Gender, Race, and Region in the Writings of Grace King, Ruth McEnery Stuart, and Kate Chopin*, Louisiana State University Press, 1989, and *Scarlett's Women*, Virago Press (forthcoming).

INDEX

INTO THE MAINSTREAM

How Feminism Has Changed Women's Writing

Nicci Gerrard

Kathy Acker, Angela Carter, Anita Desai, Margaret Drabble, Marilyn French, Doris Lessing, Joyce Carol Oates, Alice Walker, Fay Weldon and Jeanette Winterson are just some of the women who have changed the face of contemporary literature.

Nicci Gerrard has talked to more than 50 of the best-known women writing today – about how and why they write; about connections between the real worlds they live in and the imaginary worlds they create; about their political beliefs and literary ambitions; about the difficulties of living as a woman and as a writer, and having to confront age-old prejudices associated with 'women's writing'.

She gets behind the glamour of the literary world and its accolades to reveal why some writers are published and promoted whilst others are left to count their rejection letters. She asks literary agents and editors about the business of women's writing, and how feminism is influencing reading habits and shaping our culture.

Here is the evidence that women have challenged traditional literary forms and genres. Women are setting trends and winning prizes, and their books are more popular than ever before. Women's writing, and feminist writing, is entering the mainstream – it is selling, but is it 'selling out'?

0-04-440366-6

£5.99 paperback

Pandora Women Crime Writers:

THE ALWAYS ANONYMOUS BEAST

Lauren Wright Douglas

When private investigator Caitlin Reece receives a mysterious phone call from a desperate woman she sets out for their seaside rendezvous, wondering who she is going to be working for. As soon as she sets eyes on the woman it is instant recognition, for the desperate woman is Val Frazer, a news presenter, known and respected by millions of TV viewers. But the person viewers see on screen has a dark secret that is causing her a lot of heartache. For Valerie is a lesbian. She's being blackmailed and she stands to lose everything if the blackmailer is not thwarted in an attempt to ruin her life . . .

0-04-440526-X

£3.95 paperback

THE MONARCHS ARE FLYING

Marion Foster

'He'd heard it more times than he could count. I'm innocent. I didn't do it. I wasn't anywhere near the scene. They were always the hardest to do anything with, these diehards who refused to own up. And Leslie Taylor had all the earmarks. Guilty as hell.'

When radio journalist Leslie Taylor is accused of the murder of her ex-lover Marcie, it looks as though the motive for murder is obvious. After all, she's jealous of Marcie's marriage to Charles P. Denton, 'a bachelor architect who was considered by some to be a super catch.' Even when Harriet Fordham Croft, a successful attorney-at-law 'with the poise of a model and the memory of a computer' offers to defend her, Leslie can see no way out. It looks like a cut and dried case. Or is it?

0-86358-297-4

£3.95 paperback

VICTIMS

Shirley Shea

It is usually women who live in fear of multiple murderers. But when a series of particularly blood curdling and apparently unrelated killings occur, the vicitims are all men. As the murders continue, Sylvia Jennings and her successful criminal lawyer husband, David, become embroiled in their personal campaign to find a linking motive. Wading through computer statistics and aided by their enigmatic friend Craig Faron, things begin to seem clearer until suddenly the world is turned upside down and final horror of the truth reveals itself.

'For sheer suspense it is certainly the best crime story I have read this year.' – Antonia Fraser *London Daily News*

0-04-440291-0

£3.95 paperback

STUDY IN LILAC

Maria-Antonia Oliver

Translated by Kathleen McNerney

It's a hot and steamy summer in Barcelona. Lònia Guiu, private eye, and her male employee, Quim, are commissioned by a mysterious antiques dealer, Ms Gaudi, to track down three men, identities unknown. Lònia's search for the three men means combing the hot city streets of Barcelona whose opulent private estates prove for Lònia to be as dangerous as the city's seedy docklands – and risking her life in the process. This is not all she has to handle: there's the young and pregnant runaway Sebastiana whom Lònia has taken off the streets . . .

Here is a fast-paced, fast-talking thriller introducing us to a brand new, tough but likeable private eye – with a penchant for collecting lipstick.

0-04-440290-2

£3.95 paperback

STONER McTAVISH

Sarah Dreher

The first of two adventure mysteries starring lesbian romantic amateur-sleuth Stoner McTavish gets off to a promising start as Stoner is packed off by her business partner Marylou and her mystic Aunt Hermione to check out a newly-wedded man's mysterious background – to the Grand Teton National Park. Little do they know when they pack Stoner's bags that she's in for a taste of romance and adventure indeed, but served up with a large helping of corruption, cunning and death. And through her terrifying ordeal, it is only the thought of Gwen that keeps Stoner going. . . .

0-86358-241-9

£4.95 paperback

SOMETHING SHADY

Sarah Dreher

'Shady Acres posed massive and white in a lawn of dead grasses, iridescent against a washed out sky... At either end of the house, chimneys reached for the sky. The paint was chipped and peeling, the windows glinted silver.' Aunt Hermione sends Stoner McTavish off to Maine to search for a missing woman and thus starts a terrifying trip for Stoner, involving disguise, tackling the forces of that shabby white house turned mental hospital and a cliff-hanging climax.

0-86358-270-2

£4.95 paperback

AMATEUR CITY

Katherine V. Forrest

Ellen O'Neil starts her new job in a Los Angeles highrise office building – only to find herself sole witness to events surrounding a baffling murder. Detective Kate Delafield, tough and demanding leader of the homicide investigation team, soon discovers strong motives for the killing of Fergus Parker in an office united in its hatred of the murdered man. And with her own personal life in crisis, she finds her path increasingly intersecting with that of Ellen O'Neil. Here is a modern whodunnit in the best traditions of the genre.

0-86358-200-1

£3.95 paperback

MURDER AT THE NIGHTWOOD BAR

Katherine V. Forrest

'I know she's what Shakespeare thought about when he wrote that phrase – she was life's bright fire.' But Dory is dead – found lying in the parking lot of a lesbian bar, her white-blonde hair ruffled by the gentle breezes of a June evening. For homicide detective Kate Delafield, a look into the bewildered silver-blue eyes of the murdered girl is the start of a terrifying journey. A journey first to the gay city of West Hollywood where Kate uncovers shocking facts about the brief life of the murdered woman. Then an emotional trek fighting against the uncooperative silence from Dory's parents and the hostile women who should be Dory's friends – the lesbians who frequented the Nightwood Bar. Emotions run high in Kate's private life as well, with Kate see-sawing in and out of love . . .

0-86358-239-7

£3.95 paperback

Available from Pandora Press

Contemporary Crime

The Always Anonymous Beast – *Lauren Wright Douglas*	£3.95 ☐
Amateur City – *Katherine V. Forrest*	£3.95 ☐
Fieldwork – *Maureen Moore*	£3.95 ☐
The Monarchs are Flying – *Marion Foster*	£3.95 ☐
Murder and Company – *ed. Harriet Ayres*	£3.95 ☐
Murder at the Nightwood Bar – *Katherine V. Forrest*	£3.95 ☐
Something Shady – *Sarah Dreher*	£4.95 ☐
Stoner McTavish – *Sarah Dreher*	£4.95 ☐
Study in Lilac – *Maria Antonia Oliver*	£3.95 ☐
Vanishing Act – *Joy Magezis*	£4.95 ☐
Victims – *Shirley Shea*	£3.95 ☐

Classic Crime

Blood Upon the Snow – *Hilda Lawrence*	£3.95 ☐
Bring the Monkey – *Miles Franklin*	£3.95 ☐
Death of a Doll – *Hilda Lawrence*	£3.95 ☐
Duet of Death – *Hilda Lawrence*	£3.95 ☐
Easy Prey – *Josephine Bell*	£3.95 ☐
Green for Danger – *Christianna Brand*	£3.95 ☐
The Hours Before Dawn – *Celia Fremlin*	£3.95 ☐
London Particular – *Christianna Brand*	£3.95 ☐
Mischief – *Charlotte Armstrong*	£3.95 ☐
Murder's Little Sister – *Pamela Branch*	£3.95 ☐
Murder in Pastiche – *Marion Mainwaring*	£3.95 ☐
The Port of London Murders – *Josephine Bell*	£3.95 ☐
The Spinster's Secret – *Anthony Gilbert (Lucy Malleson)*	£3.95 ☐

All these books are available at your local bookshop or can be ordered direct by post. Just tick the titles you want and fill in the form below.

Name ....

Address ....

....

....

Write to Unwin Cash Sales, PO Box 11, Falmouth, Cornwall TR10 9EN.
Please enclose remittance to the value of the cover price plus:

UK: 60p for the first book plus 25p for the second book, thereafter 15p for each additional book ordered to a maximum charge of £1.90.

BFPO and EIRE: 60p for the first book plus 25p for the second book and 15p per copy for the next 7 books and thereafter 9p per book.

OVERSEAS INCLUDING EIRE: £1.25 for the first book plus 75p for the second book and 28p for each additional book.

Pandora Press reserves the right to show new retail prices on covers, which may differ from those previously advertised in the text or elsewhere. Postage rates are also subject to revision.